Orchids to Know and Grow

## UNIVERSITY PRESS OF FLORIDA

Florida A&M University, Tallahassee
Florida Atlantic University, Boca Raton
Florida Gulf Coast University, Ft. Myers
Florida International University, Miami
Florida State University, Tallahassee
University of Central Florida, Orlando
University of Florida, Gainesville
University of North Florida, Jacksonville
University of South Florida, Tampa
University of West Florida, Pensacola

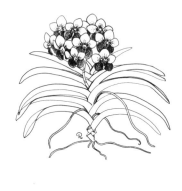

Drawings by
Marion Ruff Sheehan · Candace B. Hollinger

Color Photographs by Greg Allikas

University Press of Florida

Gainesville  Tallahassee  Tampa  Boca Raton

Pensacola  Orlando  Miami  Jacksonville  Ft. Myers

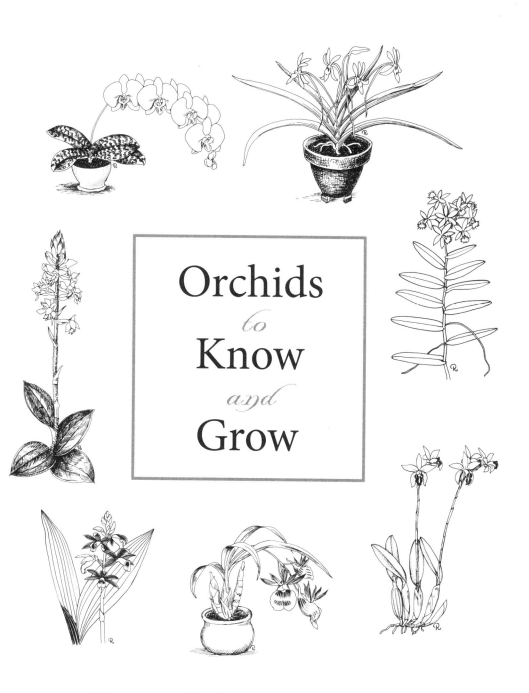

# Orchids
## *to* Know
### *and*
## Grow

Thomas J. Sheehan  ·  Robert J. Black

12  11  10  09  08  07    6  5  4  3  2  1

Library of Congress Cataloging-in-Publication Data
Sheehan, Thomas J. (Thomas John), 1924–
Orchids to know and grow / Thomas J. Sheehan, Robert J. Black; drawings by Marion Ruff
Sheehan, Candace B. Hollinger; color photographs by Greg Allikas.
p. cm.
Includes index.
ISBN 978-0-8130-3065-4 (alk. paper)
1. Orchid culture. 2. Orchids. I. Black, Robert J. (Robert John), 1942– II. Title.
SB409.S528 2007
635.9'3449–dc22        2007001302

The University Press of Florida is the scholarly publishing agency for the State University
System of Florida, comprising Florida A&M University, Florida Atlantic University, Florida
Gulf Coast University, Florida International University, Florida State University, University
of Central Florida, University of Florida, University of North Florida, University of South
Florida, and University of West Florida.

University Press of Florida
15 Northwest 15th Street
Gainesville, FL 32611-2079
http://www.upf.com

The authors dedicate this book to the late Marion Ruff Sheehan (1923–1998), who will long be remembered for her exquisite botanical illustrations, which are an integral part of this and many other books.

# Contents

# Preface

A misconception has existed from time immemorial that orchids are the play-things of the rich and famous, expensive to purchase and hard to grow. Nothing could be further from the truth today. It is obvious when one delves into the historical orchid literature how this misconception arose. One reads of Japanese feudal lords carrying plants of *Neofinetia falcata* with them on journeys. In the 1700s, the well-to-do sent explorers abroad to collect exotic plants; today, orchids are readily available in the marketplace at reasonable prices and most are easy to grow.

Depending on which taxonomists you follow there are roughly 25,000 known species of orchids worldwide. They are found in all parts of the world, except in the Arctic, Antarctica, and major deserts. Hence, no matter where you live there are orchids native to that area, so it is easy to select orchid species that will thrive in your area. If you have a greenhouse in the subtropical or temperate zones you greatly increase the range of orchids you can grow.

In addition to the myriad species available, there are more than 120,000 registered hybrids from which to select, and this number is continually increasing. With this vast array of plants, one can have orchids in bloom every month of the year in a rainbow of colors; orchids come in every color except black, and many bicolored and tricolored flowers are also available.

It has often been stated that once anyone is bitten by the "orchid bug," it's like a fatal disease, there is no cure and you are smitten for life.

It is hoped that the information contained herein will make orchid growing easier and a happy experience for the orchid hobbyist.

# Acknowledgments

We would like to express our sincere appreciation to the American Orchid Society for allowing us to use the generic line drawings by the late Marion Ruff Sheehan. We also thank the late Mary McQuerry for the use of the plates illustrating orchid insect pests originally published in *You Can Grow Cattleya Orchids* (1991).

# 1

## What Is an Orchid?

The immense orchid family is found in all parts of the world, except beyond the Arctic and Antarctic circles and in major deserts. The family, depending on which taxonomist you follow, comprises more than 800 genera, approximately 25,000 known species, and more than 120,000 registered hybrids, and these numbers continue to grow. Several new species have been identified over the past year and there are probably many more out there waiting to be named. In this multiplex of genera and species there are vast differences in plant height, ranging from 0.2 inches (*Platystele minimiflora*—a rice grain looks huge when placed next to this plant) to 27 feet (a *Sobralia* species). Plants may be leafless (*Dendrophylax*) or leafy (*Dendrobium*). They can be terrestrial (growing in soil—*Calopogon*), epiphytic (growing on trees—*Encyclia*), saprophytic (growing on decaying organic matter—*Hexalectris*), or lithophytic (growing on rocks—*Laelia crispata*). There are two major growth habits found in the orchid family, sympodial and monopodial (fig. 1.1). In sympodial orchids (e.g., *Dendrobium*) the main stem grows horizontally and produces determinate lateral branches, which when mature usually have

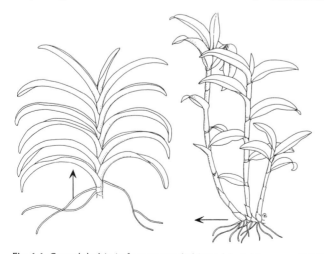

Fig. 1.1. Growth habit. Left: monopodial (*Vanda*); right: sympodial (*Dendrobium*)

terminal flowers. After flowering, the plant produces a new growth from the base of the last growth, continuing on in a horizontal direction. In monopodial orchids (e.g., *Vanda*), the main stem is perpendicular to the surface of the medium, is always vegetative at the apex (indeterminate growth), and has axillary flowering. This perpendicular or indeterminate growth can theoretically grow upward ad infinitum, assuming cultural conditions are always ideal.

Orchid flowers exhibit a very high degree of variability in size, shape, and color. Flowers range in size from 0.2 inches (*Lepanthes*) to almost 14 inches in diameter (*Brassia*). The labellum (lip) is the most prominent floral segment in many orchids (*Cochleanthes, Cattleya*), while in other genera (*Masdevallia*) the three sepals are the showy portion of the flower and the lip is miniscule. Unlike many other families in the plant kingdom, many orchid flowers are resupinate. When the buds begin to emerge, the lip is uppermost and during enlargement the buds will turn 180° before they open, placing the lip at the bottom. This turning is easy to observe in genera with spurred flowers (*Dendrobium, Vanda*). Flowers where the lip is uppermost are called nonresupinate (*Prosthechea* [= *Encyclia*] *cochleata*). In some nonresupinate flowers the lip is hinged (*Calopogon*); when the pollinating insect lands the lip falls toward the column to position the insect to ensure removal of the pollinia. A rainbow of colors can easily be found in orchid flowers—every color exists except black, and one can also find bicolor and tricolor flowers. There are very fragrant orchids (*Maxillaria tenuifolia*) and others that have less pleasant odors (*Bulbophyllum phalaenopsis, Coelogyne trinervis*). There are vines present too; of these, *Vanilla* is the most well known. This vast array of plants, regardless of point of origin, size and/or number of flowers, and a multitude of variations in vegetative growth and size, are tied together by their floral characteristics to make up the Orchidaceae.

A close look at an orchid flower will reveal which features contribute to its placement in the Orchidaceae. To be called an "orchid," a flower must have:

1. Bilateral symmetry (zygomorphic)
2. A gynandrium (column)
3. A rostellum
4. Pollinia
5. A labellum (lip)
6. An unusual seed.

Since many individuals normally do not see orchid seeds, the first five factors are the most important ones as they are always visually present. Granted, for a 0.08-inch flower of *Trichosalpinx*, at least a 10x hand lens is needed to identify the various floral segments, while in *Cattleya* and *Phalaenopsis*, the characteristics are readily visible to the naked eye.

1. Bilateral symmetry. In the plant kingdom there are two main types of flowers: regular flowers (actinomorphic), which can be divided in any plane to produce two equal halves (lilies), and irregular flowers, which cannot be divided in any plane to produce two equal halves (some cannas). The orchid flower is a special type of irregular flower in that it has bilateral symmetry (zygomorphic). It can be divided in only one plane to produce two equal halves (mirror images; see fig. 1.2). Dissecting an orchid flower vertically produces the two equal halves, cutting in any other plane will not produce two mirror images.

Fig. 1.2. Zygomorphic flower (*Cattleya*)

2. Gynandrium (column). The reproductive structures in the orchid flower are unique. In general when you look into a flower, the Easter lily as an example, there are six yellow-tipped structures (the anthers, male) around the perimeter and a white erect structure in the center with a three-lobed sticky top (the stigma, female). Many children when smelling lilies have emerged with six yellow dots (the pollen) on their faces and a sticky substance on their noses (the stigmatic fluid). During evolution of the orchid flower the male and female organs were fused together into the usually white waxy structure (sometimes the same color as the flower, e.g., *Phalaenopsis*) in the center of the flower containing the anther(s), style, and stigma (see illustration of the column, fig.

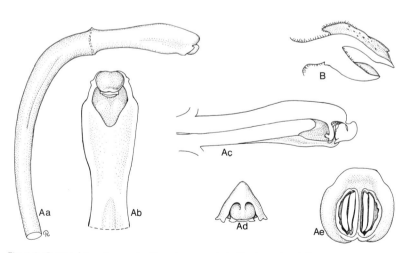

Fig. 1.3. Gynandrium (reproductive structures). A. *Cattleya*: Aa. Column and ovary, side view; Ab. Column, ventral view; Ac. Column, vertical section; Ad. Column, end view; Ae. Anther cap with pollinia in place; B. *Paphiopedilum* column, vertical section

1.3). Hence the male and female reproductive elements of the flower are all enclosed in the gynandrium.

3. Rostellum. Literally "little beak," the rostellum (fig. G.35, in the glossary) is an extension of the stigmatic tissue and serves a twofold purpose. First, it serves as a dam of tissue to separate the male portion of the flower from the female portion and thus prevents self-fertilization. There are, however, a few orchids (*Cattleya aurantica*) in which self-pollination can occur. In these species there is a self-digestion of the rostellum so self-fertilization can occur, but these are the exceptions rather than the rule. The rostellum is also a gland that exudes a very viscid substance. When the pollinating insect visits the flower and passes under the rostellum, a bead of the gluelike substance is applied to its back to assure that the insect removes the pollinia when leaving the flower. The rostellum plays a very important role in survival of the species by assuring cross-pollination rather than inbreeding.

4. Pollinia (singular, pollinium). Another very interesting feature of the orchid flower is the fact that the tetrads of pollen are not dustlike, as in pine trees,

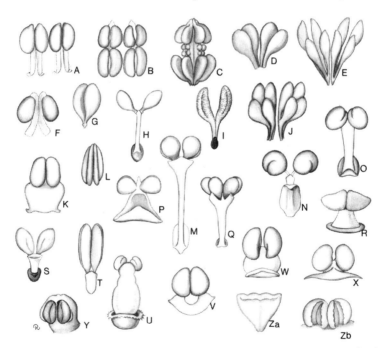

Fig. 1.4. Pollinia. A. *Broughtonia*; B. *Phaius*; C. *Brassavola*; D. *Dendrochilum*; E. *Spathoglottis*; F. *Hexisea*; G. *Masdevallia*; H. *Epidendrum*; I. *Ludisia*; J. *Calanthe*; K. *Bulbopohyllum*; L. *Dendrobium*; M. *Doritis*; N. *Rhynchostylis*; O. *Rodreguizia*; P. *Arachnis*; Q. *Trichopilia*; R. *Eulophia*; S. *Brassia*; T. *Gongora*; U. *Cycnoches*; V. *Cymbidium*; W. *Maxillaria*; X. *Ansellia*; Y. *Phragmipedium*; Z. *Vanilla*; Za. Pollen mass; Zb. Anthers

but agglutinated into little packets called pollinia (fig. 1.4). The size, shape, and number of pollinia vary among the various orchid genera. Individual orchid flowers have from two (*Phalaenopsis*) to twelve pollinia (*Brassavola cuculata*). Knowing the number of pollinia will often help in identifying flowers. *Cattleya* has four, whereas *Laelia* has eight, and although the flowers may look similar they can be easily separated by number of pollinia. The pollinia are protected by an anther cap that can be removed only when the insect leaves the flower, thus also assuring cross-pollination. Pollinia may be attached to stipes or caudicles (stalks) of various and sundry sizes and shapes. They may have a disc (viscidium) at the base of the caudicle covered with a very viscid substance to assist in the removal of the pollinia by the insect. Some orchids (*Catasetum*) have a triggering mechanism that, when tripped by the insect, fires the pollinia at the insect. The pollinia combined with their stalk and disk are referred to as the pollinarium.

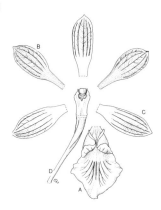

5. Labellum (lip). In orchid flowers, one petal is often highly modified into a structure called the labellum (fig. 1.5). This structure is usually at the bottom of the flower (resupinate flowers, *Cattleya*) and serves as a landing platform for the pollinator. In those flowers with the lip uppermost (nonresupinate, *Calopogon*), the lip may be hinged and falls down onto the column when the insect lands on it. These highly modified structures may contain spurs (some up to 12 inches long, *Angraecum sesquipedale*), callus tissue, or other interesting artifacts that may only attract the pollinator or in many cases also offer a reward (e.g., nectar).

Fig. 1.5. Labellum. *Epidendrum* flower dissected showing components. A. Lip (labellum); B. Petals; C. Sepals; D. Column and ovary

6. Seed (fig. 1.6). Orchid seeds may not be readily visible, but they are another interesting aspect of the orchid family. Orchid seeds are minute and measured in microns. They are almost like dust particles. If you stood orchid seeds on end, it would take approximately 300 seeds side by side to form a line 1 inch long. If you laid them end to end it would take about 50 seeds to form a 1-inch line. The seeds do not contain endosperm (a starchy substance that provides carbohydrates for germination) so they have to rely on a fungus in nature to germinate. When you eat peas, corn, or beans the majority of what you eat is endosperm, which is lacking in orchids. In order to compensate for this and to assure the survival of the species, the orchid flower produces copious

amounts of seed. An average orchid seed pod will contain somewhere between 500 thousand and 1 million seeds. The late Oakes Ames is reported to have counted the seeds in a seed capsule, on a cold wintry

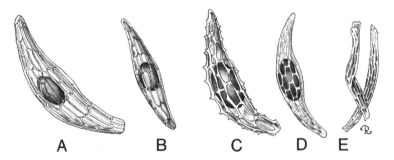

Fig. 1.6. Seed. A. *Phaius*; B. *Epidendrum*; C. *Ansellia*; D. *Dendrobium*; E. Undeveloped seed or chaff

day at Harvard University, and found more than 3.7 million! Fortunately, owing to studies by the late L. Knudson in the early 1920s at Cornell University, we now know that orchid seeds can be easily germinated in a nutrient medium under aseptic conditions.

Any flower having four or more of the above criteria falls into the orchid family. For example, *Hexisea bidentata* does not have a showy labellum, as all six floral segments are almost identical. The pollen in *Vanilla* tends to crumble rather than being in a nice packet, but these plants are still in the family because they have the other necessary characteristics.

It should also be noted that orchids, being monocotyledons, have their floral segments in threes (trimerous). The outer whorl of perianth parts consists of three sepals that are usually alike in size, shape, and color. The sepals protect the unopened buds as they emerge. The arrangement of the sepals can also be helpful in identification of some genera. In *Cattleya* flowers the sepals, arranged pinwheel fashion, are spaced equidistantly (120{dg}), while in *Maxillaria* flowers the two lateral sepals are at right angles to the dorsal sepal. The slipper orchids (*Paphiopedilum, Phragmipedium, Cypripedium, Selenipedium, Mexipedium*) have only two sepals, a dorsal sepal and a synsepal, the latter arising from the fusion of the two lateral sepals. The next inner whorl consists of the two petals and, in most orchids, one highly modified petal, the labellum. The labellum is highly variable among genera, ranging from broad and flat (*Cochleanthes*) to boot shaped (*Paphiopedilum*) and is often the dominant segment of the flower. The labellum can be helpful in identifying some orchids. In the center, surrounded by two whorls of floral segments, lies the gynandrium. The orchid is a typical monocotyledonous flower.

Getting to know orchid flowers can make a vocation or avocation only more interesting and desirable. When the flowers are starting to go by (senesce), pick one or two and dissect them. Look for the anther cap and remove the pollinia. How many are there? Is a viscidium present? Locate the stigmatic surface on the underside of the gynandrium. Check also for spurs on the labellum. There is an orchid flower (*Comparettia*) with three spurs but when you look at the flower you only see one. Where are the other two? *Broughtonia* has a spur, which many people have never noticed. Where is it? Dissecting will tell. Try making a vertical section for the proper plane to see the inner workings of the reproductive structures in the column. Orchid flowers are fascinating and really need to be looked at in detail. Then and only then will you know why it is called an orchid.

**2**

# What Is in an Orchid Name?

To name names is not to display knowledge, but how can things be known without their names? If these things are our friends, we find that familiarity with their names and origins generates greater intimacy, closer bonds and fullest pleasure in human fellowship. Orchids are close friends, indeed, to orchidists and familiarity with orchid names will inevitably enlarge their knowledge and understanding of these plants.

*Gordon W. Dillon*

Orchid growers are one of a small group of specialized plant enthusiasts who are more apt to give you the Latin name of their plants than a common name, yet there is an orchid plant out there, *Cypripedium*, with twenty-five or more common names that vary from country to country and are more apt to be used by the non-orchidists. Despite this apparent interest in knowing the Latin names of all the plants in their collection few if any orchid growers have delved into the background of **how** or **why** an individual plant got its name. This seems strange as many orchid plant names are very descriptive of the plant. For example, *Calopogon* means "beautiful beard," a reference to the bearded lip on these plants. Learning the derivation and meaning of orchid plant names will often lead to a better understanding of these plants.

There are specific international rules governing the naming of plants, whether they are found in the wild or are manmade hybrids. These rules were developed over time primarily to help taxonomists name newly discovered plants, thus preventing two different plants on opposite sides of the globe from having the same name or from having more than one genus named for the same individual.

Nontaxonomists are seldom confronted by the rules of nomenclature, but should be aware of them and how they govern the naming of a plant. This is especially true for those who are planning on naming their first hybrid orchid. Foremost, orchidists should be interested in the derivation and meaning of the plant name. Many times the names are very descriptive of distinct characteristics of the plant, or tell where the plant came from. Orchidists should thank their taxonomists for using so much descriptive terminology, as fauna taxonomists have not always followed the same approach. For example, there is a wasp genus *Lala* and a species *palusa*. One can point to that wasp and say "that's a lalapalusa." There is a clam genus *Abra* with the obvious species name of *cadabra*. Even Tom, Dick, and

Harry got into the act when it came to naming oysters, with the genera *Ptomapsis*, *Dickenapsis*, and *Arapsis*. More time could be devoted to these **cute** names, but orchid names are the topic of discussion.

## International Code of Botanical Nomenclature

The International Code of Botanical Nomenclature (ICBN) was developed to assist taxonomists in naming plants found in the wild by setting down guidelines to follow when naming new species. Basically all living organisms, including plants, are known worldwide by their Latin binomial (for example, *Vanda tricolor*), consisting of a genus name (*Vanda*) and a species name, or specific epithet (*tricolor*). In a limited number of cases, a third term may be required. The ICBN lays down the rules as to how these terms are derived and written.

First Term: Genus Name: It is always capitalized, italicized (underlined), usually descriptive (*Phalaenopsis*, mothlike), but may honor an individual (*Cattleya*, for William Cattley). If the term is descriptive it is usually derived from either Greek or Latin (*Phalaenopsis*, from Greek *phalaina* [moth] + *opsis* [appearance]). If named for an individual, then the individual's name is Latinized (William Cattley = *Cattleya*).

Second Term: Species Epithet: This term is always in lower case, italicized (underlined), usually descriptive, but may honor an individual or denote the place of origin. The derivation of the term follows the same guidelines set out for the genus name. For example, *multiflora* is descriptive and denotes many flowers, *mossiae* is named for Mrs. Moss of England, and *japonica* denotes that the plant came from Japan or vicinity. In some older books *mossiae* and *japonica* will appear as *Mossiae* and *Japonica*; this is because at one time the rules stated that specific epithets derived from names of people or countries would begin with a capital letter. However, for the past fifty-odd years only lower case has been used for all specific names so as to lessen the confusion with manmade hybrids, for which all collective epithets start with capital letters.

Third Term: Subspecies, Variety, Forma: Occasionally the need for a third term arises to describe a single characteristic that distinguishes one clone from all the others in the same species. Depending on the characteristic a taxonomist may designate it as a variety, subspecies, or forma. Many times the characteristic is a change in flower color; for example, *Cattleya labiata alba* designates the white form of the species. The third term is always italicized and in lower case.

Natural Hybrids: There are plants found in the wild that are natural hybrids between two species in the vicinity. These plants are named following the same rules set down for species. In order to designate these plants as natural hybrids a mathematical × is placed between the generic and specific names (*Phalaenopsis* ×*intermedia*).

## International Code of Nomenclature for Cultivated Plants

The International Code of Nomenclature for Cultivated Plants (ICNCP) is similar to the ICBN in some aspects but differs sufficiently to make it easy to distinguish between species and manmade hybrids.

First Term: Genus Name: Orchids are unique in the sense that the Orchidaceae is the only family in the plant kingdom in which multigeneric hybrids are commonplace. Therefore, special rules had to be established to identify these hybrids. The hybrids are named as follows:

1. Seedlings derived from crosses between species and/or hybrids within the same genus will bear the generic name of the parents.
   Example:   *Cattleya trianaei* × *Cattleya mossiae* = *Cattleya* Trimos

The genus name is always capitalized and italicized (underlined) as in ICBN.

2. Bigeneric crosses. When combining two genera to make a hybrid, the resulting offspring are given a genus name that is a combination of the parental generic names.
   Example:   *Epidendrum* × *Cattleya* = *Epicattleya*
   *Vanda* × *Ascocentrum* = *Ascocenda*

Once a bigeneric cross has been registered all future crosses between species and/or hybrids in those two genera will always carry that combination of generic names.

3. Trigeneric crosses. Seedlings produced from combinations of three genera used to produce a hybrid can be named in two possible ways.
   a. The hybridizer can combine the three generic names.
   Example:   *Brassavola* × *Laelia* × *Cattleya* = *Brassolaeliocattleya*
   b. The hybridizer can opt to name it after an individual and add the Latin ending -*ara*.
   Example:   *Cochlioda* × *Odontoglossum* × *Oncidium* = *Wilsonara*
4. Multigeneric crosses. Hybrids with four or more genera in their background are all given generic names ending in -*ara*. Frequently they are named after individuals. Today there are combinations among the more than 150 registered -*ara* genera involving up to nine individual genera involved in one offspring.
   Example:   *Brassavola* × *Cattleya* × *Laelia* × *Schomburgkia* × *Sophronitis*
   = *Fergusonara*.

Once a multigeneric name has been registered, all ensuing hybrids that have the same generic makeup will carry that name.

Second Term: Collective Grex (Specific Epithet): The differences between ICBN and ICNCP are most evident in the **collective epithet**. Roman type is used and all names begin with a capital letter. The name should be a "fancy" name (Trimos, Delightful, Orchid World, Trick or Treat, Fuch's Delight).

Combining the generic name and the collective epithet produces the binomial by which the orchid plant will be known.

Third Term: Cultivar Name: When an individual plant from a manmade grex has a characteristic that sets the plant off from all the rest of the grex it is given a cultivar name. In addition, orchid plants, whether manmade hybrids or species, that receive flower quality awards from orchid societies (American Orchid Society [AOS]) are given cultivar names. The cultivar name is always in roman type, starts with a capital letter, and is offset by either single quotes (' ') or preceded by cv. The initials of the award and granting organization are appended (*Phalaenopsis* Limestone 'Zuma Canyon' AM/AOS).

Individuals are often confused as to when a Latin word should be italicized. Latin (*Cattleya*) words are always italicized (underlined in handwriting or if italic font is not available) in the genus and species names; however, when the word is anglicized (cattleyas) it is not italicized or capitalized unless it is the first word of a sentence. Family names are not italicized. Some examples follow:

1. This is the genus *Cattleya.*
2. I have many cattleyas and cymbidiums.
3. We have *Cattleya skinneri* in the greenhouse.
4. Do you have *Cattleya* Bob Betts 'The Virgin'?
5. Cattleyas have beautiful flowers.

## What Orchid Names Mean

The following orchids exemplify the descriptive nature of many of the generic and specific names.

*Ancistrochilus rothschildianus*—The generic name comes from two Greek words *ankistron* (hook) and *cheilos* (lip). The specific name honors Mr. Rothschild. Hence, Rothschild's flower with the hooked lip.

*Arachnis flos-aëris*—The generic name is derived from the Greek word *arachne* (spider). The specific name comes from two Latin words *flos* (flower) and *aëris* (airy). This plant has airy, spiderlike flowers.

*Ascocentrum miniatum*—Two Greek words *ascos* (bag) and *kentron* (spur) have been combined to form the generic name. The specific name is Latin for "vermilion" (*miniatum*). This name is very descriptive of these plants with vermilion flowers with spurred lips.

*Catasetum barbatum*—The generic name is derived from two Greek words *kata* (down) and *seta* (bristle). The Latin word *barbatum* (bearded) is used to denote the specific name. Freely translated, these are the bearded flowers with bristly appendages.

*Cymbidium floribundum*—The Greek word *kymbes* (boat shaped) defines this genus. Specifically, the Latin word *floribundum* (many flowers) typifies this plant. These easy blooming plants have flowers with boat-shaped lips.

*Disa uniflora*—This plant name combines the Greek word *dis* (rich) and the Latin word *uniflora* (one flower) to describe the rich, single flower found in this species.

*Gastrochilus bellinus*—The genus name is a combination of two Greek words *gaster* (belly) and *cheilos* (lip), while the specific name is derived from the Latin word *bellinus* (pretty). This plant has pretty flowers with belly-like lips.

*Ionopsis utricularioides*—*Ion* (violet) and *opsis* (appearance), derived from Greek, depict this genus. The specific name comes from the Latin word *ultricularioides* (bladderlike). Thus, the plant can be described as having bladderlike, violet flowers.

*Octomeria grandiflora*—The two Greek words *octo* (eight) and *meros* (part) are combined to form the generic name and the Latin word *grandiflora* (large flowers) denote the specific name. Freely translated, it means large flowers with eight parts (pollinia), although the flowers are small in comparison to many other orchids.

*Polycycnis muscifera*—The Greek words *polys* (many) and *kyknos* (swan) are used to describe this genus. The Latin word *muscifera* (fly-carrying) forms this specific name. Many swans bearing flies would be a free translation of the above names. When first seen in the wild the spotting had the appearance of a swarm of flies, inspiring *muscifera* as the specific name.

*Psygmorchis pusilla*—*Psygma* (fan) and *orchis* (orchid) from Greek are united to form the generic name, while the Latin word *pusillo* (tiny) is used for the specific name. Hence, we have the tiny, fan-shaped orchid.

*Sophronitis coccinea*—The generic name is the diminutive form of the Greek word *sophronia* (chaste, modest). The specific name comes from the Latin word *coccinea* (scarlet, red). The small, modest plant with red flowers is a good descriptive name for this plant.

Genus Names: Most genus names are derived from either Greek or Latin, but occasionally a word from another language may be used (*Vanda* from Sanskrit, *Vanilla* from Spanish) or the Latinized name of an individual may be used (*Finetia* for Achille Finet). The derivation and meaning of a random selection of genus names follows:

| | |
|---|---|
| *Angraecum* | from Malayan *angurek*, the word for epiphytes. |
| *Ascocentrum* | from Greek *ascos* (bag) + *kentron* (spur), spurred lip |
| *Cattleya* | after William Cattley |
| *Cypripedium* | from Greek *Cypros*, an island sacred to Venus, + *pedilum* (slipper) |
| *Cymbidiella* | *Cymbidium*-like |

| | |
|---|---|
| *Dendrobium* | from Greek *dendros* (tree) + *bios* (life), living on trees |
| *Disa* | from Latin *dis* (*dives*) (rich), referring to beauty of the flowers |
| *Domingoa* | from Santa Domingo, now Dominican Republic |
| *Doritis* | from Greek *dory* (spear), referring to lip shape, or to the goddess Doritis |
| *Dresslerella* | after Robert Dressler |
| *Encyclia* | from Greek *enkykein* (to encircle), referring to lip lobes folded over the column |
| *Epidendrum* | from Greek *epi* (upon) + *dendron* (tree), growing on a tree |
| *Ionopsis* | from Greek *ion* (violet) + *opsis* (appearance), referring to flowers |
| *Neomoorea* | the new Moore, since there was already a genus named *Moorea* |
| *Paphiopedilum* | from Greek *Paphos*, a city dedicated to Venus, + *pedilum* (slipper), hence Venus slipper |
| *Phalaenopsis* | from Greek *phalaina* (moth) + *opsis* (appearance), mothlike |
| *Pleurothallis* | from Greek *pleuron* (rib) + *thallos* (short, branch), short stem |
| *Psygmorchis* | from Greek *psygma* (fan) + *orchis* (orchid), fanlike orchid |
| *Sarcochilus* | from Greek *sarx* (flesh) + *cheilos* (lip), referring to the fleshy lip |
| *Sobennikoffia* | Schlechter's wife's maiden name |
| *Tridactyle* | from Greek *tri* (three or trice) + *daktylos* (finger), trilobed lip |
| *Vanda* | Sanskrit, referring to plants with monopodial growth like *Vanda tessellata* |
| *Zootrophion* | from Greek *zootrophion* (menagerie), flowers likened to animals |

Species Epithets: Species names may be descriptive, honor an individual, or denote the location where the plant was discovered. A random selection of specific names and their meanings follow:

| | |
|---|---|
| *africana* | from Africa |
| *albiflora* | white flowered |
| *arachnites* | spiderlike |
| *bambusifolia* | bamboo-like foliage |
| *brevis* | short |
| *bidentata* | two teeth |
| *cinnabarina* | orange red |
| *concolor* | one color |
| *cordifolia* | heart-shaped leaves |
| *cyanea* | blue |

| | |
|---|---|
| *flava* | yellow |
| *grandiflora* | large flowers |
| *javanica* | from Java |
| *labiata* | having a lip |
| *linearis* | linear, usually refers to leaves |
| *miniatum* | small |
| *purpurata* | purple |
| *palmifolia* | palmlike leaves |
| *rigida* | stiff, rigid |
| *spectabilis* | showy |
| *sanguinea* | red |
| *tetragonium* | having four sides, or four angled |
| *uniflora* | single flowered |
| *variabilis* | variable |

Knowing the Latin binomial of a plant is good, but not sufficient. Orchidists should also be cognizant of the meaning of both the **genus name** and the **specific epithet** for their plants.

## Why Do Orchid Names Change?

Many people wonder why taxonomists keep changing plant names. Is it really necessary? There are valid reasons to change some names and not very valid reasons for others. When considering the circumstances the early taxonomists faced when they were naming the world's plants in the 1700s and 1800s it becomes obvious that the chances for error were high. Early taxonomists often worked from a single dry specimen, using only a small microscope or hand lens to aid in identification. At times they did not have the entire plant. In many cases, they were not completely aware of the variability among plants in a single species population (e.g., *Catasetum*, with male flowers very different from female flowers). Conceivably, then, plants at either extreme of the population might be identified as different species. Once they named the plant, they published the name, often in a local botanical journal. In addition, communication between and among taxonomists was, by today's standards, minimal; thus taxonomists did not get to see all the small journals published in those days and were not always in communication with other taxonomists who might be trying to name the same plant. It is easy to see that confusion could have arisen very easily in this period. Today, times have changed, taxonomists have better tools, and there is much better communication among the international groups. Electronic communication allows taxonomists to be in instant contact with their colleagues worldwide; questions can be readily answered or computer databases searched to be sure a plant is not being misnamed as plants are still being discovered in the wild. Also, as scientists learn more and more about plants (e.g., by DNA fingerprinting), additional changes in classification and nomenclature may be required. There is no doubt that taxonomic changes will continue to take place. Since taxonomists follow a set of international rules, the ICBN, when studying a genus they are sometimes obliged to change a generic or specific name after discovering in an old journal that a plant was identified and a name published earlier than publication of its present name. According to the rules of nomenclature the earliest published name takes precedence, hence there is a need for the name change. Consequently, with better communication and travel, more taxonomists are looking into older herbaria and literature and occasionally discovering prior names. As taxonomists learn more about given genera and species, including their native populations, variability, and breeding habits, they may find that a plant has been misnamed or that what has been known as a variety is in reality a species (e.g., *Cattleya dowiana* var. *aurea* is in reality *Cattleya aurea*).

Today, as biotechnologists and taxonomists delve more into the inner sanctums of plants, the potential for additional name changes will increase. Could it be, as some have proposed, that what we are calling genera in the Orchidaceae are in reality species? Yes, that might be the ultimate extreme, possibly exaggerated, but only time will tell.

## Suggested References for Orchid Nomenclature

Bechtel, H., P. Cribb, and E. Launert. 1992. *The manual of cultivated orchids*, 3rd ed. Boston: MIT Press.

Cribb, P. J., J. Greatwood, and P. F. Hunt. 1992. *The handbook on orchid nomenclature and registration*, 4th ed. London: Royal Horticultural Society.

Dressler, R. 1993. *Phylogeny and classification of the orchid family*. Portland, Ore.: Discorides.

Gledhill, D. 1985. *The names of plants*. Cambridge: Cambridge University Press.

Mayr, H. 1998. *Orchid names and their meanings*. Germany: A.R.G. Gantner Verlag K.-G.

Pridgeon, A. (ed.). 1992. *The illustrated encyclopedia of orchids*. Portland, Ore.: Timber Press.

Schultes, R. E., and A. S. Pease. 1963. *Generic names of orchids*. Orlando, Fla.: Academic.

Sheehan, T., and M. Sheehan. 1995. *An illustrated survey of orchid genera*. Portland, Ore.: Timber Press.

Stern, W. T. 1983. *Botanical Latin*, 3rd ed. London: David and Charles.

# 3

## Orchid Classification

The first major classification of the orchid family (Orchidaceae) came in 1825 as the results of the efforts of John Lindley, who continued to work on and modify it for the next forty years. He was followed by other taxonomists such as Reichenbach, Pfitzer, Rolf, and Ames, who continued updating it. Later, Pfitzer's work was the basis for the reclassification of the orchid family by Schlechter, who basically followed Pfitzer but increased the number of subtribes. Since 1930, continual modification has taken place and is continuing today at an even more rapid pace on the basis of DNA studies. Some of the taxonomists presently working on the family include Carlyle Luer, Robert Dressler, Calaway Dodson, Mark Clements, Philip Cribb and Finn Rasmussen.

Because of its size and complexity, the Orchidaceae always has been and will continue to be a challenge to taxonomists. It consists of more than 800 genera and 25,000 species and, to say the least, is a very complex family. Unfortunately, not all taxonomists agree on the entire classification of the orchid family, and the hobbyist is faced with the dilemma of choosing among the various classifications found in the literature.

Dr. Robert Dressler's classification of the Orchidaceae (1993) will be followed herein. Dr. Dressler began reclassifying the family in the 1960s and is still actively working on the family and fine-tuning his work. As of 2006, most changes have been minor and have not altered the major classifications; however, this may change when all of the DNA studies are completed, with genera possibly being merged in some cases.

Large complex families like the Orchidaceae require taxonomists to develop a way of dividing the family into segments in an orderly fashion. The breakdown of the family, governed by the International Rules of Nomenclature and outlined in the appendix, is delineated as follows.

*Family (example, Orchidaceae)*

The family category is a natural unit combining a number of characteristics that occur in the members of this group. The plant kingdom is divided into many families, with more than 300 families of flowering plants. Many family names end in *-aceae*.

## Subfamily (example, Orchidoideae)

Large families such as Orchidaceae are often divided into a number of sections, called subfamilies, that comprise genera believed to have a common origin. The Orchidaceae family is composed of at least four subfamilies. All subfamily designations end in *-oideae*.

## Tribe (example, Epidendreae)

Large subfamilies are often further divided into more composite groups called tribes, a group of genera that are more alike than dissimilar. There are ten tribes in the subfamily Orchidoideae. Tribe designations end in *-eae*.

## Subtribe (example, Laeliinae)

Often tribes are subdivided into one or more subtribes, with each subtribe containing one or more genera. The designated ending for subtribe nomenclature is *-inae*.

## Genus (example, Encyclia)

A genus is a group of plants that have more characteristics in common with one another than they do with other members of the family. There are more than 800 genera in Orchidaceae. Generic names have a variety of endings such as *-a*, *-um*, *-us*, etc.

## Species (example, cordigera)

A species is a group of plants that are nearly alike and differ only in very minor characteristics. The species designation ending should agree with the gender of the genus ending (e.g., *Encyclia cordigera*). There are more than 200 species of *Encyclia*.

## Subspecies (example, alba)

Within some species there are groups of individuals that vary slightly, but not significantly enough to be designated as another species. Subspecies names have endings that follow gender of the genus and species such as *Encyclia cordigera alba*.

## Variety (example, alba)

Often used to designate characteristics similar to those of subspecies. It is widely used by horticulturists, sometimes erroneously, to designate any variant of the species. Again, the ending of the designated term, such as *alba*, must agree with the gender of the genus and species.

*Forma (example, alba)*

Usually forma is used to designate a color variation, such as *alba* (i.e., white). However, because of variations in taxonomy, one taxonomist could list *alba* as a subspecies, while another will designate it as a variety and still another as a forma. Forma is usually the smallest sector in any taxonomic grouping.

Figure 3.1. The taxonomic classification of *Encyclia cordigera alba* within the plant kingdom.

Plant Kingdom
Division: Spermatophyta
    Subdivision: Angiospermae
        Class: Monocotyledoneae
            Family: Orchidaceae
                Subfamily: Orchidoideae
                    Tribe: Epidendreae
                        Subtribe: Laeliinae
                            Genus: *Encyclia*
                              Species: *cordigera*
                                Variety: *alba*

# 4

# A Selection of Orchid Genera

## Orchid Nomenclature

Orchid nomenclature is currently in a state of flux as a result of myriad DNA studies being undertaken by plant taxonomists around the world; many generic names are in the process of being changed or will possibly be changed in the near future. Consequently, the question arises as to which name is correct. For example, *Laelia purpurata* was first identified in 1825 and was known by that name until 2000 when it was changed to *Sphronitis purpurata* by Chase at Kew Gardens. However, since 2000 it has been changed three more times, becoming *Hadrolaelia purpurata*, then *Brazilaelia purpurata*, and then *Chironiella purpurata*, making it very confusing for the average horticulturist to know which name to put on the label in the pot. These changes will continue to take place for the next few years. Consequently, the final decisions are yet to come in many cases. Therefore, since there is so much fluctuation in orchid nomenclature, it was decided for this book to follow basically the nomenclature of Dressler, with slight modifications. The generic names contained therein are the ones with which most horticulturists and orchid hobbyists are familiar and have labeled their plants, so hopefully we will not add to the confusion. Previous experience indicates that horticulturists are often reluctant to change names as rapidly as taxonomists; however, for those who are interested in the latest nomenclature changes and want to keep relabeling their plants, they can go to the Kew World Monocot List on the Web pages of the Royal Botanic Garden, Kew, London, at www.kew.org/wcsp, where the list is maintained and constantly updated. Type in any orchid species name and you will know immediately if it is still the accepted name or a synonym and, if the latter, it will appear under its new name with the old name in synonymy.

Hopefully, in the near future the DNA studies will be completed and the final list of accepted generic names will be available; then the new names may be added to the plant labels if so desired by the orchidists.

# Growth and Cultural Icons

## Growth Habit

Terrestrial

Epiphyte

Lithophyte

## Growth Pattern

Sympodial

Monopodial

# Light

Full Sun

Partial Shade

Moderate Shade

Heavy Shade

# Temperature

Cool

Intermediate

Warm

# Container/Mount

Pot

Plaque

Hanging Basket

Tree Limb

## Acanthephippium

**Genus**: *Acanthephippium* Blume (uh-can-the-FIP-ee-um)
**Tribe:** Arethuseae
**Subtribe:** Bletiinae
**Etymology:** From the Greek words *akantha* (thorn) and *ephippion* (saddle), a reference to the saddle-shaped lip.
**Native habitat:** Taiwan and the Philippines, west to India.
**Number of species:** 15
**Commonly grown species:** *bicolor, javanica, mantinianum* (color plate 1), *striatum, yamotoi.*
**Hybridizes with:** None recorded.
**Generic description**: Although these terrestrial sympodial plants resemble *Calanthe* and *Phaius*, they are easily separated. *Acanthephippium* has taller, multinoded pseudobulbs. Each dark green,

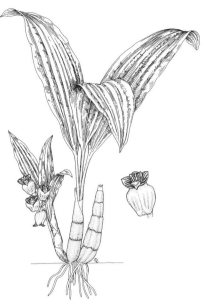

Fig. 4.1. *Acanthephippium mantinianum*

slightly fluted pseudobulb is topped by 2 or more soft, pleated, often wrinkled deciduous leaves. The almost urn-shaped 2-inch flowers are borne on erect inflorescences on the newly developing growth. The few flowers per inflorescence are dull yellow or pink, often spotted or striped.
**Flowering season**: Spring and summer.
**Culture**

    **Medium:** Any well-drained, terrestrial mix containing 40% or more organic matter.

    **Fertilizers and fertilization:** Use a balanced fertilizer as directed on the container.

    **Watering:** Keep moist during the growing season.

    **Propagation:** Seed or division.

    **Repotting:** Should be repotted every 2 years.

## Acineta

**Genus:** Acineta Lindley (ah-sin-EE-tuh)
**Tribe:** Maxillarieae
**Subtribe:** Stanhopeinae
**Etymology:** From the Greek word *akinetos* (immovable), a reference to the rigid lip.
**Native habitat:** Southern Mexico to northern South America.
**Number of species:** 15
**Commonly grown species:** *alticola*; *barkeri*; *chrysantha*; *erythroxantha*; *superba*.
**Hybridizes with:** *Embreea* and *Stanhopea*.
**Generic description:** *Acineta* plants are typified by their tight clusters of furrowed pseudobulbs, to 4 inches tall, topped by as many as 4 plicate leaves. The large pendent inflorescences arise from the base of the pseudobulbs on these sympodial epiphytes. Each pendent inflorescence bears up to 20 mostly yellow flowers often 2 inches in diameter. The colorful floral segments are thick and fleshy.
**Flowering season:** Spring and summer.
**Culture**

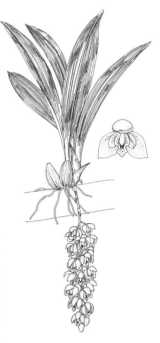

Fig. 4.2. *Acineta chrysantha*

> **Medium:** Bark mixes; peat and perlite or sphagnum moss.
> **Fertilizers and fertilization:** Will depend on the medium. Use a 3-1-1 for bark and 1-1-1 for the other media, fertilize monthly.
> **Watering:** Water thoroughly and not again until the surface becomes dry to the touch.
> **Propagation:** Seed, division, or meristem.
> **Repotting:** After flowering every 2 years.

## Ada

**Genus:** *Ada* Lindley (A-duh)
**Tribe:** Maxillarieae
**Subtribe:** Oncidiinae
**Etymology:** Named for the sister of Artemisia, a character in ancient history.
**Native habitat:** Costa Rica south to northern South America.
**Number of species:** 8
**Commonly grown species:** *aurantiaca, glumacea, ishmanii, keiliana.*
**Hybridizes with:** *Aspasia, Brassia, Cochlioda, Gomesa, Miltonia, Odontoglossum, Oncidium.*
**Generic description:** Vegetatively, *Ada* species resemble *Brassia* with their flattened pseudobulbs covered by the clasping leaf bases of the 5–7 leaves on each pseudobulb. The inflorescence of these sympodial epiphytes (rarely terrestrial) arises from the leaf axil of the new growth as it matures. The 1.5-inch flowers range from orange through red to almost brown. Some flowers barely open (*A. aurantiaca*) while others are full blown (*A. glumacea*).

Fig. 4.3. *Ada aurantiaca*

**Flowering season:** Winter, spring, and summer.
**Culture**
   **Medium:** Tree fern, peat and perlite, or bark mixes.
   **Fertilizers and fertilization:** Monthly, ratio depends on the medium.
   **Watering:** Water thoroughly and not again until the surface becomes dry to the touch.
   **Propagation:** Seed or division.
   **Repotting:** Preferably every 2 years.

## Aerangis

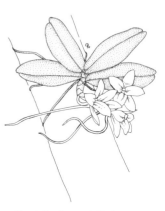

**Genus:** *Aerangis* Reichenbach f. (air-ANG-giss)
**Tribe:** Vandeae
**Subtribe:** Aerangidinae
**Etymology:** Comes from two Greek words *aer* (air) and *angos* (vessel) and refers to the pronounced spurs.
**Native habitat:** Central Africa.
**Number of species:** 120
**Commonly grown species:** *brachycarpa, citrate, fastuosa, kotschyana, luteoalba* var. *rhodosticta, thomsonii, ugandensis.*

Fig. 4.4a. *Aerangis fastuosa*

**Hybridizes with:** *Aeranthes, Ansellia, Angraecum, Cyrtorchis, Jumellea, Vanda.*
**Generic description:** These delightful monopodial epiphytic plants have two distinct habits of vegetative growth; some species resemble *Phalaenopsis* (*A. brachycarpa*) while others resemble *Vanda* (*A. thomsonii*). The inflorescences arise from the leaf axils, are mostly pendent, and bear up to 10 whitish flowers with very long spurs at the base of the lip. One variety, *A. luteoalba* var. *rhodostichta*, is very popular because of its bright orange-red column in the center of the creamy white flowers.
**Flowering season:** All year depending on species.
**Culture**

> **Medium:** Tree fern, bark mixes, or mounted on a plaque.
> **Fertilizers and fertilization:** Monthly, use a 3-1-1 for bark and 1-1-1 for all other media.
> **Watering:** Water thoroughly and again when medium feels dry to the touch. Plants on plaques may require daily watering.
> **Propagation:** Seed, cuttings, and meristems.
> **Repotting:** When medium decomposes or the plant becomes too large for the container.

Fig. 4.4b. *Aerangis kotschyar*

## Aeranthes

**Genus:** *Aeranthes* Lindley (air-ANN-theez)
**Tribe:** Vandeae
**Subtribe:** Angraecinae
**Etymology:** From two Greek words *aer* (air) and *anthos* (flower), to denote the single flower on the long inflorescence that appears to be suspended in air.
**Native habitat:** Madagascar.
**Number of species:** 30
**Commonly grown species:** *arachnites, denticulate, filipes, grandiflora, henrici, imerinensis, longipes, peyrotii, ramosa.*
**Hybridizes with:** *Aerangis, Angraecum, Jumellea, Vanda.*

Fig. 4.5. *Aeranthes grandiflora*

**Generic description:** The monopodial epiphytic plants of the genus *Aeranthes* are easy to distinguish as the leathery leaves are unequally lobed at the apex, clasp the stem, and have a joint a short distance above where they clasp. The white to green flowers are borne on axillary inflorescences. Some inflorescences are long, green, and wiry (*A. grandiflora*) and bear a single flower at a time with additional flowers blooming in succession over several weeks. Depending on species, some flowers can be up to 5 inches in diameter.
**Flowering season:** All year depending on species.
**Culture**
    **Medium:** Bark mixes or any coarse, epiphytic mix.
    **Fertilizers and fertilization:** Monthly using a balanced fertilizer.
    **Watering:** Water thoroughly and not again until dry to the touch.
    **Propagation:** Seed or tip cuttings.
    **Repotting:** When plants become too large for their containers or medium decomposes.

## Aerides

**Genus:** *Aerides* Loureiro (AIR-ih-deez)

**Tribe:** Vandeae

**Subtribe:** Aeridinae

**Etymology:** From the Greek words *aer* (air) and *eides* (resembling), often translating literally as "children of the air."

**Native habitat:** Taiwan and Philippines, west to India including Indonesia.

**Number of species:** 60

**Commonly grown species:** *crassifolia*, *crispa*, *falcata*, *flabellata*, *lawrenciae* (color plate 2), *odorata*, *quinquevulnera*, *rosea*.

**Hybridizes with:** *Arachnis*, *Ascocentrum*, *Doritis*, *Neofinetia*, *Phalaenopsis*, *Renanthera*, *Rhynchostylis*, *Trichoglottis*, *Vanda*, *Vandopsis*.

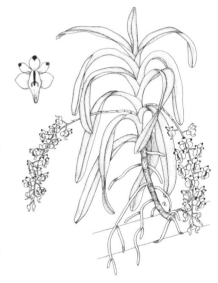

Fig. 4.6. *Aerides odorata*

**Generic description:** The mostly pendent multiflowered inflorescences on these monopodial epiphytes are adorned with mostly white and pink spurred, often fragrant (*A. odorata*) flowers. Occasionally white flowers have been found. The mostly erect stems are round and seldom thicker than a pencil. The leathery leaves, with bilobed apices, are borne in a loose fan-shaped arrangement and the plants climb by their thick aerial roots, attaching to the tree or object they are growing against.

**Flowering season:** Spring, summer, and fall.

**Culture**

    **Medium:** Tree fern or charcoal.

    **Fertilizers and fertilization:** Monthly using a balanced fertilizer.

    **Watering:** Keep medium moist.

    **Propagation:** Seed and keikis

    **Repotting:** Every two years or when it becomes too large for its container.

## Ancistrochilus

**Genus:** *Ancistrochilus* Rolfe (an-sis-tro-KYE-luss)
**Tribe:** Arethuseae
**Subtribe:** Bletiinae
**Etymology:** From the two Greek words *ankistron* (hook) and *cheilos* (lip), referring to the hooklike nature of the lip midlobe.
**Native habitat:** Africa.
**Number of species:** 2
**Commonly grown species:** *rothschildianus*.
**Hybridizes with:** None recorded.
**Generic description:** *Ancistrochilus* is a unique genus in several ways. The vegetative growth more closely resembles the Asian orchids (*Pleione*) than African species. Also, the flowers, although delicate looking, are long lasting, often for several weeks. These sympodial terrestrial plants have unusual, almost cormlike pseudobulbs topped by usually 2 lancelike soft leaves. The erect inflorescences arise from the base of the pseudobulbs and bear up to 7 lavender flowers with the midlobe of the lip being almost hooklike. The basic flower color is rose pink.
**Flowering season:** Spring.
**Culture**
  **Medium:** Most terrestrial mixes.
  **Fertilizers and fertilization:** Use a balanced fertilizer monthly.
  **Watering:** Keep medium moist during growing season.
  **Propagation:** Seed and division.
  **Repotting:** Every 2 years.

Fig. 4.8. *Ancistrochilus rothschildianus*

## Angraecum

**Genus:** *Angraecum* Bory (an-GRAY-kum)
**Tribe:** Vandeae
**Subtribe:** Angraecinae
**Etymology:** Derived from the Malayan word *angrek*, describing plants of vandaceous growth habit.
**Native habitat:** Central Africa and Madagascar.
**Number of species:** Approximately 200
**Commonly grown species:** *compactum, distichum, eburneum, erectum, germinyanum, infundibulare, leonis, magdalenae, montanum, scottianum, sesquipedale, superbum*.
**Hybridizes with:** *Aerangis, Aeranthes, Ascocentrum, Ceratocentron, Cyrtorchis, Eurychone, Neofinetia, Oeoniella, Plectrelminthus, Rhynchostylis, Sobennikoffia, Tuberolabium*.

Fig. 4.7a. *Angraecum eburneum*

**Generic description:** *Angraecum* species are known for their very distinct white to almost greenish star-shaped flowers with long spurs on the lip. *Angraecum sesquipedale* has a spur that is 12–14 inches long. These monopodial epiphytic species can vary in height among species, from 2 to 3 inches to more than 6 feet. The leaves are leathery and strap shaped in many species. The axillary inflorescences may be erect to pendent with 1 or more flowers, some up to 7 inches in diameter (*A. sesquipedale*).
**Flowering season:** Species can be in flower every month of the year.

**Culture**

Fig. 4.7b. *Angraecum sesquipedale*

    **Medium:** Tree fern or bark mixes.
    **Fertilizers and fertilization:** Monthly, apply 3-1-1 to bark mixes and 1-1-1 to tree fern.
    **Watering:** Maintain uniform moisture throughout the year.
    **Propagation:** Seed, tip cuttings, or keikis.
    **Repotting:** When plants become too large for container or medium decomposes.
**Note:** *Angraecum sesquipedale* is often called the Star of Bethlehem as the plants flower around Christmastime and the star-shaped flowers with their long spurs are likened to shooting stars.

## Ansellia

**Genus:** *Ansellia* Lindley (an-SELL-ee-uh)
**Tribe:** Cymbidieae
**Subtribe:** Cyrtopodiinae
**Etymology:** Named for John Ansell, who discovered the first plant in Niger around 1840.
**Native habitat:** Central Africa.
**Number of species:** 1
**Commonly grown species:** *africana* (color plate 3).
**Hybridizes with:** *Catasetum*, *Cycnoches*, *Cymbidium*, *Cyrtopodium*, *Galeandra*, *Graphorkis*, *Promenaea*.
**Generic description:** The highly variable flower color ranges from almost lemon yellow to heavily covered with red-brown spots that merge and almost cover the entire floral segments. This has led some taxonomists to divide the genus into three species just on the basis of flower color. These sympodial epiphytic plants have tight clusters of multinoded, reedlike pseudobulbs, up to 2 feet or more tall. The lower portion of the stem

Fig. 4.9. *Ansellia africana*

is covered with papery bracts and has 5 or more leaves near the apex. The large, branched, mostly erect, multiflowered inflorescences arise from the apex and the upper nodes. A well-grown *Ansellia* plant can be a handsome specimen.
**Flowering season:** Winter, spring, and summer.
**Culture**
    **Medium:** Bark mixes.
    **Fertilizers and fertilization:** Monthly, using a 3-1-1 fertilizer.
    **Watering:** Keep medium moist, but do not overwater.
    **Propagation:** Seed and division.
    **Repotting:** Pot in a larger container every 2–3 years to obtain a specimen plant.

## Spider or Scorpion Orchid

**Genus:** *Arachnis* Blume (uh-RAK-niss)
**Tribe:** Vandeae
**Subtribe:** Aeridinae
**Etymology:** From the Greek word *arachne* (spider), a reference to the spiderlike flowers.
**Native habitat:** Indonesia and Malay Peninsula.
**Number of species:** 15
**Commonly grown species:** *flos-aeris, hookeriana.*
**Hybridizes with:** *Acampe, Aerides, Ascocentrum, Paraphalaenopsis, Phalaenopsis, Renanthera, Rhynchostylis, Trichoglottis, Vanda, Vandopsis.*

Fig. 4.10. *Arachnis flos-aeris*

**Generic description:** *Arachnis* is closely related to *Renanthera* and *Vanda* but is readily separated by the lack of a spur on the lip and the fact that the lip is hinged. These monopodial epiphytes when well grown can attain a height of 15 feet or more. The canelike growths have alternate, clasping, leathery leaves and produce aerial roots at the nodes, usually opposite the leaf. The inflorescence, also arising from the node opposite the leaf blade, is mostly erect, to 2 feet long, and bears 6–10 spiderlike flowers that are mostly cream or yellow with brownish purple spots. The flowers are long lasting and may stay fresh for up to three weeks after cutting.
**Flowering season:** Spring, summer, fall.
**Culture**
    **Medium:** Any epiphytic mix.
    **Fertilizers and fertilization:** Monthly, with any balanced fertilizer.
    **Watering:** Water thoroughly and not again until dry to the touch.
    **Propagation:** Seed, tip cuttings, or keikis.
    **Repotting:** When the medium decomposes or plants become too tall for their containers.

## Bamboo Orchid

**Genus:** *Arundina* Blume (ar-un-DEE-nuh)

**Subtribe:** Arundinae

**Etymology:** From the Greek word *arundo* (reed), denoting the bamboo-like growth.

**Native habitat:** Southeast Asia.

**Number of species:** 1

**Commonly grown species:** *graminifolia*.

**Hybridizes with:** None recorded.

**Generic description:** *Arundina* plants form large dense clumps of bamboo-like growths topped by pale lavender *Catteya*-like flowers that have dark purple lips. These sympodial terrestrials have rigid, often 2-ranked, curved leaves that clasp the stem, making the stem almost invisible. The erect inflorescences arise from the tip of each growth and continue to elongate and branch, producing flowers for several months. Vegetative offsets often form at the base of the spent inflorescences and can be removed and potted after the little bulblike growth forms at the base of the keikis.

Fig. 4.11. *Arundina graminifolia*

**Flowering season:** All year.

**Culture**

    **Medium:** Coarse terrestrial mix.

    **Fertilizers and fertilization:** Monthly, using a 1-1-1 fertilizer.

    **Watering:** Do not let the soil dry out completely.

    **Propagation:** Seed, division, or keikis.

    **Repotting:** When plants become too large for their containers.

## Ascocentrum

**Genus:** *Ascocentrum* Schlechter (ass-koh-SEN-trum)
**Tribe:** Vandeae
**Subtribe:** Aeridinae
**Etymology:** From two Greek words *ascos* (bag) and *kentron* (spur), denoting the large floral spur.
**Native habitat:** Southeast Asia.
**Number of species:** 10
**Commonly grown species:** *ampullaceum, curvifolium, garayi* (color plate 4), *hendersonianum, miniatum.*
**Hybridizes with:** *Aerides, Angraecum, Arachnis, Doritis, Gastrochilus, Holcoglossum, Ludisia, Neofinetia, Paraphalaenopsis, Phalaenopsis, Renanthera, Trichoglottis, Vanda.*

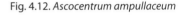

Fig. 4.12. *Ascocentrum ampullaceum*

**Generic description:** The monopodial habit of these small epiphytic plants resembles that of a small *Vanda* species. The narrow strap-shaped leaves of *A. mimiatum* are stiff and erect while those of *A. curvifolia* are soft and curved. The short inflorescences arise from leaf axils and bear many closely packed 1-inch mostly yellow or lavender flowers. The compact growth of these species makes them ideal for growers with limited space.
**Flowering season:** All year depending on species.
**Culture**
    **Medium:** Any well-aerated, epiphytic mix or plaque.
    **Fertilizers and fertilization:** Monthly, ratio depends on the medium.
    **Watering:** Maintain uniform moisture throughout the year.
    **Propagation:** Seed or keikis.
    **Repotting:** Approximately every 2–3 years.
**Note:** Several *Ascocentrum* species have been the backbone of the myriad of colorful *Ascocenda* hybrids produced since 1960 and are still very popular today.

## *Barkeria*

**Genus:** *Barkeria* Knowles & Westcott (bar-KER-ee-uh)
**Tribe:** Epidendreae
**Subtribe:** Laeliinae
**Etymology:** In honor of George Barker, who imported the first plant into England.
**Native habitat:** Mexico and Central America.
**Number of species:** 12
**Commonly grown species:** *chinensis, cyclotella, elegans, lindleyana, skinneri, spectabilis.*
**Hybridizes with:** *Brassavola, Cattleya, Diacrium, Encyclia, Epidendrum, Laelia, Leptotes, Sophronitis, Tetramicra.*
**Generic description:** This close relative of *Epidendrum* has been included by some taxonomists as a section of this genus; however, there are small taxonomic differences that separate them. *Barkeria* flower lips are not attached to the column and the reed-type growth is often swollen at the base. The leaves are clustered near the apex. The leaves of these sympodial epiphytes are

Fig. 4.13. *Barkeria lindleyana*

leathery, often recurved with wavy margins. The delicate flowers, up to 3 inches in diameter, are red, lavender, or yellow and borne on an erect terminal inflorescence.
**Flowering season:** All year depending on species.
**Culture**
    **Medium:** Tree fern or cork plaques.
    **Fertilizers and fertilization:** At least monthly using 1-1-1 fertilizer.
    **Watering:** Daily for best growth.
    **Propagation:** Seed or division.
    **Repotting:** Only after the plaque decomposes.

## Bifrenaria

**Genus:** *Bifrenaria* Lindley (bye-fren-AIR-ee-uh)
**Tribe:** Maxillarieae
**Subtribe:** Lycastinae
**Etymology:** From two Greek words *bi* (two) and *frenum* (strap), referring to the 2-stalked pollinia.
**Native habitat:** Northern and central South America.
**Number of species:** 11
**Commonly grown species:** *atropurpurea, bicornaria, harrisoniae, inodora, longicornis, minuta, tetragona, tyrianthina, vitellina.*
**Hybridizes with:** *Aganisia, Cymbidium, Lycaste, Rudolfiella.*
**Generic description:** *Bifrenaria* plants are typified by their tight clusters of ovate, 4-angled pseudobulbs, each topped by a large (up to 18 inches), leathery, lanceolate leaf. The inflorescence arises from the base of the pseudobulb and bears 1–3 flowers. The slightly spurred flowers are variable in color, ranging from yellow green to wine red. The 3-lobed lip is covered with hairs, including the yellow crest.

Fig. 4.14. *Bifrenaria harrisoniae*

**Flowering season:** Winter, spring, and summer.
**Culture**
    **Medium:** Any well-drained, epiphytic mix.
    **Fertilizers and fertilization:** Monthly, using a balanced fertilizer.
    **Watering:** Thoroughly and not again until the surface is dry.
    **Propagation:** Seed or division.
    **Repotting:** At least every 2 years after flowering.

## Bletia

**Genus:** *Bletia* Ruiz-Pavón (BLEE-tee-uh)
**Tribe:** Arethuseae
**Subtribe:** Bletiinae
**Etymology:** Named in honor of Don Luis Blet, an eighteenth-century Spanish botantist.
**Native habitat:** Florida south to Argentina, including the West Indies.
**Number of species:** 26
**Commonly grown species:** *florida*, *patula*, *purpurea*.
**Hybridizes with:** *Chysis*, *Spathoglottis*.
**Generic description:** *Bletia* species have pseudobulbs that are almost cormlike. Each pseudobulb of this sympodial terrestrial is topped by one or more, long (up to 36 inches), soft, lanceolate-like, deciduous leaves. The erect (sometimes lax) inflorescence arises from the base of the pseudobulb and may be up to 40 inches tall, although heights of 80 inches have been reported in literature. Each many-flowered inflorescence has its showy flowers clustered near the apex. The basic flower colors are red, purple, and pink.
**Flowering season:** Spring and summer.
**Culture**
    **Medium:** Any well-drained, terrestrial mix.
    **Fertilizers and fertilization:** Monthly during growing season with 1-1-1.
    **Watering:** Keep medium moist during growing season, reduce watering when dormant.
    **Propagation:** Seed.
    **Repotting:** Every 2–3 years.

Fig. 4.15. *Bletia purpurea*

## Bletilla

**Genus:** *Bletilla* Reichenbach f. (bleh-TILL-uh)
**Tribe:** Arethuseae
**Subtribe:** Bletiinae
**Etymology:** The diminutive form of *Bletia*, due to their close resemblance.
**Native habitat:** Southern Japan and eastern China.
**Number of species:** 6
**Commonly grown species:** *striata*.
**Hybridizes with:** None recorded.
**Generic description:** *Bletilla* comprises one species, *B. striata*, one of a very few orchids sold as garden perennials. This small genus of sympodial terrestrial orchids is typified by underground, cormlike structures that are produced every year. As the new leaves develop in early spring, the inflorescence develops in the center of the unfolding leaves and flowers before the deciduous leaves mature. Each growth has 3 or more soft, pleated leaves, whose bases clasp the stem. The 2-inch flowers are either lavender, yellow, or white.
**Flowering season:** Spring.
**Culture**

Fig. 4.16a. *Bletilla striata*

   **Medium:** A well-drained terrestrial mix.
   **Fertilizers and fertilization:** Monthly, using a 1-1-1 fertilizer.
   **Watering:** Keep medium moist during the growing season, reduce watering when dormant.
   **Propagation:** Cormlike growths or seed.
   **Repotting:** When plants become too crowded in their containers.

## Bollea

**Genus:** *Bollea* Reichenbach f. (BOH-lee-uh)
**Tribe:** Maxillarieae
**Subtribe:** Zygopetalinae
**Etymology:** Named in honor of the German botanist Carl Boll.
**Native habitat:** Northern South America (Colombia to Guyana).
**Number of species:** 6
**Commonly grown species:** *coelestis* (color plate 5), *lawnenceana*, *violacea*.
**Hybridizes with:** *Aganisia*, *Chondrorhyncha*, *Cochleanthes*, *Kefersteinia*, *Pescatoria*, *Zygopetalum*.
**Generic description:** Reichenbach established the genus in 1852, removing plants from *Huntleya*. Although closely related to *Huntleya* and *Pescatoria*, *Bollea* is easily separated by the hooded column. These sympodial epiphytes

Fig. 4.16b. *Bollea violacea*

have fans of 6–10 leaves. The lanceolate leaves, up to 12 inches long, are long lasting and most plants contain several fans. The single-flowered inflorescences, one to several per fan, arise from the lower leaf axils. The flowers, up to 4 inches in diameter, are borne close to the base of the fan and may be reddish purple, bluish purple, or white.
**Flowering season:** Spring, summer, and fall.
**Culture**
    **Medium:** Most good epiphytic mixes.
    **Fertilizers and fertilization:** Monthly, use a balanced fertilizer.
    **Watering:** Keep medium moist all year.
    **Propagation:** Seed or division.
    **Repotting:** Every 2 to 3 years.

## Bonatea

**Genus:** *Bonatea* Willdenow (boh-NAH-tee-uh)
**Tribe:** Orchideae
**Subtribe:** Habenariinae
**Etymology:** Named in honor of M. Bonat, an Italian professor of botany.
**Native habitat:** Tropical and South Africa, also found in North Yemen.
**Number of species:** 10
**Commonly grown species:** *antennifera, speciosa.*
**Hybridizes with:** None recorded.
**Generic description:** The picturesque, green and white flowers of *Bonatea* species are similar to *Habenaria*, but are easily separated by different floral characteristics. Like typical herbaceous perennials, *Bonatea* species are dormant for 4–6 months. These large, sympodial, terrestrial plants have fleshy, elongated tubers that sustain the plants during dormancy. In spring, the erect, leafy stems emerge. The thin leaves, at first measuring 2 x 6 inches, decrease in size as the stem elongates, becoming almost bract-like below the flowers. The terminal inflorescence has a cluster of large flowers at the apex. Individual plants when in flower may be up to 40 inches tall.

Fig. 4.17. *Bonatea speciosa*

**Flowering season:** Spring and summer.
**Culture**
    **Medium:** Coarse sand for best growth.
    **Fertilizers and fertilization:** Monthly during growing season using a 1-1-1.
    **Watering:** Keep medium moist during growing season, do not water dormant plants until new growth begins in spring.
    **Propagation:** Seed or division.
    **Repotting:** Every 2–3 years.

## Brassavola

**Genus:** *Brassavola* R. Brown (bra-suh-VOH-luh)
**Tribe:** Epidendreae
**Subtribe:** Laeliinae
**Etymology:** Named for a Venetian botanist, Antonio Musa Brassavole.
**Native habitat:** Mexico south through tropical South America.
**Number of species:** 15
**Commonly grown species:** *acualis*, *cordata* (color plate 6), *cucullata*, *martiana*, *nodosa*.
**Hybridizes with:** *Barkeria*, *Broughtonia*, *Cattleya*, *Diacrium*, *Encyclia*, *Epidendrum*, *Laelia*, *Schomburgkia*, *Sophronitis*.
**Generic description:** The narrow, stemlike pseudobulbs, each topped by a single, terete leaf, make *Brassavola* species easy to identify. The inflorescences arise from the apex of the pseudobulb on these sympodial epiphytes, and

Fig. 4.18. *Brassavola cordata*

bear up to 12 long-lasting, very fragrant flowers. The fragrance is nocturnal. The white to creamy green flowers have narrow sepals and petals with very distinct, large, white lips. The lip margin may be entire or fringed.
**Flowering season:** All year depending on species.
**Culture**
    **Medium:** Plaques or any well-drained, epiphytic mix or mounted.
    **Fertilizers and fertilization:** Monthly, ratio depends on media.
    **Watering:** Do not let the medium dry out excessively.
    **Propagation:** Seed, division, or meristems
    **Repotting:** Every 2 years or when the medium decomposes.
**Note:** *Brassavola nodosa* is known as Lady of the Night because of its powerful nocturnal fragrance.

## Brassia

**Genus:** *Brassia* R. Brown (BRASS-ee-uh)
**Tribe:** Maxillarieae
**Subtribe:** Oncidiinae
**Etymology:** Named for William Brass, a British botanical enthusiast.
**Native habitat:** South Florida and Cuba, south to Venezuela.
**Number of species:** 30
**Commonly grown species:** *arcuigera, caudata, gireoudiana, lanceana, maculata, pumila* (color plate 7), *verrucosa*.
**Hybridizes with:** *Ada, Aspasia, Cattleya, Cochlioda, Miltonia, Odontoglossum, Oncidium*.
**Generic description:** The long, at-

Fig. 4.19. *Brassia verrucosa*

tenuated sepals and petals are the hallmark of *Brassia* species. The pale, yellow-green flowers with their varying degrees of brownish red spotting may be as much as 21 inches in diameter. These sympodial epiphytes have flattened pseudobulbs, each topped by up to three leathery leaves and subtended by one or more leafy bracts. The inflorescences, bearing up to 12 flowers, arise from the base of the pseudobulb.
**Flowering season:** All year depending on species.
**Culture**
    **Medium:** Plaque or bark mixes.
    **Fertilizers and fertilization:** Monthly using a balanced fertilizer.
    **Watering:** Frequency depends on medium; water plaques daily for best growth.
    **Propagation:** Seed and division.
    **Repotting:** Every 2–3 years or when the plaque decomposes.

## Bulbophyllum

**Genus:** *Bulbophyllum* Thouars (bul-boh-FILL-um)
**Tribe:** Dendrobieae
**Subtribe:** Bulbophyllinae
**Etymology:** From two Greek words *bulbus* (bulb) and *phyllon* (leaf), denoting the pseudobulb with a single leaf found throughout this genus.
**Native habitat:** Worldwide in the Tropics.
**Number of species:** Approximately 1,100
**Commonly grown species:** *bandischii, barbigerum, coccinium, craveolens, falcatum, grandiflorum, lepidum, lobbii, medusae* (color plate 8), *phalaenopsis, polystictum* (color plate 9), *rothchildianum, umbellatum, wendlandianum.*

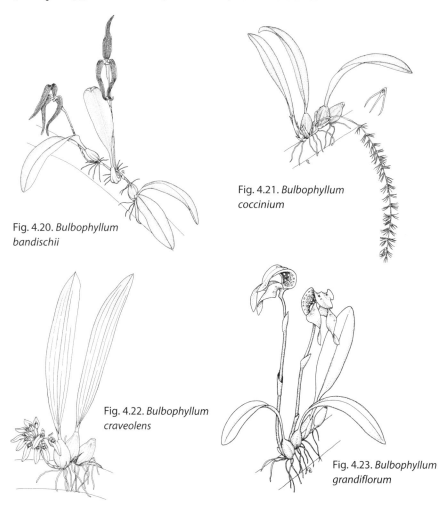

Fig. 4.20. *Bulbophyllum bandischii*

Fig. 4.21. *Bulbophyllum coccinium*

Fig. 4.22. *Bulbophyllum craveolens*

Fig. 4.23. *Bulbophyllum grandiflorum*

Fig. 4.24. *Bulbophyllum wendlandianum*          Fig. 4.25. *Bulbophyllum lepidum*

**Hybridizes with:** *Cirrhopetalum, Mastigion, Trias.*

**Generic description:** There is great variation in this genus of sympodial epiphytes in both vegetative and floral characteristics. The pseudobulbs, usually containing one leaf, vary in size and shape and may be closely spaced or some distance apart along the rhizome. The leaves, some thick and leathery, range from 0.5 inches to more than 40 inches long. The inflorescences and flowers are also highly variable among the species, with many having interesting and unusual configurations (see illustrations). Many flowers have a strong fetid odor (*B. phalaenopsis*).

**Flowering season:** Varies among species, but can be found in bloom every month.

**Culture**

> **Medium:** Sphagnum moss, tree fern, cork plaques or any epiphytic medium.
>
> **Fertilizers and fertilization:** Monthly, depending on medium. Use a balanced fertilizer on sphagnum moss and plaques and a 3-1-1 on media containing mostly bark.
>
> **Watering:** Water thoroughly and not again until dry to the touch. Frequency will depend on the container used and the medium in the container.
>
> **Propagation:** Seed, division, or meristems.
>
> **Repotting:** When the plants outgrow their containers or plaques decompose.

## Calanthe

**Genus:** *Calanthe* R. Brown (kal-ANN-thee).
**Tribe:** Arethuseae
**Subtribe:** Bletiinae
**Etymology:** From two Greek words *kalos* (beautiful) and *anthe* (flower), to denote the showy flowers.
**Native habitat:** Africa, Southeast Asia, and Central America.
**Number of species:** 150
**Commonly grown species:** *biloba, discolor, masuca, rosea, rubens, triplicata, vestita.*
**Hybridizes with:** *Phaius.*

Fig. 4.26. *Calanthe triplicata*

**Generic description:** *Calanthe* species flowers are all very similar, but there are two distinctive vegetative growths in this sympodial, terrestrial genus. The evergreen group (*C. masuca*) has small cormlike pseudobulbs, while the deciduous group (*C. rosea*) has large angular pseudobulbs sometimes constricted at the midpoint. Each pseudobulb is topped by several soft, pleated leaves that may be up to 3 feet long. The erect inflorescence arises from the base of the pseudobulb and bears up to 20 mauve, red, or white flowers.
**Flowering season:** All year depending on species.
**Culture**
  **Medium:** One part peat moss, one part perlite, and one part soil.
  **Fertilizers and fertilization:** Monthly during growing season using a 1-1-1.
  **Watering:** Keep medium moist especially during growing season.
  **Propagation:** Seed, division, or meristems.
  **Repotting:** At least every 2–3 years.

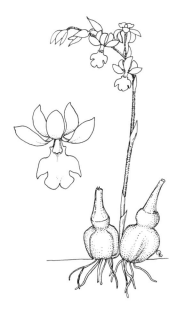

Fig. 4.27. *Calanthe vestita*

**Note:** *Calanthe* was the first orchid to be hybridized by humans. J. Dominy in the 1850s crossed *C. masuca* × *C. furcata* (*triplicata*) to produce *C.* Dominy, which flowered in 1856.

## Calopogon

**Genus:** *Calopogon* R. Brown (kal-oh-POH-gon)
**Tribe:** Arethuseae
**Subtribe:** Bletiinae
**Etymology:** In Greek this name signifies a beautiful (*kalos*) beard (*pugon*), a reference to the hairy lip.
**Native habitat:** Eastern United States and Canada.
**Number of species:** 5
**Commonly grown species:** *pallidus, tuberosus.*
**Hybridizes with:** *Arethusa, Eleorchis.*
**Generic description:** Calopogons, like the spring migration of the robins, are the heralds of spring when their colorful flowers arise above the grasses in meadows and along roadsides. These sympodial, terrestrial plants have underground, cormlike structures that are renewed and produce one set of grasslike leaves annually. The terminal inflorescence, up to 30 inches tall, bears from a few to as many as 25 nonresupinate (upside down) flowers in shades of rose pink and white.
**Flowering season:** Spring and summer.
**Culture**
　**Medium:** Any rich, organic, terrestrial mix.
　**Fertilizers and fertilization:** Once or twice during the growing season using a 1-1-1.
　**Watering:** Keep medium moist at all times.
　**Propagation:** Seed.
　**Repotting:** Approximately every 3 years.

Fig. 4.28. *Calopogon tuberosus*

## Catasetum

**Genus:** *Catasetum* L. C. Richard *ex* Kunth (kat-uh-SEE-tum)
**Tribe:** Cymbidieae
**Subtribe:** Catasetinae
**Etymology:** From two Greek words *kata* (down) and *seta* (bristle), to describe the antenna-like projections on the column of the male flower.
**Native habitat:** Cuba and Mexico, south to southern Brazil.
**Number of species:** 50
**Commonly grown species:** *barbatum, discolor, expansum, fimbriatum, integerrimum, longifolium, maculatum, pileatum* (color plate 10), *saccatum, viridiflavum.*

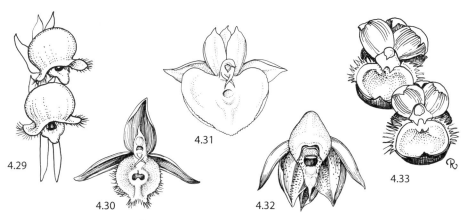

Fig. 4.29. *Catasetum discolor* ♀; Fig. 4.30. *Catasetum saccatum* ♂; Fig. 4.31. *Catasetum pileatum* ♂; Fig. 4.32. *Catasetum maculatum* ♀; Fig. 4.33. *Catasetum longifolium* ♀

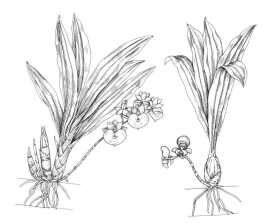

Fig. 4.34. *Catasetum expansum* ♂ and *Catasetum expansum* ♀

**Hybridizes with:** *Cycnoches, Cymbidium, Galeandra, Mormodes.*

**Generic description:** The flowers of *Catasetum* are not only highly variable, but also dimorphic, making the genus quite interesting to grow. These sympodial epiphytes are sometimes found growing in small pockets of organic matter on the ground just like terrestrials. Up to 7 deciduous soft pleated leaves with clasping bases hide the conical pseudobulbs. The inflorescence arises from the base or lower leaf axils and bears 3 or more flowers. The male flowers are borne in larger numbers and come in a wide range of colors. The female flowers are green and fleshy, with an urn-shaped lip. Flowers of both sexes are borne on the same plant but on different inflorescences.

**Flowering season:** All year depending on species.

**Culture**

    **Medium:** Any proven mix for epiphytes. Grows well on palm trees and fence posts.

    **Fertilizers and fertilization:** Monthly during the growing season, ratio depends on the medium.

    **Watering:** Keep medium moist during growing season.

    **Propagation:** Seed, division, and meristems.

    **Repotting:** At least every 2 years.

**Note:** Catasetums have an unusual pollinating system. When the insect enters the flower it triggers a mechanism that shoots the pollinarium at the forehead of the insect, ensuring its removal when the insect departs. *Catasetum pileatum* is the national flower of Venezuela. It has been reported that high light levels tend to induce the production of female flowers while male flowers tend to be more plentiful at very low light levels.

## Cattleya

**Genus:** *Cattleya* Lindley (KAT-lee-uh)
**Tribe:** Epidendreae
**Subtribe:** Laeliinae
**Etymology:** Named for William Cattley, who flowered the first *Cattleya* plant in England.
**Native habitat:** Mexico south to southern Brazil.
**Number of species:** 65
**Commonly grown species:** *amethystoglossa, aurantiaca, bicolor, dowiana, forbeii, harrisoniana* (color plate 11), *intermedia, labiata, loddigesii, luteola, maxima, mossiae, nobilior, percivaliana* (color plate 12), *trianaei, violacea, walkeriana, warscewiczii.*
**Hybridizes with:** *Barkeria, Brassavola, Broughtonia, Caularthron, Encyclia, Epidendrum, Laelia, Leptotes, Myrmecophila, Rhyncholaelia, Sophronitis.*
**Generic description:** These epiphytic, sympodial plants have two distinct vegetative growth habits. The unifoliate species *(C. mossiae)* have 1 large, leathery leaf at the apex of the pseudobulb and bears 1–5 large flowers. Flower colors are basically lavender, white, or yellow. The bifoliate species *(C. violacea)* have 1–3 smaller leathery leaves atop usually more reedlike pseudobulbs and bear 1–15 smaller flowers in similar colors. Both vegetative forms have erect, terminal inflorescences.
**Flowering season:** All year depending on species.
**Culture**
    **Medium:** Any well-drained, epiphytic mix.
    **Fertilizers and fertilization:** Monthly, ratio depends on medium.
    **Watering:** Water thoroughly and then not again until the surface of the medium is dry to the touch. Frequency will depend on the container used and the medium.
    **Propagation:** Seed, division, or meristems.
    **Repotting:** Every 2 years or when the rhizome grows over the rim of the container.

Fig. 4.35. *Cattleya percivaliana*

Fig. 4.36. *Cattleya violacea*

## Caularthron

**Genus:** *Caularthron* Rafinesque (call-ARR-thron)
**Tribe:** Epidendreae
**Subtribe:** Laeliinae
**Etymology:** From two Greek words *kaulos* (stem) and *arthron* (joint), referring to the persistent leaf bases.
**Native habitat:** Costa Rica south to northern Brazil.
**Number of species:** 6
**Commonly grown species:** *bicornutum* (color plate 13), *bilamellatum.*
**Hybridizes with:** *Laelia, Sophronitis.*
**Generic description:** These interesting sympodial epiphytic plants have hollow pseudobulbs and are often found in the wild growing in ant nests. The tightly clustered pseudobulbs have 3 leaves near the apex and up to 4 persistent bracts. The erect inflorescence arises from the apex of the pseudobulb and bears up to 12 white flowers measuring 3 inches across. The 3-lobed white lip is speckled with purplish dots.
**Flowering season:** Spring.
**Culture**
  **Medium:** Equal volumes of peat moss and perlite or any bark mix.
  **Fertilizers and fertilization:** Monthly, ratio depends on the medium.
  **Watering:** Do not let medium dry out excessively.
  **Propagation:** Seed or division.
  **Repotting:** When the plant becomes too large for the container or the medium decomposes.

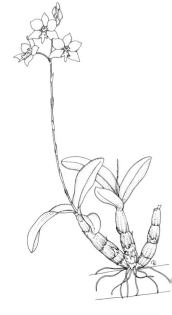

Fig. 4.37. *Caularthron bicornutum*

## Chiloschista

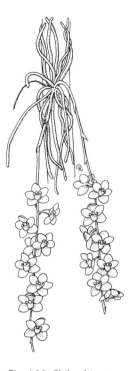

**Genus:** *Chiloschista* Lindley (ki-loh-SHIS-tuh)
**Tribe:** Vandeae
**Subtribe:** Aeridinae
**Etymology:** From two Greek words *cheilos* (lip) and *schistos* (cleft), to denote the cleft lip on the flower.
**Native habitat:** Southeast Asia.
**Number of species:** 7
**Commonly grown species:** *lunifera, usneoides.*
**Hybridizes with:** None recorded.
**Generic description:** For the major portion of the year, plants of this monopodial epiphyte are composed of a mass of roots that wrap around whatever supports it. Occasionally 2–4 very short-lived leaves arise from the small crown in the midst of the roots. In early spring, 1 or more pendent inflorescences arise from the crown and bear from a few to many flowers. The very attractive, small (0.5 inch) flowers vary in color from creamy white to greenish yellow to reddish brown.
**Flowering season:** Spring.
**Culture**

Fig. 4.38. *Chiloschista usneoides*

    **Medium:** Mount on tree fern plaques or tree limbs, or place in a small clay pot with no medium.
    **Fertilizers and fertilization:** At least monthly with a weak, balanced fertilizer.
    **Watering:** Daily for best growth.
    **Propagation:** Seed.
    **Repotting:** Only when the plaque decomposes.

## Chondrorhyncha

**Genus:** *Chondrorhyncha* Lindley (con-dro-RINK-uh)
**Tribe:** Maxillarieae
**Subtribe:** Zygopetalinae
**Etymology:** From two Greek words *chondros* (cartilege) and *rhynchos* (beak or snout), denoting the beaklike rostellum found in these flowers.
**Native habitat:** Mexico, Central America, and tropical South America.
**Number of species:** 35
**Commonly grown species:** *bicolor*, *flaveola*, *lendyana*, *reichenbachiana*, *rosea*.
**Hybridizes with:** *Cochleanthes*.
**Generic description:** There has always been confusion between *Chondrorhyncha* and *Cochleanthes*, with the same plant being sold under both names. However, they are readily separated on the basis of floral characteristics. *Chondrorhyncha* has a long column foot and basal callus on the lip while *Cochleanthes* has a short claw on the column base and a lunate callus on the lip. Vegetatively, these sympodial epiphytes consist of loosely arranged leaves in fanlike forms. The 4–5 soft leaves, up to 12 inches long, have clasping leaf bases and wavy margins. The single-flowered inflorescence arises from the leaf axil. The 1–1.5-inch flowers are white to ivory to light yellow. The lip may be darker and have varying degrees of reddish to dark brown markings.
**Flowering season:** Spring, summer, and fall.
**Culture**
  **Medium:** Any proven epiphytic mix.
  **Fertilizers and fertilization:** Monthly, ratio depends on medium.
  **Watering:** Water thoroughly and not again until medium is dry to the touch.
  **Propagation:** Seed or division.
  **Repotting:** Every 2–3 years.

Fig. 4.39. *Chondrorhyncha reichenbachiana*

## Chysis

**Genus:** *Chysis* Lindley (KYE-siss)
**Tribe:** Arethuseae
**Subtribe:** Chysinae
**Etymology:** From the Greek *chysis* (melt), denoting the fusion of the pollinia upon self-pollination.
**Native habitat:** Mexico to Venezuela.
**Number of species:** 3
**Commonly grown species:** *aurea, bractescens* (color plate 14), *laevis.*
**Hybridizes with:** *Bletia.*
**Generic description:** This small genus of sympodial epiphytes has several very unique growth habits, making it an interesting subject for hobbyists. The 12-inch-long, cigar-shaped, pendent pseudobulbs are topped by 5

Fig. 4.40. *Chysis bractescens*

or more soft, pleated deciduous leaves to 18 inches long. The bases of the pseudobulbs are covered by papery bracts. The inflorescence arises from the base of the newly emerging growth and finishes blooming before the growth matures. The long-lived 3-inch flowers are white, cream, or yellowish with various amounts of pink or brown marking.
**Flowering season:** Spring and summer.
**Culture**
    **Medium:** Any coarse, well-drained, epiphytic mix.
    **Fertilizers and fertilization:** Monthly, ratio depends on medium.
    **Watering:** Keep medium moist during growing season, reduce water when deciduous.
    **Propagation:** Seed or division.
    **Repotting:** Only when the medium decomposes.

## Clowesia

**Genus:** *Clowesia* Lindley (klo-EES-ee-uh)
**Tribe:** Cymbidieae
**Subtribe:** Catasetinae
**Etymology:** Named in honor of Reverend Clowes, an English horticulturist who first flowered this genus.
**Native habitat:** Mexico south to Venezuela and Colombia.
**Number of species:** 5
**Commonly grown species:** *rosea, russelliana, warscewiczii.*
**Hybridizes with:** *Cycnochoes, Cymbidium, Mormodes.*
**Generic description:** At first glance *Clowesia* plants look like *Catasetum* vegetatively, but they

Fig. 4.41. *Clowesia russelliana*

are easily separated by floral characteristics. *Clowesia* has bisexual flowers and a different method of pollination. These sympodial epiphytes have tightly clustered, several-noded pseudobulbs with up to 5 soft, pleated deciduous leaves that ensheathe pseudobulbs. The ensheathing portions remain and become papery after leaf blades fall off. The pendent, multiflowered (up to 25) inflorescences arise from the base of the pseudobulb. The 2.5-inch flowers may be green or rose.
**Flowering season:** Summer, fall, and winter.
**Culture**
    **Medium:** Any coarse epiphytic mix.
    **Fertilizers and fertilization:** Monthly during the growing season, ratio depends on the medium.
    **Watering:** Keep medium moist during the growing season.
    **Propagation:** Seed or division.
    **Repotting:** Infrequently or when the medium decomposes.

## Cochleanthes

**Genus:** *Cochleanthes* Rafinesque (kock-lee-ANN-theez)
**Tribe:** Maxillarieae
**Subtribe:** Zygopetalinae
**Etymology:** From two Greek words *kochlias* (shell) and *anthos* (flower), denoting the shell-like character of some flowers.
**Native habitat:** Cuba and Mexico south to southern Brazil.
**Number of species:** 12
**Commonly grown species:** *amazonica, aromatica, discolor, flabelliformis, marginata* (color plate 15).
**Hybridizes with:** *Aganisia, Bollea, Chondrorhyncha, Colax, Huntleya, Lycaste, Pescatoria, Promenaea, Stenia, Zygopetalum, Zygosepalum.*

Fig. 4.42. *Cochleanthes discolor*

**Generic description:** *Cochleanthes* is very similar to *Chondrorhyncha*, but the two are easily separated by floral characteristic. Although easy to grow, this plant has one small disadvantage in that it forms large clumps and flowers may be concealed among the leaves. These sympodial epiphytes lack pseudobulbs, hence each lateral growth will have approximately 6–8 soft, elongated, lanceolate leaves (up to 10 inches) with basal joints. The upright, sometimes lax inflorescence arises from the axil of a leaf. Each naked flower spike is topped by a single flower. Each 2-inch flower is subtended by a papery bract and is basically whitish to creamy yellow with lips and other floral segments adorned with various degrees of purple markings.
**Flowering season:** Spring, summer, and fall.
**Culture**
    **Medium:** Any proven epiphytic mix.
    **Fertilizers and fertilization:** Monthly, ratio depends on medium.
    **Watering:** Keep medium moist at all times for best growth.
    **Propagation:** Seed or division.
    **Repotting:** Every 2–3 years.

## Cochlioda

**Genus:** *Cochlioda* Lindley (kok-lee-OH-duh)
**Tribe:** Maxillarieae
**Subtribe:** Oncidiinae
**Etymology:** From the Greek word *kochlioides* (spiral or snail shell), to denote the snail-like callus tissue on the lip.
**Native habitat:** Peru, Bolivia, Equador, and western Brazil.
**Number of species:** 5
**Commonly grown species:** *noezliana, rosea, vulcanica.*
**Hybridizes with:** *Ada, Aspasia, Brassia, Gomesa, Miltonia, Odontoglossum, Oncidium.*

Fig. 4.43. *Cochlioda rosea*

**Generic description:** The delicate flowers carried above the foliage are an attractive feature of these cool-growing plants. Vegetatively, *Cochlioda* species, with their tight clusters of ovoid pseudobulbs each topped by 1 or 2 leaves, resemble *Oncidium* plants. The leaves on these sympodial epiphytes may be up to 10 inches long, lanceolate, and often folded at the base. Each erect or sometimes pendent inflorescence arises from the base of a pseudobulb and bears from a few to many 2-inch scarlet or magenta flowers.
**Flowering season:** All year depending on species.
**Culture**
    **Medium:** Any proven epiphytic mix.
    **Fertilizers and fertilization:** Monthly, ratio depends on medium.
    **Watering:** Keep medium moist for best growth.
    **Propagation:** Seed or division.
    **Repotting:** Every 2–3 years.

## Coelia

**Genus:** *Coelia* Lindley (SEE-lee-uh)
**Tribe:** Epidendreae
**Subtribe:** Coeliinae
**Etymology:** From the Greek word *koilos* (hollow), referring to a condition of the pollinia that was later determined to be nothing more than an artifact in the original illustration.
**Native habitat:** Mexico to Guatemala and West Indies.
**Number of species:** 1
**Commonly grown species:** *triptera*.
**Hybridizes with:** None recorded.

Fig. 4.44. *Coelia triptera*

**Generic description:** This monotypic genus of sympodial epiphytes has its single-noded pseudobulbs tightly clustered. Each pseudobulb is topped by up to 5 linear-lanceolate leaves up to 30 inches long. The short, erect or sometimes lax inflorescence arises from the base of the pseudobulb and has a number of bracts at the base. Each inflorescence will have several to many flowers, usually tightly arranged. Each flower is subtended by a prominent bract that is longer than the flower. The white flowers have a strong scent.
**Flowering season:** Spring and summer.
**Culture**
    **Medium:** Any well-drained epiphytic mix.
    **Fertilizers and fertilization:** Monthly, ratio depends on medium.
    **Watering:** Keep medium moist at all times.
    **Propagation:** Seed or division.
    **Repotting:** Every 2–3 years.

## Coelogyne

**Genus:** *Coelogyne* Lindley (see-LOJ-in-ee)
**Tribe:** Coelogyneae
**Subtribe:** Coelogyninae
**Etymology:** From two Greek words *koilos* (hollow) and *gyne* (female), describing the hollow stigmatic area on the column.
**Native habitat:** India east to Borneo.
**Number of species:** Approximately 125
**Commonly grown species:** *asperata, cristata, fimbriata, lactea, massangeana, nervosa, pandurata, speciosa, tomentosa.*
**Hybridizes with:** None recorded.
**Generic description:** Although this popular genus consists mostly of sympodial epiphytes, there are also a few terrestrials. Species vary in size and arrangement of the pseudobulbs on the rhizome. The somewhat flattened, usually medium green pseudobulbs are usually topped by 2 either soft and pleated or thick and leathery leaves. The inflorescences arise from the apex of the newly developing growth. Depending on species, flowers may be up to 5 inches across. The basic flower color is white or greenish white with yellow or darker-colored markings that are almost black on the lip of *C. asperata.*

Fig. 4.45. *Coelogyne asperata*

**Flowering season:** All year depending on species.
**Culture**

    **Medium:** Tree fern mix, peat and perlite, bark mix, or terrestrial mix.
    **Fertilizers and fertilization:** Monthly, ratio depends on the medium.
    **Watering:** Do not allow medium to dry out excessively.
    **Propagation:** Seed or division.
    **Repotting:** At least every 2 years.

Fig. 4.46. *Coelogyne tomentosa*

## Comparettia

**Genus:** *Comparettia* Poeppig & Endlicher (kom-puh-RET-ee-uh)
**Tribe:** Maxillarieae
**Subtribe:** Oncidiinae
**Etymology:** Named in honor of the well-known plant physiologist Andreas Comparetti, working at Padua.
**Native habitat:** Mexico south to Brazil.
**Number of species:** 12
**Commonly grown species:** *coccinea, falcata, macroplectron, speciosa.*
**Hybridizes with:** *Ada, Gomesa, Ionopsis, Miltonia, Odontoglossum, Oncidium, Rodriguezia.*

Fig. 4.47. *Comparettia macroplectron*

**Generic description:** The showy, delicate flowers of these species are very deceiving, appearing to have 1 spur attached to the lip, when actually there are 3, with 2 inserted inside the outer spur. These sympodial epiphytes have narrow, almost pencil-like pseudobulbs covered by papery bracts and topped by 1 to 3 leathery leaves. The bracts are often shed at maturity. The inflorescences arise from the base of the pseudobulbs and bear 5–7 flowers. The 1-inch flowers are red, orange, or purple and may have magenta or white spots.
**Flowering season:** Summer, fall, and winter.
**Culture**
    **Medium:** Fir bark or a 1:1 mix of peat and perlite.
    **Fertilizers and fertilization:** Monthly, ratio depending on medium.
    **Watering:** Keep medium moist at all times for best growth.
    **Propagation:** Seed or division.
    **Repotting:** Every 2 years.

## Bucket Orchid

**Genus:** *Coryanthes* Hooker (kor-ee-ANN-theez)
**Tribe:** Maxillarieae
**Subtribe:** Stanhopeinae
**Etymology:** From two Greek words *korys* (helmet) and *anthos* (flower), denoting the helmet-like hypochile of the lip.
**Native habitat:** Mexico to southern Brazil.
**Number of species:** 15
**Commonly grown species:** *biflora*, *macrantha* (color plate 16), *maculata*, *speciosa*.
**Hybridizes with:** *Stanhopea*.
**Generic description:** Many consider *Coryanthes* flowers to be the most unique in the orchid family. The "bucket" is a portion of the lip that is filled with a watery substance from two glands. The pollinator must swim through this to pollinate the flower. These sympodial epiphytes are often found growing in ant nests in the wild. They have clusters of grooved pseudobulbs that resemble those of *Gongora*, and

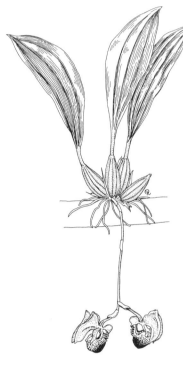

Fig. 4.48. *Coryanthes macrantha*

are topped by 2 large soft pleated leaves. The pendent inflorescence arises from the base of the pseudobulb and bears 2 large, fragrant flowers measuring 5 inches across. The flower color varies, often being cream colored with varying degrees of reddish markings.
**Flowering season:** All year depending on species.
**Culture**
    **Medium:** Grow in a basket in any epiphytic mix.
    **Fertilizers and fertilization:** Monthly, ratio depends on medium.
    **Watering:** Keep medium moist at all times.
    **Propagation:** Seed or division.
    **Repotting:** Every 3–5 years or when the medium or basket decomposes.

## Corybas

**Genus:** *Corybas* Salisbury (CORE-ee-bus)
**Tribe:** Diurideae
**Subtribe:** Acianthinae
**Etymology:** From the Greek word *Korybas*, a priest of the goddess Cybele, or a drunken man, a reference to the unique flowers.
**Native habitat:** Southeast Asia west to the Himalayas and south to Australia, including Pacific Islands.
**Number of species:** 100
**Commonly grown species:** *aconitiflorus, fimbratus, pruinosus.*
**Hybridizes with:** None recorded.

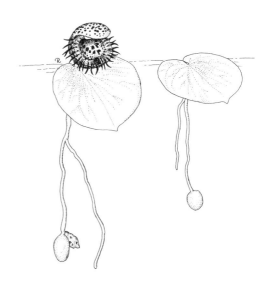

Fig. 4.49. *Corybas fimbriatus*

**Generic description:** *Corybas* species are attractive not only for their unique flowers, but also for the variegated leaves in some species. These sympodial, terrestrial, herbaceous plants can form large colonies. The deciduous, mostly heart-shaped leaves are often prostrate on the soil and may be green or variegated with white or red veins. The solitary flower is borne on a very short inflorescence and usually rests on the leaf blade. At first glance, all that is seen of the flower is the hooded, dorsal sepal and the large lip, which obscure the other floral segments. Flower color varies among species.
**Flowering season:** Spring and summer.
**Culture**
> **Medium:** Forest litter or a mix of soil, partially decayed leaves, and wood shavings.
> **Fertilizers and fertilization:** Monthly during the growing season using 1-1-1.
> **Watering:** Keep medium moist during growing season, reduce water during dormancy.
> **Propagation:** Seed or division.
> **Repotting:** Every 2–3 years.

## Swan Orchid

**Genus:** *Cycnoches* Lindley (sik-NOH-cheez)
**Tribe:** Cymbidieae
**Subtribe:** Catasetinae
**Etymology:** From two Greek words *kyknos* (swan) and *auchen* (neck), denoting the unique arrangement of the lip and column in these flowers, which resemble swans.
**Native habitat:** Mexico to southern Brazil.
**Number of species:** 12
**Commonly grown species:** *chlorochilon, egertonianum, loddigesii, ventricosum, warscewiczii.*
**Hybridizes with:** *Ansellia, Catasetum, Galeandra, Mormodes.*
**Generic description:** Early taxonomists, unfamiliar with the dissimilar male and female flowers on separate plants, named them as different species. Even today there is some

Fig. 4.50. *Cycnoches chlorochilon*

confusion regarding the species in this genus. Vegetatively, *Cycnoches* species are similar. The large (18-inch) club-shaped pseudobulbs of these sympodial epiphytes may have a few or many large (18-inch), soft, pleated, deciduous leaves. The leafless pseudobulbs are green and covered with papery bracts. The often curved inflorescence develops from an upper node and bears few to many flowers. The large flowers, up to 7 inches across, come in a variety of colors, with the base color greenish or yellowish.
**Flowering season:** All year depending on species.
**Culture**
> **Medium:** Any well-drained epiphytic mix.
> **Fertilizers and fertilization:** Monthly during growing season.
> **Watering:** Keep medium moist when plants are in active growth, reduce watering when dormant.
> **Propagation:** Seed or division.
> **Repotting:** At least every 2 years, some growers repot annually.

## Cymbidiella

**Genus:** *Cymbidiella* Rolfe (sym-bid-ee-ELL-uh)
**Tribe:** Cymbidieae
**Subtribe:** Cyrtopodiinae
**Etymology:** The name is the diminutive form of *Cymbidium* based on resemblances between the two genera.
**Native habitat:** Madagascar.
**Number of species:** 3
**Commonly grown species:** *falcigera, flabellata, pardalina.*
**Hybridizes with:** *Eulophiella, Graphorkis.*
**Generic description:** This small Madagascar genus is unique not only when it comes to host plants (see note), but also for its spectacular flowers. The showy green flowers, with almost black spotted petals and a brilliant red lip, are a sight to behold. Vegetatively, these sympodial epiphytes are similar to *Cymbidium* except for their narrower and taller pseudobulbs. Each pseudobulb will have up to 40 deciduous leaves, 40 inches

Fig. 4.51. *Cymbidiella pardalina*

long, in a fan-shaped arrangement. The erect many-flowered inflorescence arises from the base of the pseudobulb. The flowers, up to 2.5 inches in diameter, are yellowish green to pale green, with green, orange, or red lips and dark reddish brown markings.
**Flowering season:** Spring and summer.
**Culture**
  **Medium:** A coarse, well-drained epiphytic mix.
  **Fertilizers and fertilization:** Monthly, ratio depends on medium.
  **Watering:** Do not allow medium to dry out excessively.
  **Propagation:** Seed or division.
  **Repotting:** Every 2 years.
**Note:** In the wild, *C. pardalina* grows in association with staghorn ferns (*Platycerium madagascariense*), *C. flabellata* is found on heathlike shrubs, and *C. falcigera* grows on a palm trunk (*Raphia ruffia*).

## Cymbidium

**Genus:** *Cymbidium* Swartz (sym-BID-ee-um)
**Tribe:** Cymbidieae
**Subtribe:** Cyrtopodiinae
**Etymology:** From the Greek word *kymbes* (boat), a reference to some lips that resemble a boat in some species.
**Native habitat:** Japan west to India and south to Australia.
**Number of species:** 70
**Commonly grown species:** *atropurpureum, caniculatum, devonianum, eburneum, ensifolium* (color plate 17), *finlaysonianum, grandiflorum, lowianum, tracyanum, virescens.*
**Hybridizes with:** *Ansellia, Bifrenaria, Catasetum, Eulophiella, Grammatophyllum, Phaius.*
**Generic description:** The wide array of pastel colors found in the large *Cymbidium* hybrids make them popular for Easter and Mother's Day corsages. There is great variation in plant and flower sizes in this genus. Vegetatively, aside from size, these sympodial epiphytes or terrestrial plants are much alike with their pseudobulbs ensheathed by the leaves, which are lanceolate and either soft or leathery. The inflorescences arise from the base of the pseudobulb and may be erect or pendent. The flowers, up to 12 or more per inflorescence, range from 0.5 to 5 inches in diameter and include most of the pastel colors.
**Flowering season:** All year depending on species.

**Culture**
   **Medium:** Cymbidiums grow well in most epiphytic or terrestrial mixes.
   **Fertilizers and fertilization:** Monthly, ratio depends on the medium.
   **Watering:** Keep medium moist all year.
   **Propagation:** Seed, division, or meristem.
   **Repotting:** For best growth, every 2–3 years.

Fig. 4.52. *Cymbidium finlaysonianum*

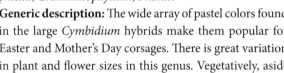

Fig. 4.53. *Cymbidium tracyanum*

## Cynorkis

**Genus:** *Cynorkis* Thouars (syn-OR-kiss)
**Tribe:** Orchideae
**Subtribe:** Habenariinae
**Etymology:** From two Greek words *kynos* (dog) and *orkis* (testicle), referring to the small tubers that resemble testicles.
**Native habitat:** Africa, Madagascar, and Mascarene Islands.
**Number of species:** 125
**Commonly grown species:** *gibbosa, purpurascens, uncinata.*
**Hybridizes with:** None recorded.
**Generic description:** *Cynorkis*, like many perennial plants, are dormant for 4–6 months each year; hence their containers appear to be plantless, tempting helpers to toss them out. However, when they are in flower, they make up for their dormancy. These sympodial, ter-

Fig. 4.54. *Cynorkis purpurascens*

restrial, herbaceous plants have tuberous roots. The soft, usually dark green radial leaves are usually borne singly. The inflorescence arises from the leaf base and is erect or sometimes lax. The colorful flowers may appear individually or in clusters atop the inflorescence. The flowers are very similar to those of *Habenaria*, differing only in minor floral characteristics, but entirely different in color. Lavender and pink are the base colors.
**Flowering season:** Spring and summer.
**Culture**
    **Medium:** Any well-drained terrestrial mix or sphagnum moss.
    **Fertilizers and fertilization:** Monthly during growing season using a 1-1-1.
    **Watering:** Keep medium moist during growing season. Reduce water when dormant.
    **Propagation:** Seed or division.
    **Repotting:** Every 2–3 years.

## Lady's Slipper Orchid

**Genus:** *Cypripedium* Linnaeus (sip-rih-PEE-dee-um)

**Subfamily:** Cypripedioideae

**Etymology:** From two Greek words *kypris* (Venus) and *pedi(l)on* (slipper), a reference to the slipper-like lip.

**Native habitat:** North temperate regions around the world.

**Number of species:** 25

**Commonly grown species:** *acaule* (color plate 18), *calceolus*, *candidum*, *japonicum*, *reginae*.

**Hybridizes with:** None listed.

**Generic description:** *Cypripedium* is one of four genera affectionately called "Slipper Orchid" because of bootlike lips on the flow-

Fig. 4.55. *Cypripedium acaule*

ers. This genus completely encircles the globe in the north temperate zone, where the various species are also popular in gardens. Unfortunately, this popularity has led to the demise of some wild populations. These sympodial, deciduous, terrestrial plants have underground rhizomes and fibrous roots. There are two distinct vegetative types: one has only two leaves, either stemless or with a short stem (*C. acaule*), and the other a leafy stem having one or more flowers (*C. reginae*). The leaves are soft and often heavily pubescent. The slipper-like flowers, up to 5 inches in diameter, come in white, pink, yellow, or brown. There may be two or more colors on a flower.

**Flowering season:** Spring.

**Culture**

    **Medium:** Rich organic soil.

    **Fertilizers and fertilization:** In spring when growth begins, using a balanced fertilizer

    **Watering:** Keep medium moist during growing season.

    **Propagation:** Seed.

    **Repotting:** Every 3 to 5 years.

**Note:** Native North American Indians boiled roots of *Cypripedium* plants, added a sweetening such as maple sugar, and drank the solution as a cure for headaches.

## Cowhorn or Cigar Orchid

**Genus:** *Cyrtopodium* R. Brown (sir-toh-POH-dee-um)
**Tribe:** Cymbidieae
**Subtribe:** Cyrtopodiinae
**Etymology:** From two Greek words *kyrtos* (curved) and *podion* (foot), to describe the curve on the foot of the column.
**Native habitat:** Florida, Mexico, and Cuba south to Argentina.
**Number of species:** 30
**Commonly grown species:** *andersonii, gigas, parviflorum, punctatum.*
**Hybridizes with:** *Ansellia, Grammatophyllum.*
**Generic description:** *Cyrtopodium* plants can become massive specimens, with erect pseudobulbs to 3 feet or more topped by 3–4-foot, branched, colorful inflorescences. These sympodial plants may be either epiphytic or terrestrial. An individual pseudobulb has up to 7 soft pleated leaves clustered near the apex. The leaves have 3 prominent veins. Each flower and each lateral branch on the inflorescence is subtended by a leafy bract in the same color combination as the flower. Yellow and yellow green are the base flower colors, adorned with varying amounts of reddish brown markings.
**Flowering season:** All year depending on species.
**Culture**
  **Medium:** Mounted on cypress knees or potted in any epiphytic mix.
  **Fertilizers and fertilization:** Monthly, ratio depending on the medium.
  **Watering:** Water thoroughly and not again until the surface of the medium is dry.
  **Propagation:** Seed or division.
  **Repotting:** Only when the medium or cypress knee decomposes.
**Note:** In Brazil *Cyrtopodium* is a source of glue used mainly in the manufacture of musical instruments.

Fig. 4.56. *Cyrtopodium punctatum*

## Dendrobium

**Genus:** *Dendrobium* Swartz (den-DROH-bee-um)
**Tribe:** Dendrobieae
**Subtribe:** Dendrobiinae
**Etymology:** From two Greek words *dendron* (tree) and *bios* (life), describing the epiphytic nature of the genus.
**Native habitat:** Japan west to India and south to Australia.
**Number of species:** 1,500
**Commonly grown species:** *anosmum, antennatum, aphyllum, bigibbum, canaliculatum, chrysotoxum, crumenatum, dearei, farmeri, formosum* (color plate 19), *kingianum, leonis, lindleyi, loddigesii, lowii, nobile, parishii, phalaenopsis, secundum, speciosum, spectabile, superbum, teretifolium, tetragonum, victoriae-reginae* (color plate 20).
**Hybridizes with:** *Flickingeria.*

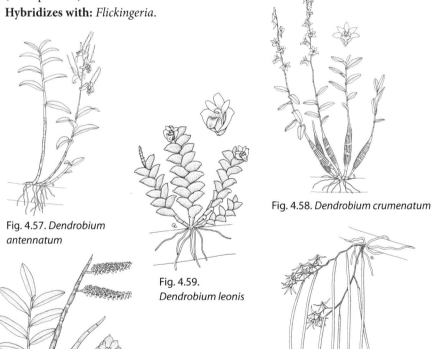

Fig. 4.57. *Dendrobium antennatum*

Fig. 4.58. *Dendrobium crumenatum*

Fig. 4.59. *Dendrobium leonis*

Fig. 4.60. *Dendrobium secundum*

Fig. 4.61. *Dendrobium teretifolium*

**Generic description:** This large genus native to the Pacific Basin is highly variable in both vegetative and flowering characteristics. The longevity of its individual flowers ranges from 1 day (*D. crumenatum*) to 8–10 months (*D. cuthbertonsonii*). These sympodial epiphytes have pseudobulbs that range from small, round, and 1 inch tall to canelike bulbs to 5 feet tall, usually forming tightly clustered plants. The leaves may be deciduous or evergreen with great variation in leaf substance and size. Inflorescences are either terminal (*D. phalaenopsis*) or axillary (*D. nobile*) and bear one to many spurred flowers in a range of colors.

**Flowering season:** All year depending on the species.

**Culture**

    **Medium:** Most coarse bark mixes.

    **Fertilizers and fertilization:** Monthly, using a 3-1-1.

    **Watering:** Water thoroughly and not again until the medium is dry to the touch.

    **Propagation:** Seed, division, keikis, or meristems.

    **Repotting:** When plants become too large for their containers or the medium decomposes.

**Note:** Over the years *Dendrobium* hybrids have played a major role in the orchid cut-flower industry. *Dendrobium phalaenopsis* and its hybrids, with their long, arching sprays bearing up to 15 flowers, lend themselves readily to floral arrangements, and the flowers are long lasting. Primitive tribes in New Guinea wove baskets using the reedlike stems of *D. utile*. Other species are used to weave baskets in the Philippines and Java.

Fig. 4.62. *Dendrobium tetragonum*

Fig. 4.63. *Dendrobium bigibbum*

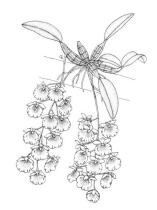

Fig. 4.64. *Dendrobium lindleyi*

## Dendrochilum

**Genus:** *Dendrochilum* Blume (den-droh-KYE-lum)
**Tribe:** Coelogyneae
**Subtribe:** Coelogyninae
**Etymology:** From two Greek words *dendron* (tree) and *cheilos* (lip), referring to the epiphytic nature and variability in the lip of this genus.
**Native habitat:** Malay Peninsula southeast to New Guinea.
**Number of species:** 100+
**Commonly grown species:** *album, cobbianum, filiforme, longifolium, uncatum, wenzelii.*
**Hybridizes with:** None recorded.
**Generic description:** Affectionately called the

Fig. 4.65. *Dendrochilum cobbianum*

Necklace Orchid to depict the gracefully arching, long sprays of delicate closely arranged flowers. There are two distinct vegetative growths in *Dendrochilum*. One section has tightly clustered, ovoid pseudobulbs with one terminal leaf and an inflorescence that develops from the base of the newly developing growth. The other section has similar pseudobulbs, but they are widely spaced on the rhizome, which is often branched. The inflorescence arises from a separate flowering spur. The basic colors of these small flowers, borne in chainlike fashion, are cream to yellowish cream.
**Flowering season:** Spring, summer, and fall.
**Culture**
    **Medium:** Any well-drained epiphytic mix.
    **Fertilizers and fertilization:** Monthly, ratio depends on the medium.
    **Watering:** Do not let medium dry out excessively.
    **Propagation:** Seed or division.
    **Repotting:** When plants become too large for their containers or when the medium decomposes.

## Ghost or Frog Orchid

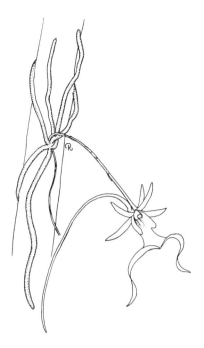

**Genus:** *Dendrophylax* Reichenbach f. (den-DROH-fie-lax)
**Tribe:** Vandeae
**Subtribe:** Angraecinae
**Etymology:** From two Greek words *dendron* (tree) and *phylas* (guard), denoting the aerial roots that clasp tree limbs.
**Native habitat:** South Florida and the West Indies.
**Number of species:** 6 to 8
**Commonly grown species:** *funalis*, *lindenii* (color plate 21).
**Hybridizes with:** None recorded.
**Generic description:** These most interesting monopodial epiphytes have become very popular of late owing to publicity surrounding the book *Orchid Thief* and movies where *Dendrophylax* (= *Polyradicion*) holds center stage. These leafless plants, with their clasping roots winding around

Fig. 4.66. *Dendrophylax lindenii*

branches, often go undetected in their native habitat. The masses of roots radiate from a very short stem that often looks like a small dry bud in the center of the mass. The dark, thin, short inflorescence arises from this stem and bears up to 10 flowers that open one at a time over several weeks. The 5-inch flowers are greenish white. In their native habit the flowers appear to be floating in air, giving them a ghostly appearance.
**Flowering season:** Winter, spring, and summer.
**Culture**
　**Medium:** Tree limbs or tree fern totems.
　**Fertilizers and fertilization:** Monthly using a weak, balanced fertilizer.
　**Watering:** Daily for best growth.
　**Propagation:** Seed.
　**Repotting:** Only when absolutely necessary.

## Dichaea

**Genus:** *Dichaea* Lindley (dye-KEY-uh)
**Tribe:** Maxillarieae
**Subtribe:** Zygopetalinae
**Etymology:** From the Greek word *diche* (twofold), to describe the 2-ranked foliage in this genus.
**Native habitat:** West Indies, Central America, and tropical South America.
**Number of species:** 100+
**Commonly grown species:** *glauca, hystricina, muricata.*
**Hybridizes with:** None recorded.
**Generic description:** *Dichaea* species are unique and an interesting group to work with. Vegetatively, these sympodial epiphytes without pseudobulbs are variable, but have two characteristics that tie them together. The stems elongate over the course of several years, as though the plant were monopodial, and all have distichous leaves. The stems may be erect or pendent. The small colorful flowers

Fig. 4.67. *Dichaea glauca*

are borne singly in the axils of the upper leaves. The base flower colors are white to greenish white with varying degrees of purplish brown markings. Some lips are lavender.
**Flowering season:** All year depending on species.
**Culture**
    **Medium:** Mounted or any well-drained epiphytic mix.
    **Fertilizers and fertilization:** Monthly, ratio depends on medium.
    **Watering:** Water mounted plants daily and keep medium moist for best growth.
    **Propagation:** Seed or division.
    **Repotting:** When mount decomposes, epiphytic mix every 2–3 years.

## Dimorphorchis

**Genus:** *Dimorphorchis* (Lindley) Rolfe (die-morph-OR-kiss)
**Tribe:** Vandeae
**Subtribe:** Aeridinae
**Etymology:** From three Greek words *di* (two), *morphe* (shape), and *orchis* (orchid), to denote the two distinct flowers types on each inflorescence.
**Native habitat:** Borneo.
**Number of species:** 3
**Commonly grown species:** *lowii*.
**Hybridizes with:** None recorded.
**Generic description:** The unique flowering characteristics of *Dimorphorchis* have long made these easy to grow plants a conversation piece, but unfortunately the plants are a little large for small greenhouses. These monopodial epiphytes have large stems (30 inches) and

Fig. 4.68. *Dimorphorchis lowii*

large leaves (up to 28 inches long) that clasp at the base. The pendent, many-flowered inflorescences arise from the leaf axils. Each inflorescence has two types of flowers: the lower two or three very fragrant flowers are yellowish green and weakly spotted with maroon, while the remaining upper flowers are less fragrant and heavily blotched with maroon.
**Flowering season:** Spring and summer.
**Culture**
 **Medium:** Any well-drained epiphytic mix.
 **Fertilizers and fertilization:** Monthly, ratio depends on medium.
 **Watering:** Keep medium moist all year.
 **Propagation:** Seed or tip cuttings.
 **Repotting:** When plants become too large for their containers or medium decomposes.
**Note:** *Dimorphorchis* species should be repotted only when absolutely necessary for best growth, as disturbing roots can be detrimental.

## Disa

**Genus:** *Disa* Bergius (DEE-suh)
**Tribe:** Diseae
**Subtribe:** Disinae
**Etymology:** From the Latin word *dis*, meaning "rich," a reference to the intense color of *Disa uniflora* flowers.
**Native habitat:** Central Africa and eastern South Africa.
**Number of species:** 100
**Commonly grown species:** *capricornis, draconis, longicornu, racemosa, stolzii, uniflora*.
**Hybridizes with:** *Herschelia*.
**Generic description:** The showy flowers in an array of vivid colors have made *Disa* a very popular genus. These sympodial terrestrials have fleshy roots and vary vegetatively. Some species have both fertile (flowering) and sterile (flowerless) stems. The leaves on the fertile stems are often reduced to bracts. The flowers on erect inflorescences are subtended by a leafy bract and have spurred dorsal sepals that form a hood. The flowers, up to 5 inches in diameter, may be lavender, blue, orange red or white.

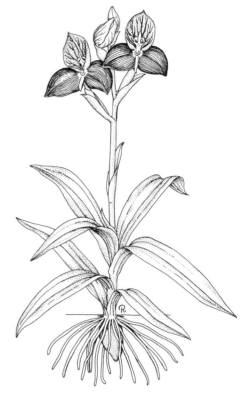

Fig. 4.69. *Disa uniflora*

**Flowering season:** All year depending on species.
**Culture**
    **Medium:** Bog-type soils or live sphagnum moss for some species.
    **Fertilizers and fertilization:** Bimonthly with a 1-1-1.
    **Watering:** Keep medium moist at all times as some species are found growing in running water.
    **Propagation:** Seed.
    **Repotting:** When plants become too large for their containers.

## Dracula

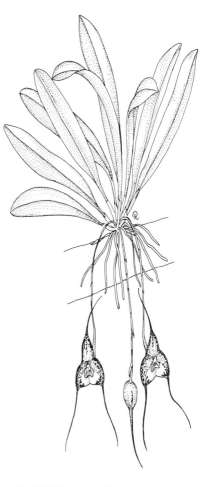

**Genus:** *Dracula* Luer (DRA-kue-luh)
**Tribe:** Epidendreae
**Subtribe:** Pleurothallidinae
**Etymology:** From the Latin word *draco* (dragon), denoting some of the grotesque flowers found in this genus.
**Native habitat:** Colombia.
**Number of species:** 80
**Commonly grown species:** *bella, caderi, chimaera, marsupialis* (color plate 22), *simia, vampira.*
**Hybridizes with:** *Masdevallia.*
**Generic description:** These sympodial, epiphytic orchids are so unique that they are conversation topics whenever they are in bloom. *Dracula simia* flowers have the likeness of an ape's face in the center. It is so real that people have been accused of doctoring photographs (see color plate 22). *Dracula* species produce tight clusters of short ramicauls, each topped by a single leaf. The soft leaf blades have a distinct midrib. The usually single-flowered inflorescence arising from the base of the ramicaul is usually pendent, but may sometimes be erect. The flowers may be several inches wide when measured from sepal tips. Color varies among the species.

Fig. 4.70. *Dracula bella*

**Flowering season:** All year depending on species.
**Culture**
   **Medium:** Any well-drained epiphytic mix.
   **Fertilizers and fertilization:** Monthly, ratio depending on medium.
   **Watering:** Keep medium moist at all times for best growth.
   **Propagation:** Seed or division.
   **Repotting:** Every 2–3 years.

 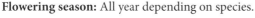

## Elleanthus

**Genus:** *Elleanthus* Presl (ell-ee-ANTH-us)
**Tribe:** Epidendreae
**Subtribe:** Sobraliinae
**Etymology:** From the Greek *anthos* (flower) and Helle, the mythological heroine Hellespont, hence Helle's flower.
**Native habitat:** Tropical America.
**Number of species:** 50
**Commonly grown species:** *capitatus, furfuraceus, hymenophorus, longibracteatus.*
**Hybridizes with:** None recorded.
**Generic description:** These sympodial epiphytic or terrestrial plants form dense clumps of reedlike stems and resemble *Sobralia* plants when not in flower. The erect stems are supported by thick fleshy roots and often adorned with purplish spots. The usually 2-ranked leaves, with clasping leaf bases, are heavily veined or pleated and often diminish in size near the inflorescence. A head or raceme inflorescence tops each reed. The small flowers, depending on species, may be tightly clustered or loosely arranged. The flower color varies widely from white to yellow through orange, red, and purple.

Fig. 4.71. *Elleanthus capitatus*

**Flowering season:** Spring, summer, and fall.
**Culture**
    **Medium:** Most terrestrial or epiphytic mixes.
    **Fertilizers and fertilization:** Monthly using a 1-1-1.
    **Watering:** Keep medium moist for best growth.
    **Propagation:** Seed or division.
    **Repotting:** When plant outgrows its container.

## Encyclia

**Genus:** *Encyclia* Hooker (en-SIK-lee-uh)
**Tribe:** Epidendreae
**Subtribe:** Laeliinae
**Etymology:** From the Greek *enkyklein* (encircle), to describe the partial encircling of the column by the lateral lobes of the lip.
**Native habitat:** Florida, Mexico, and south to Brazil.
**Number of species:** Approximately 150
**Commonly grown species:** *adenocarpum*, *alata* (color plate 23), *belizensis*, *bractescens*, *cordigera*, *hanburyi*, *phoenicea*, *tampensis*.
**Hybridizes with:** *Barkeria*, *Brassavola*, *Broughtonia*, *Cattleya*, *Diacrium*, *Laelia*, *Rhyncholaelia*, *Schomburgkia*, *Sophronitis*.

Fig. 4.72. *Encyclia cordigera*

**Generic description:** *Encyclia* is closely related to *Epidendrum* but easily separated by its pseudobulbous growth and the floral lips being partially adnate to the column. The pyriform pseudobulbs of these sympodial epiphytes are tightly clustered and topped by 2 or more mostly lanceolate leaves. The terminal and often branched inflorescences may be up to 3 feet tall. The size and color of the flowers are highly variable in this genus, with the lips often large and very colorful.
**Flowering season:** All year depending on species.
**Culture**
   **Medium:** Tree fern or cork plaques or any well-drained epiphytic medium.
   **Fertilizers and fertilization:** Monthly, ratio depends on medium.
   **Watering:** Plaques will require frequent or in some cases daily watering.

Fig. 4.73. *Encyclia tampensis*

   **Propagation:** Seed, division, or meristems.
   **Repotting:** Every 3–5 years or when the medium or plaque decomposes.

## Epidendrum

**Genus:** *Epidendrum* Linnaeus (ep-ih-DEN-drum)
**Tribe:** Epidendreae
**Subtribe:** Laeliinae
**Etymology:** From two Greek words *epi* (upon) and *dendron* (tree), to describe these epiphytic species.
**Native habitat:** North Carolina south to Brazil.
**Number of species:** Several hundred
**Commonly grown species:** *anceps, ciliare, cinnabarinum, difforme, ibaguense, magnoliae* (= *conopseum*), *nocturnum, paniculatum, pseudepidendrum* (color plate 24), *radicans, stamfordianum.*
**Hybridizes with:** *Barkeria, Brassavola, Broughtonia, Cattleya, Diacrium, Encyclia, Laelia, Schomburgkia, Sophronitis.*
**Generic description:** *Epidendrum* is the oldest American genus, having been identified by Linnaeus in 1753. Actually, Linnaeus used it as a catchall genus for all epiphytes; over the years the number of species has declined as taxonomists split off groups (*Encyclia*). Despite the removal of various groups there is still vegeta-

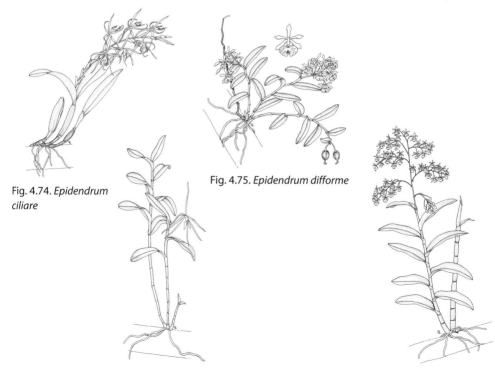

Fig. 4.74. *Epidendrum ciliare*

Fig. 4.75. *Epidendrum difforme*

Fig. 4.76. *Epidendrum nocturnum*

Fig. 4.77. *Epidendrum paniculatum*

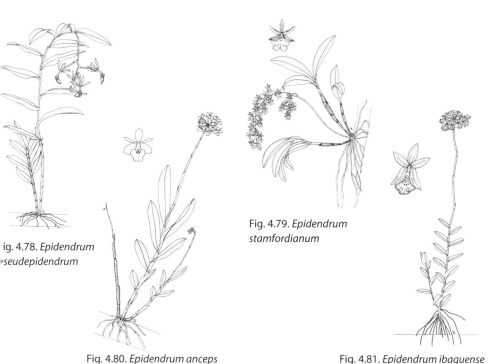

Fig. 4.78. *Epidendrum pseudepidendrum*

Fig. 4.79. *Epidendrum stamfordianum*

Fig. 4.80. *Epidendrum anceps*

Fig. 4.81. *Epidendrum ibaguense*

tive variation in this sympodial, epiphytic genus. They have either reedlike growth with many leaves (*E. radicans*) or tall pseudobulbs topped by 2 leaves (*E. stamfordianum*). The inflorescence usually arises from the apex and bears 1 to many flowers, but may also arise as a separate flowering branch (*E. stamfordianum*). The attractive flowers come in a wide range of colors.

**Flowering season:** All year depending on species.

**Culture**

    **Medium:** Tree fern or cork plaques or any well-drained epiphytic mix.

    **Fertilizers and fertilization:** Monthly, ratio depends on medium.

    **Watering:** Plaques require frequent or in some cases daily watering.

    **Propagation:** Seed, division, keikis, or meristems.

    **Repotting:** When the plant becomes too large for its container or the medium decomposes.

*Epigeneium*

**Genus:** Epigeneium Gagnepain (eh-pih-JEEN-ee-um)
**Tribe:** Dendrobieae
**Subtribe:** Dendrobiinae
**Etymology:** From two Greek words *epi* (upon) and *geneion* (chin), describing the method by which the sepals and petals are attached to the column foot.
**Native habitat:** India east to the Philippines and New Guinea.
**Number of species:** 35
**Commonly grown species:** *acuminatum, amplum, coelogyne, cymbidioides, lyonii, stella-silvae, treacherianum.*
**Hybridizes with:** None listed.
**Generic description:** Removed from *Dendrobium* in 1932 by Gagnepain because of differences in floral and vegetative characteristics. These sympodial epiphytes have ovoid pseudobulbs covered with papery bracts and often spaced up to 2 inches apart on distinct rhizomes. Each pseudobulb is topped by 1 or 2 short-petioled, somewhat fleshy leaves with very small lobes at the apex. The terminal inflorescences, depending on species, will bear 1 (*E. coelogyne*) to 20 (*E. acuminatum*) bright, almost star-shaped flowers in white, yellow, or reddish maroon.

Fig. 4.82. *Epigeneium treacherianum*

**Flowering season:** Fall, winter, and spring.
**Culture**
    **Medium:** Mount on cork, tree fern, or tree limbs.
    **Fertilizers and fertilization:** Biweekly, using a half-strength balanced fertilizer.
    **Watering:** Daily for best growth.
    **Propagation:** Seed or division.
    **Repotting:** When the mount no longer supports the plant.

## Eria

**Genus:** *Eria* Lindley (EHR-ee-uh)
**Tribe:** Podochileae
**Subtribe:** Eriinae
**Etymology:** From the Greek *erion* (wool), referring to the heavy pubescence on some species.
**Native habitat:** India east to New Guinea and Philippines.
**Number of species:** Approximately 350
**Commonly grown species:** *bractescens, coronaria, cylindrostachya, densa, javanica, longissima, spicata, veluntina.*
**Hybridizes with:** None listed.
**Generic description:** Variations are paramount in this Old World genus. Vegetatively taxonomists divide *Eria* into 15 divisions based on pseudobulb differences. The pseudobulbs of these sympodial epiphytes have one to many thin to leathery leaves, sometimes clustered near the apex, and some pseudobulbs are covered by hairs. Inflorescences arise from the pseudobulb's base or may be lateral or terminal. In some, the inflorescence bursts from the side of the pseudobulb (*E. cylindrostachya*), leaving a hole when the spike falls off. The flowers, up to 2 inches in diameter, are often hairy and in dominant colors of white, creamy yellow, or pink striped.
**Flowering season:** All year depending on species.
**Culture**
    **Medium:** Any epiphytic mix, cork or tree fern plaque.
    **Fertilizers and fertilization:** Monthly using a balanced fertilizer.
    **Watering:** Depends on medium, but do not allow the medium to dry out excessively.
    **Propagation:** Seed or division.
    **Repotting:** Approximately every 2 years.

Fig. 4.83. *Eria densa*

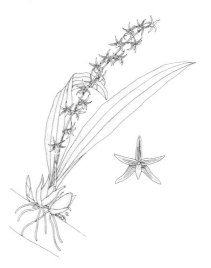

Fig. 4.84. *Eria javanica*

## Eulophia

**Genus:** *Eulophia* R. Brown (you-LOH-fee-uh)
**Tribe:** Cymbidieae
**Subtribe:** Eulophiinae
**Etymology:** From the Greek words *eu* (well) and *lophos* (plume), referring to the crested lip.
**Native habitat:** Tropical areas around the world.
**Number of species:** 300
**Commonly grown species:** *alta, angolensis, bicarinata, guineensis, horsfallii, macrostachya, rosea, stricta.*
**Hybridizes with:** *Oeceoclades.*
**Generic description:** *Eulophia* contains some outstanding species. Vegetatively, these sympodial, mostly terrestrial orchids may have either subterranean (*E. bicarinata*) or aboveground (*E. guineensis*) pseudobulbs topped by 3–5 leathery or soft pleated leaves. The clasping

Fig. 4.85. *Eulophia alta*

leaves make the plants appear to have stems. The tall (up to 7 feet), erect inflorescences have many flowers, which open sequentially from the base upward. Since the flowers open slowly, plants are in flower for long periods. Most flowers are yellowish or greenish with reddish or purple marks.
**Flowering season:** All year depending on species.
**Culture**
    **Medium:** Most well-drained terrestrial mixes.
    **Fertilizers and fertilization:** Monthly with a balanced fertilizer.
    **Watering:** Water thoroughly and not again until the medium surface is dry.
    **Propagation:** Seed or division.
    **Repotting:** When plants become too large for their containers.

## Flickingeria

**Genus:** *Flickingeria* A. D. Hawkes (flick-in-GEER-ee-uh)
**Tribe:** Dendrobieae
**Subtribe:** Dendrobiinae
**Etymology:** Named in honor of Edward A. Flickinger, a friend of Hawkes.
**Native habitat:** Southeast Asia south to Australia and the Pacific Islands.
**Number of species:** 60
**Commonly grown species:** *comata, fugax.*
**Hybridizes with:** *Dendrobium.*
**Generic description:** This very interesting, sympodial epiphyte (sometimes lithophyte) has erect or pendent stems that form clumps. The usually unifoliate *Flickingeria* stems, which may be up to 40 inches long, are often branched near the tip. In some species the apical node on the stem is swollen. The flowers are borne individually in the upper leaf axils. Each flower is short lived, usually less than a day. The flowers are thin and almost translucent. Colors vary and many flowers are spotted purple and/or have a purple anther cap.

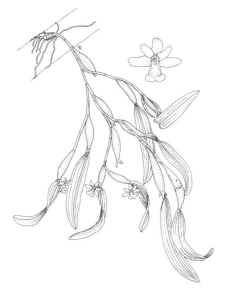

Fig. 4.86. *Flickingeria fugax*

**Flowering season:** Spring and summer.
**Culture**
  **Medium:** Any well-drained epiphytic mix.
  **Fertilizers and fertilization:** Monthly, ratio depends on medium.
  **Watering:** Keep medium moist at all times.
  **Propagation:** Seed or division.
  **Repotting:** Every 2–3 years.

## Galeandra

**Genus:** *Galeandra* Linley (gal-ee-ANN-druh)
**Tribe:** Cymbidieae
**Subtribe:** Cyrtopodiinae
**Etymology:** From two Greek words *galea* (helmet) and *andr* (anther), referring to the anther cap in this genus.
**Native habitat:** West Indies, Mexico south to southern Brazil.
**Number of species:** 25
**Commonly grown species:** *baueri, beyrichii, claesiana, devoniana, lucustris, pubicentrum.*
**Hybridizes with:** *Catasetum, Cycnoches, Oncidium.*
**Generic description:** Vegetatively, these sympodial epiphytic species have tightly clustered, spindle-like pseudobulbs. Each *Galeandra* pseudobulb has 6 or more soft, arching, lancelike leaves

Fig. 4.87. *Galeandra baueri*

with ensheathing leaf bases. The short inflorescence that arises from the apex is slightly curved and bears up to 12 flowers up to 3 inches in diameter. In these species, the flowering is prolonged because a secondary or even tertiary inflorescence develops on the original inflorescence. The base flower color is creamy white with variable reddish brown and lavender markings.
**Flowering season:** All year depending on species.
**Culture**
    **Medium:** Any well-drained epiphytic medium.
    **Fertilizers and fertilization:** Monthly, ratio will depend on the medium.
    **Watering:** Keep medium moist at all times.
    **Propagation:** Seed or division.
    **Repotting:** At least every 2 years.

## Galeottia

**Genus:** *Galeottia* A. Richard (gal-ee-OT-tee-uh)
**Tribe:** Maxillarieae
**Subtribe:** Zygopetalinae
**Etymology:** In honor of Richard's colleague, nineteenth-century Italian botanist H. Galeotti.
**Native habitat:** Mexico south to Brazil and Peru.
**Number of species:** 11
**Commonly grown species:** *burkei, fimbriata, grandiflora, marginata.*
**Hybridizes with:** *Cochleanthes, Colax, Zygopetalum, Zygosepalum.*
**Generic description:** *Galeottia* species maybe either sympodial epiphytes (*G. fimbriata*) or terrestrial (*G. burkei*). The tightly clustered,

Fig. 4.88. *Galeottia grandiflora*

large, smooth, slightly ribbed pseudobulbs are topped by two leaves. The leaves are large (6–8 inches), soft, and plicate. The many-flowered inflorescence arises from the base of the newly developing pseudobulb. Each inflorescence bears a few large showy flowers. The base flower color is yellowish green with heavy spotting or barring of reddish brown. The lip may be white with distinct reddish brown lines (*G. fimbriata*).
**Flowering season:** Spring and summer.
**Culture**
    **Medium:** Depending on species, any well-drained epiphytic or terrestrial mix.
    **Fertilizers and fertilization:** Monthly, ratio depends on medium.
    **Watering:** Do not allow medium to dry.
    **Propagation:** Seed or division.
    **Repotting:** Every 2–3 years.
**Note:** In 1963, Hawkes transferred *Galeottia* species to the genus *Mendoncella* as he thought *Galeottia* had already been published for a species of grass. The publication was not valid, hence *Galeottia* is the proper name; however, some plants may still be listed as *Mendoncella.*

## Little Man Orchid

**Genus:** *Gomesa* R. Brown (go-MEE-suh)
**Tribe:** Maxillarieae
**Subtribe:** Oncidiinae
**Etymology:** Named in honor of Bernardino Antonio Gomes, a Portuguese botanist.
**Native habitat:** Southeastern Brazil.
**Number of species:** 13
**Commonly grown species:** *crispa, glaziovii, laxiflora, planifolia, recurva, sessilis, verboonenii.*
**Hybridizes with:** *Ada, Aspasia, Cochlioda, Comparettia, Lockhartia, Odontoglossum, Oncidium.*

Fig. 4.89. *Gomesa crispa*

**Generic description:** At first glance the pale green flowers of *Gomesa* lined up on the inflorescence look like a row of little men, hence the common name Little Man Orchid. The flattened, almost elliptical pseudobulbs of these sympodial epiphytic orchids are tightly arranged along the rhizome. They are subtended by leafy bracts and topped by two lancelike curved leaves. The short, usually curved inflorescence arises from the base of the pseudobulb and bears up to 25 small flowers. The fragrant flowers' base color is yellow green.
**Flowering season:** Spring, summer, and fall.
**Culture**
    **Medium:** Any well-drained epiphytic mix.
    **Fertilizers and fertilization:** Monthly, ratio depends on medium.
    **Watering:** Water thoroughly and not again until the surface of the medium is dry.
    **Propagation**: Seed or division.
    **Repotting:** At least every 2 years.

## Gongora

**Genus:** *Gongora* Ruiz & Pavón (gon-GOR-uh)
**Tribe:** Maxillarieae
**Subtribe:** Stanhopeinae
**Etymology:** Named in honor of the Bishop of Cordoba, Don Antonio Caballero y Gongora.
**Native habitat:** Mexico to northern South America.
**Number of species:** 12
**Commonly grown species:** *armeniaca*, *fulva* (color plate 25), *galeata*, *quinquenervis*, *truncata*.
**Hybridizes with:** *Houlletia*, *Stanhopea*.
**Generic description:** Ease of growth, unique flowers, and pleasing fragrance all favor *Gongora*'s being in everyone's collection. These sympodial epiphytes have short, tightly, clustered, ridged pseudobulbs topped by up to 3 large (10-inch) soft pleated leaves. The long (3 feet or more), pendent inflorescences bear from a few to many 2-inch flowers. *Gongora* flowers can be described as "strange" or "unlike other orchids" and the colors and fragrance of the flowers only enhance their uniqueness.

Fig. 4.90. *Gongora quinquenervis*

**Flowering season:** All year depending on species.
**Culture**
  **Medium:** Well-drained epiphytic mix.
  **Fertilizers and fertilization:** Monthly, ratio depends on medium.
  **Watering:** Several times weekly to keep medium moist.
  **Propagation:** Seed or division.
  **Repotting:** Only when medium or container breaks down.

## Goodyera

**Genus:** *Goodyera* R. Brown (good-YER-uh)
**Tribe:** Cranichideae
**Subtribe:** Goodyerinae
**Etymology:** Named in honor of John Goodyer (1592–1664), an English botanist.
**Native habitat:** North America's north temperate zone south to Mexico; Australia north through the Pacific Islands to southeast Asia.
**Number of species:** 40
**Commonly grown species:** *hispida, pubescens, repens.*
**Hybridizes with:** *Anoectochilus, Dossinia, Ludisia.*
**Generic description:** *Goodyera* is one of a group of orchid genera often affectionately referred to as Jewel Orchids, not because they have pearly white flowers, but because they all have excellent variegated foliage. These sympodial terrestrial plants have creeping rhizomes and produce lateral branches with the leaves usually in a cluster or rosette at the base. The soft leaves are often variegated green and white. The erect inflorescence arises from the center of the rosette and bears a few to many flowers. The flowers are small, basically white, and by some standards insignificant.

Fig. 4.91. *Goodyera pubescens*

**Flowering season:** Spring and summer.
**Culture**
> **Medium:** Any proven terrestrial mix.
> **Fertilizers and fertilization:** Monthly during growing season using a 1-1-1.
> **Watering:** Keep medium moist during growing season and reduce watering when dormant.
> **Propagation:** Seed.
> **Repotting:** Every 3–5 years.

## Grammangis

**Genus:** *Grammangis* Richenbach f. (gram-MANG-iss)
**Tribe:** Cymbidieae
**Subtribe:** Cyrtopodiinae
**Etymology:** From two Greek words *gramma* (mark) and *angos* (vessel), denoting the distinct purple lines on the lip.
**Native habitat:** Madagascar.
**Number of species:** 2
**Commonly grown species:** *ellisii*.
**Hybridizes with:** None recorded.
**Generic description:** *Grammangis* species are large sympodial epiphytes with extensive root systems. There are reports of plants growing in the wild with thick, succulent roots several

Fig. 4.92. *Grammangis ellisii*

meters long. The large pseudobulbs are ensheathed by up to 5 leaves. The 16-inch leaves are grayish green and have rounded apices. The erect inflorescence arises from the base of the newly developing pseudobulb, may be up to 26 inches tall, and bears up to 40 flowers. The large flowers are waxy, usually with a brown base color and spotted yellow.
**Flowering season:** Spring and summer.
**Culture**
    **Medium:** Any well-drained epiphytic mix.
    **Fertilizers and fertilization:** Monthly, ratio depends on medium.
    **Watering:** Water thoroughly and not again until medium feels dry to the touch.
    **Propagation:** Seed or division.
    **Repotting:** Every 3–5 years.

## Grammatophyllum

**Genus:** *Grammatophyllum* Blume (grah-mat-oh-FILL-um)
**Tribe:** Cymbidieae
**Subtribe:** Cyrtopodiinae
**Etymology:** From two Greek words *gramma* (marked) and *phyllon* (leaf), probably referring to spots on the petals and sepals.
**Native habitat:** Indochina southeast to New Guinea.
**Number of species:** 5–8
**Commonly grown species:** *measuresianum*, *scriptum* (color plate 26), *speciosum*.
**Hybridizes with:** *Catasetum*, *Cymbidium*, *Cyrtopodium*.
**Generic description:** Vegetatively there are two distinct growth types in this sympodial epiphytic genus. One has short, stout pseudobulbs with up to 5 large leathery leaves (*G. scriptum*). The other (*G. speciosum*) has thick, almost bamboo-like pseudobulbs up to 7 feet long, with leaves to 24 inches long. The thick, long (up to 8 feet), mostly erect inflorescences bear as many as 100 flowers 2–6 inches in diameter. The base floral color is greenish yellow with varying degrees of brownish purple spotting.
**Flowering season:** Spring, summer, and fall.
**Culture**
    **Medium:** Any coarse, well-drained, epiphytic mix.
    **Fertilizers and fertilization:** Monthly, ratio depends on the medium.
    **Watering:** Keep medium moist at all times.
    **Propagation:** Seed or division.
    **Repotting:** When plant becomes too large for the container.
**Note:** *Grammatophyllum speciosum* is one species that can rapidly outgrow a greenhouse as plants as large as 42.5 feet in circumference and 21 feet in diameter have been recorded. Moluccan natives considered the seeds of *Grammatophyllum* to be a love potion.

Fig. 4.93. *Grammatophlyllum scriptum*

## *Habenaria*

**Genus:** *Habenaria* C. L. Willdenow (hab-in-AIR-ee-uh)
**Tribe:** Orchideae
**Subtribe:** Habenariinae
**Etymology:** From the Latin word *habena* (reins), referring to the long strap shapes of some petals and lips.
**Native habitat:** Pantropical.
**Number of species:** About 600
**Commonly grown species:** *carnea, dentata, repens, rhodocheila, splendens.*
**Hybridizes with:** None recorded.
**Generic description:** *Habenaria* plants emerge in late spring, flower in midsummer, then set seed and die back in the fall, a typical life cycle for a perennial. The plants are sustained while dormant by their tubers and fleshy roots, which are also renewed annually. The soft smooth leaves

Fig. 4.94. *Habenaria rhodocheila*

are borne on stems up to 3 feet tall. The erect terminal inflorescence bears from a few to many flowers up to 2 inches in diameter. Flower color varies; many species have white or green flowers.
**Flowering season:** Spring and summer.
**Culture**
    **Medium:** Any well-drained terrestrial mix.
    **Fertilizers and fertilization:** Monthly during growing season with a balanced fertilizer.
    **Watering:** Minimal watering during the dormant season.
    **Propagation:** Seed or division of fleshy roots.
    **Repotting:** Every 3–5 years.
**Note:** Although many *Habenaria* species have very colorful flowers (*H. rhodocheila*), they are not widely grown because, as typical deciduous perennials, they are dormant for 6–8 months of the year, leaving empty-looking pots in the greenhouse. *Habenaria repens* is a wetland species and makes an attractive pond-side plant.

## Holcoglossum

**Genus:** *Holcoglossum* Schlechter (hole-koh-GLOSS-um)
**Tribe:** Vandeae
**Subtribe:** Aeridinae
**Etymology:** From two Greek words *holkos* (strap) and *glossa* (tongue), describing the spurred lip on these flowers.
**Native habitat:** Myanmar, Thailand, and Indochina.
**Number of species:** 1
**Commonly grown species:** *quasipinifolium*.
**Hybridizes with:** *Ascocentrum*.
**Generic description:** This miniature genus of monopodial epiphytes consists of delightful plants with long lasting flowers. Vegetatively, the plants have 6–10

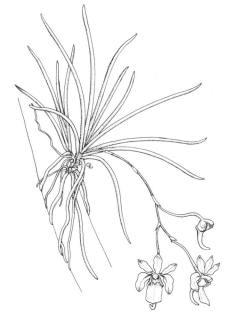

Fig. 4.95. *Holcoglossum quasipinifolium*

needlelike leaves about 6 inches long usually clustered near the top of the stem. The inflorescences arise between two leaf bases or at the base of the stem. The pendent, purplish inflorescenses bear 1 to several flowers that may not open until six months after they emerge. The long-lasting (2 wks) 1-inch flowers, borne individually, are distinctly spurred and white to pinkish purple. The flowers unfold very slowly but are well worth the wait.
**Flowering season:** Spring.
**Culture**
    **Medium:** Mounted on tree fern or cork bark plaques.
    **Fertilizers and fertilization:** Monthly using a balanced fertilizer.
    **Watering:** For best growth water daily.
    **Propagation:** Seed.
    **Repotting:** When the mounts decompose.
**Note:** Occasionally some taxonomists break this genus into three species: *amesianum*, *kimballianum*, and *quasipinifolium*.

## Huntleya

**Genus:** *Huntleya* Bateman *ex* Lindley (HUNT-lee-uh)
**Tribe:** Maxillarieae
**Subtribe:** Zygopetalinae
**Etymology:** Named in honor of the Reverend J. T. Huntley in 1837.
**Native habitat:** Eastern South America from Colombia to Brazil.
**Number of species:** 4
**Commonly grown species:** *meleagris* (color plate 27).
**Hybridizes with:** *Cochleanthes.*
**Generic description:** This genus is easy to recognize: the fan of soft

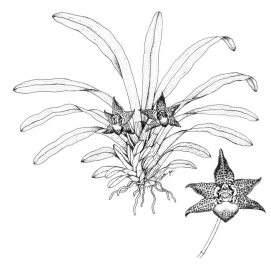

Fig. 4.96. *Huntleya meleagris*

leathery lanceolate leaves, up to 12 inches long, not only reflexes but also has a distinct mark about one-third of the way up from the leaf base. The single-flowered inflorescence arises from the lower leaves of the fans of these sympodial epiphytes. The large, (up to 5-inch) flowers are held in the lower half of the fan and often go undetected when the plants are crowded. The base color of these fragrant flowers is brown. Flower color varies and in some cases gives the flowers a checkerboard appearance.

**Flowering season:** Summer and fall.
**Culture**
    **Medium:** Any proven epiphytic medium
    **Fertilizer and fertilization:** Monthly using a balanced fertilizer.
    **Watering:** Water thoroughly and not again until the top of the medium is dry to the touch.
    **Propagation:** Seed or division.
    **Repotting:** Every 2 years.

## Ionopsis

**Genus:** *Ionopsis* Humboldt, Bonpland, & Kunth (eye-oh-NOPP-siss)

**Tribe:** Maxillarieae

**Subtribe:** Oncidiinae

**Etymology:** From two Greek words *opsis* (apearing) and *ion* (violet), denoting the violet-like characteristics of these flowers.

**Native habitat:** Mexico south to southern Brazil.

**Number of species:** 10

**Commonly grown species:** *satyrioides*, *utricularioides* (color plate 28).

**Hybridizes with:** *Comparettia*, *Notylia*, *Oncidium*, *Rodriguezia*.

**Generic description:** The delightful, delicate flowers borne on long inflorescences make these plants very attractive, but belies the fact that the plants are difficult to maintain in greenhouses. The small pseudobulbs of

Fig. 4.97. *Ionopsis utricularioides*

these sympodial epiphytes are hidden by the clasping leaf bases so they appear to lack them. The thick leathery leaves are folded and have pronounced keels. The branched, wiry inflorescence arises from the leaf axil. Most are 24 inches long, but have been reported as long as 3 feet. The flowers, borne in large numbers, are usually white or violet and the white flowers may have dark violet stripes.

**Flowering season:** All season depending on species.

**Culture**

    **Medium:** Mount on tree branches.

    **Fertilizers and fertilization:** Monthly with a weak, balanced fertilizer.

    **Watering:** Daily for best growth.

    **Propagation:** Seed or division.

    **Repotting:** When the branch decomposes.

## Isochilus

**Genus:** *Isochilus* R. Brown (eye-soh-KYE-luss)
**Tribe**: Epidendreae
**Subtribe:** Laeliinae
**Etymology:** From two Greek words *isos* (equal) and *cheilos* (lip); the lip is almost equal to the petals in size.
**Native habitat:** Mexico to southern Brazil.
**Number of species:** 2
**Commonly grown species:** *linearis* (color plate 29), *major*.
**Hybridizes with:** None recorded.
**Generic description:** One species in this small genus, *Isochilus major*, has a very unique characteristic, found elsewhere only in bromeliads. When the plants develop their inflorescences the upper leaves on the stem turn lavender, becoming

Fig. 4.98. *Isochilus major*

green again after flowering. These sympodial epiphytic plants' reedlike growth can form dense clumps. Each reed has its upper two thirds clothed in soft, flat leaves with clasping leaf bases. The terminal inflorescences may have 1 to several small (0.3-inch) pink or magenta flowers.
**Flowering season:** All year.
**Culture**
    **Medium:** Tree fern, bark mixes, or peat and perlite.
    **Fertilizers and fertilization:** Monthly, ratio depends on medium.
    **Watering:** Do not allow medium to dry out excessively.
    **Propagation:** Seed or division.
    **Repotting:** When plant becomes too large for its container or the medium decomposes.

## Jumellea

**Genus:** *Jumellea* Schlechter (joo-MELL-ee-uh)
**Tribe:** Vandeae
**Subtribe:** Angraecinae
**Etymology:** Named in honor of Henri Jumelle, a French botanist who studied the flora of Madagascar.
**Native habitat:** Madagascar, Mascarene Islands, and eastern Africa.
**Number of species:** 40
**Commonly grown species:** *fragrans, gracilipes, sagittata*.
**Hybridizes with:** *Aeranthes, Angraecum*.

Fig. 4.99. *Jumellea gracilipes*

**Generic description:** This angraecoid has long white spurred flowers that typify the group. Vegetatively, these monopodial plants may be either epiphytic or grow on mossy rocks (lithophytic). The plants usually have 2-ranked, thin, leathery, bilobed leaves with clasping leaf bases. The dark green, wiry inflorescences arise from the lower leaf axils and usually bear 1 delicate white flower that can be up to 5 inches in diameter, depending on species.
**Flowering season:** Winter and spring.
**Culture**
    **Medium:** Any coarse, epiphytic mix.
    **Fertilizers and fertilization:** Monthly, ratio depends on medium.
    **Watering:** Keep medium moist at all times.
    **Propagation:** Seed or offsets.
    **Repotting:** Every 2–3 years.

## Laelia

**Genus:** *Laelia* Lindley (LAY-lee-uh)

**Tribe:** Epidendreae

**Subtribe:** Laeliinae

**Etymology:** Probably named for the female members of the Roman family Laelius.

**Native habitat:** Mexico, Central America, and Brazil.

**Number of species:** Varies from 35 to 75 depending on taxonomist

**Commonly grown species:** *anceps, autumnalis, cinnabarina, flava, grandis, harpophylla, lobata, lundii, milleri, pumila, purpurata* (color plate 30), *rubescens, tenebrosa.*

**Hybridizes with:** *Barkeria, Brassavola, Broughtonia, Cattleya, Caularthron, Encyclia, Epidendrum, Schomburgkia, Sophronitis.*

**Generic description:** Vegetatively, *Laelia* can be divided into sections based on pseudobulbs. They range from round and flat (*L. rubescens*) to egg shaped (*L. anceps*) to reedlike (*L. harpophylla*). Each pseudobulb bears one or more stiff, leathery leaves. The terminal inflorescences of these sympodial epiphytes are also variable, ranging in length from 1 inch to 6 feet and bearing from 1 to 20 flowers. The 1–6-inch flowers, depending on species, may be purple, white, reddish, or yellow.

**Flowering season:** All year depending on species.

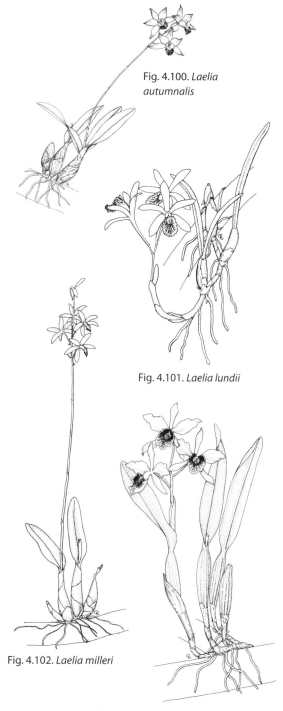

Fig. 4.100. *Laelia autumnalis*

Fig. 4.101. *Laelia lundii*

Fig. 4.102. *Laelia milleri*

Fig. 4.103. *Laelia purpurata*

### Culture

**Medium:** Any proven epiphytic mix.

**Fertilizers and fertilization:** Monthly, ratio depends on medium.

**Watering:** Water thoroughly and not again until the medium feels dry to the touch.

**Propagation:** Seed, division, or meristems.

**Repotting:** Approximately every 2 years.

**Note:** *Laelia* is closely related to *Cattleya* but easily separated on the basis of number of pollinia (*Laelia* has 8, *Cattleya* has 4) and *Laelia* has been widely used as parent stock for thousands of hybrids. Recent DNA studies have indicated that the large flowered laelias (*L. purpurata*) are likely to be transferred to the genus *Sophronitis*.

## Lepanthes

**Genus:** *Lepanthes* Swartz (luh-PAN-theez)
**Tribe:** Epidendreae
**Subtribe:** Pleurothallidinae
**Etymology:** From two Greek words *lepis* (scale) and *anthos* (flower) denoting the very small flowers found in this genus.
**Native habitat:** Central and South America and West Indies at high elevations.
**Number of species:** 100+ (up to 800 in some texts); many new species are still being discovered annually
**Commonly grown species:** *calodictyon, escobariana, lindleyana, obtusa, puchella.*
**Hybridizes with:** *Lepanthopsis.*

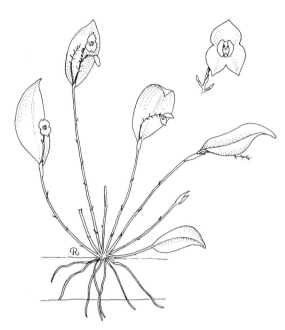

Fig. 4.104. *Lepanthes obtusa*

**Generic description:** When it comes to delicate, delightful, miniature orchids the genus *Lepanthes* has it all. One outstanding species, *L. calodictyon*, has small (less than 1 inch), almost circular leaves that are green heavily overlaid with reddish brown, also making it an attractive miniscule foliage plant. The thin stems (ramicauls) of these sympodial epiphytic plants are usually tightly clustered and topped by a single, sessile leaf. The axillary inflorescence bears 1 to many flowers, the latter usually 2-ranked. The small, delicate flowers come in a variety of colors and are sometimes borne prone on the leaf blade.
**Flowering season:** All year depending on species.
**Culture**
    **Medium:** Plaques or sphagnum moss.
    **Fertilizers and fertilization:** Monthly using a 1-1-1.
    **Watering:** Keep medium moist at all times.
    **Propagation:** Seed or division.
    **Repotting:** Only when plaque or medium decomposes.

## Leptotes

**Genus:** *Leptotes* Lindley (lep-TOH-teez)
**Tribe:** Epidendreae
**Subtribe:** Laeliinae
**Etymology:** From the Greek word *leptotes* (delicateness), denoting the small size of these plants.
**Native habitat:** Southeastern Brazil.
**Number of species:** 5
**Commonly grown species:** *bicolor, unicolor.*
**Hybridizes with:** *Barkeria, Brassavola, Cattleya, Encyclia, Epidendrum, Laelia, Sophronitis.*

Fig. 4.105. *Leptotes bicolor*

**Generic description:** When it comes to attractive miniature plants, *Leptotes* species are high on the list. Vegetatively, *Leptotes* could be diminutive *Brassavola* plants with their thin, tightly clustered pseudobulbs, 1 inch or less in height, each topped by a small (usually less than 5 inches long), terete, green leaf that may sometimes have a purplish cast. A very short inflorescence arises from the apex of the pseudobulb bearing 2–12 1-inch flowers. The base flower colors are white and rose in these sympodial epiphytes.
**Flowering season:** Winter and spring.
**Culture**
    **Medium:** Tree fern plaques or tree limbs.
    **Fertilizers and fertilization:** Monthly using a weak, balanced fertilizer.
    **Watering:** Daily for best growth.
    **Propagation:** Seed or division.
    **Repotting:** Only when the plaque or limb decomposes.
**Note:** The seed pods have a high vanillin content and in its native habitat the local inhabitants use them for flavoring.

## Liparis

**Genus:** *Liparis* I. C. Richard (LIP-per-iss)
**Tribe:** Malaxideae
**Etymology:** From the Greek word *liparos* (fat, greasy, or shiny), denoting the often shiny, almost greasy look of the leaves.
**Native habitat:** Tropical and temperate regions of the world, most common in Southeast Asia.
**Number of species:** 250
**Commonly grown species:** *nervosa, nugentea, nutans, reflexa.*
**Hybridizes with:** None recorded.
**Generic description:** Most descriptions of the genus *Liparis* characterize it as "highly variable" because of the diversity of vegetative features. These sympodial plants may be terrestrial, epiphytic, or lithophytic depending on the species. The tightly

Fig. 4.106. *Liparis nervosa*

clustered pseudobulbs may be small (pyriform) to tall and slender, the latter looking more like a herbaceous stem than a pseudobulb. Leaves vary from soft and plicate to smooth and leathery, with one to several per pseudobulb. The terminal inflorescence may be erect or lax and bears a few to many flowers up to 0.75 inch across. Flower color varies widely and includes yellow green, green, purple, and rusty orange.
**Flowering season:** All year depending on species.
**Culture**
    **Medium:** Any proven terrestrial or epiphytic mix, depending on species.
    **Fertilizers and fertilization:** Monthly, ratio depends on medium.
    **Watering:** Water thoroughly and not again until the surface of the medium is dry.
    **Propagation:** Seed or division.
    **Repotting:** Every 2–3 years.

## Lockhartia

{Fig. 4.107 here}

**Genus:** *Lockhartia* Hooker (lock-HART-ee-uh)

**Tribe:** Maxillarieae

**Subtribe:** Oncidiinae

**Etymology:** Named in honor of David Lockhart, superintendent of the Royal Botanical Gardens in Trinidad.

**Native habitat:** Mexico south to Brazil.

**Number of species:** 25

**Commonly grown species:** *acuta, elegans, oerstedii, serra.*

Fig. 4.107. *Lockhartia oerstedii*

**Hybridizes with:** *Comparettia, Gomesa, Leochilus, Oncidium, Trichopilia.*

**Generic description:** In the literature *Lockhartia* is described as "distichous" or having its small clasping leaves in two ranks such that they appear to be braided. Vegetatively, the stems of these sympodial epiphytes elongate for several years, and the plant continues to have axillary flowering during this period. Hence, a novice might think they are monopodial instead of sympodial. The small inflorescences that arise from the leaf axils just below the stem apex have several buds, but only one flower opens at a time. The 0.75-inch flowers are yellow with reddish purple markings on the lip.

**Flowering season:** All season depending on species.

**Culture**

    **Medium:** Any proven epiphytic mix or mounted on plaques.

    **Fertilizers and fertilization:** Monthly, ratio depends on medium.

    **Watering:** Keep medium moist at all times and water plaque daily.

    **Propagation:** Seed or division.

    **Repotting:** Every 3–5 years or when plaques decompose.

## Ludisia

**Genus:** *Ludisia* A. Richard (loo-DISS-ee-uh)
**Tribe:** Cranichideae
**Subtribe:** Goodyerinae
**Etymology:** Origin of the name is unknown, possibly named for a person.
**Native habitat:** Southeast Asia and Indonesia.
**Number of species:** 1
**Commonly grown species:** *discolor.*
**Hybridizes with:** *Anoectochilus, Macodes.*
**Generic description:** *Ludisia* is one of the so-called Jewel Orchids, a name given to a variety of terrestrial orchids whose colorful, often variegated foliage makes them attractive all season. Vegetatively, these sympodial plants have succulent, brittle stems that may be procumbent or erect and red in color. Each stem is topped by up to 6 leaves, usually tightly clustered. The reddish green leaf blade may have either bright (*L. discolor* var. *dawsoniana*) or dull red veins. The apical, erect, hairy inflorescence bears up to 12 flowers, each

Fig. 4.108. *Ludisia discolor*

subtended by a purplish leafy bract. The white flowers, with yellow anther cap, each have a lip with 2 twisted lobes and the anther cap is also slightly twisted.
**Flowering season:** Fall and winter.
**Culture**
    **Medium:** Equal parts of peat, perlite, and soil.
    **Fertilizers and fertilization:** Monthly using a 1-1-1 fertilizer.
    **Watering:** Do not allow medium to dry out excessively.
    **Propagation:** Seed, division, or tip cuttings.
    **Repotting:** When the plants become too large for their containers.

## Lycaste

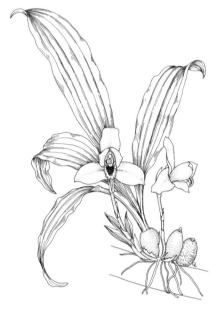

**Genus:** *Lycaste* Lindley (lye-KASS-tee)
**Tribe:** Maxillarieae
**Subtribe:** Lycastinae
**Etymology:** Could be in honor of Lycaste, the lovely daughter of Priam, king of Troy, or from the Greek word *lycaste* (nymph).
**Native habitat:** Mexico and northwestern South America.
**Number of species:** Approximately 35
**Commonly grown species:** *aromatica, brevispatha, crinita, curenta, dowiana* (color plate 31), *leucantha, longipetala, skinneri, tricolor.*
**Hybridizes with:** *Anguloa, Bifrenaria, Cochleanthes, Colax, Maxillaria, Zygopetalum.*
**Generic description:** Showy, colorful flowers of *Lycaste*, often borne in large numbers on well-grown plants, are the hallmark of

Fig. 4.109. *Lycaste skinneri*

this genus. Vegetatively, *Lycaste* species are very similar. These sympodial epiphytes form tight clusters of often furrowed pseudobulbs, each topped by 1–3 leaves. The soft, thin, lanceolate leaves last a little more than a year and may be up to 30 inches long. One or more erect inflorescences arise from the base of the pseudobulbs and have a single flower up to 5 inches in diameter. There is a wide range of flower colors, including yellow, pale green, olive green, pink, and brownish green.
**Flowering season:** All year depending on species.
**Culture**
    **Medium:** Most well-drained epiphytic mixes.
    **Fertilizers and fertilization:** Monthly, ratio depends on the medium.
    **Watering:** Keep moist during the growing season, but do not allow medium to dry out excessively in the dormant season.
    **Propagation:** Seed or division.
    **Repotting:** At least every 2–3 years.
**Note:** The white form of *Lycaste skinneri* is the national flower of Guatemala.

## Macradenia

**Genus:** *Macradenia* R. Brown (mac-ruh-DEEN-ee-uh)
**Tribe:** Maxillarieae
**Subtribe:** Oncidiinae
**Etymology:** From two Greek words *makros* (long) and *aden* (gland), denoting the long stipe in these flowers.
**Native habitat:** Florida, West Indies, Mexico south to northern South America.
**Number of species:** 12
**Commonly grown species:** *brassavolae, lutescens, multiflora.*
**Hybridizes with:** *Gomesa, Oncidium, Rodriguezia.*
**Generic description:** *Macradenia* is an interesting genus when it comes to flowering. When the erect inflorescence emerges the flowers are nonresupinate, but this does not present a pollination problem because when the inflorescence elongates it becomes pendent putting the flower in a resupinate position. These sympodial epiphytes have almost round pseudobulbs, up to 2 inches tall, that form dense clumps. The pseudobulbs have basal, green

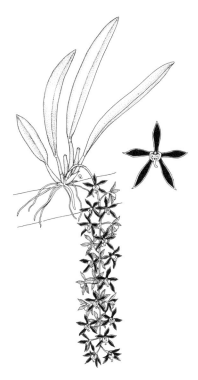

Fig. 4.110. *Macradenia lutescens*

sheaths that become dry and papery with age. There is a single, thick, almost leathery 7-inch leaf atop each pseudobulb. The pendent inflorescence may bear as many as 25 1-inch flowers in yellow, maroon, or white.
**Flowering season:** Spring and summer.
**Culture**
    **Medium:** Best mounted on branches or plaques.
    **Fertilizers and fertilization:** Monthly using a 1–1–1.
    **Watering:** Daily for best growth.
    **Propagation:** Seed or division.
    **Repotting:** Only when the mount decomposes.

## Malaxis

**Genus:** *Malaxis* Swartz (mal-axe-is)
**Tribe:** Malaxideae
**Etymology:** From the Greek word *malaxis* (softening), probably a reference to the soft, somewhat succulent leaves.
**Native habitat:** Worldwide, except Africa. Southeast Asia has the largest concentration of species.
**Number of species:** 300
**Commonly grown species:** *calophylla, latifolia, monophyllos, ophrydis, paludosa.*
**Hybridizes with:** None recorded.
**Generic description:** Although *Malaxis* species vary considerably as far as vegetative growth is concerned, they all have one thing in common: these sympodial epiphytes, sometimes terrestrial,

Fig. 4.111. *Malaxis ophrydis*

are blessed with large numbers of miniature flowers. Depending on species, these plants may be quite small, less than 6 inches with pseudobulbs measuring 0.5 inch or less (*M. paludosa*), while others have 6-inch pseudobulbs hidden by 12-inch pleated leaves with clasping leaf bases (*M. latifolia*). The erect terminal inflorescence may bear up to 100 small flowers. Since the flowers open slowly and sequentially from base to apex, the plants are in flower for a long period. The base flower colors are green and shades of cream; a few species have pinkish purple flowers.
**Flowering season:** All year depending on species.
**Culture**
    **Medium:** Most proven epiphytic mixes.
    **Fertilizers and fertilization:** Monthly during growing season, ratio depends on medium.
    **Watering:** Keep medium moist during growing season and water less frequently during dormant period.
    **Propagation:** Seed, division, or keikis.
    **Repotting:** Every 2–3 years.
**Note:** In the fall, the leaves of some deciduous species (*M. latifolia*) turn grayish, become soft and collapse making the plant very unsightly and causing the novice to fear the worst. However bad the plants look, this is a natural occurrence and they will produce normal growth the next spring.

## Masdevallia

**Genus:** *Masdevallia* Ruiz & Pavón (maz-deh-VAL-ee-uh)
**Tribe:** Epidendreae
**Subtribe:** Pleurothallidinae
**Etymology:** Named in honor of the Spanish botanist José Masdevall.
**Native habitat:** Mexico to southern Brazil.
**Number of species:** 300
**Commonly grown species:** *attenuata, bicolor, caudata, coccinea, elephanticeps, militaris, princeps* (color plate 32), *rosea, uniflora, veitchiana.*
**Hybridizes with:** *Dracula, Porroglossum.*
**Generic description:** When it comes to an array of vivid colors the genus *Masdevallia* is hard to surpass. These sympodial orchids may be epiphytic or terrestrial, but they are all very similar vegetatively. The plants lack pseudobulbs. Tight clusters of leathery leaves form atop short, lateral branches (ramicauls). The inflorescences arise from the top of the ramicauls and usually bear one flower up to 12 inches across, depending on species. Three large sepals, often with long attenuated apices, are the showiest part of the flower. The petals, lip, and column are hidden in the sepaline tube. Flower colors are bright red, orange, purple, and white.
**Flowering season:** All year depending on species.
**Culture**
    **Medium:** A terrestrial or epiphytic mix, depending on species.
    **Fertilizers and fertilization:** Monthly, ratio will depend on the medium.
    **Watering:** Medium should never be allowed to dry out.
    **Propagation:** Seed or division.
    **Repotting:** When plants become too large for their containers or medium decomposes.

Fig. 4.112. *Masdevallia caudata*

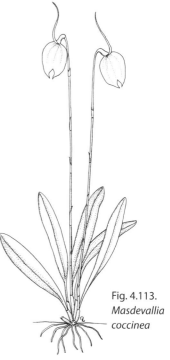

Fig. 4.113. *Masdevallia coccinea*

## Maxillaria

**Genus:** *Maxillaria* Ruiz & Pavón (max-ih-LARE-ee-uh)
**Tribe:** Maxillarieae
**Subtribe:** Maxillariinae
**Etymology:** From the Latin word *maxilla* (jawbone), because the lips and columns reminded Ruiz & Pavón of insect jaws.
**Native habitat:** Florida, Cuba, and Mexico south to southern Brazil.
**Number of species:** 300
**Commonly grown species:** *acuminata, brunnea, crassifolia, cucullata, friedrich-sthallii, fulgens, grandiflora, inaudita, neglecta, ochroleuca, rufescens, sanderiana, sophronitis* (color plate 33), *tenuifolia* (color plate 34), *valenzuelana, variabilis, venusta.*
**Hybridizes with:** *Lycaste, Xylobium.*
**Generic description:** This large group of sympodial epiphytes can easily be divided into two groups vegetatively. One group has the pseudobulbs arranged in tight clusters (*Maxillaria cucullata*), while the other group has the pseudobulbs arranged in chainlike fashion on the rhizome (*M. tenuifolia*). The mostly flattened pseudobulbs are sheathed by one or more leafy bracts. The leathery, persistent leaves vary in number and size per pseudobulb. The erect, bracted inflorescences, up to 3 or 4 per pseudobulb, arise from the base of the pseudobulb and bear a single flower. Individual flowers range from 1 to 6 inches in diameter and the predominant base colors are white, yellow, and red, often spotted with other colors.

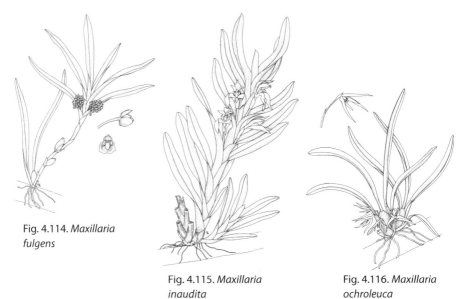

Fig. 4.114. *Maxillaria fulgens*

Fig. 4.115. *Maxillaria inaudita*

Fig. 4.116. *Maxillaria ochroleuca*

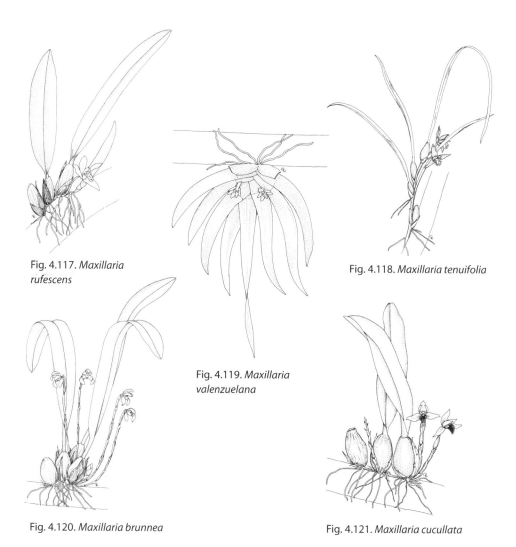

Fig. 4.117. *Maxillaria rufescens*

Fig. 4.118. *Maxillaria tenuifolia*

Fig. 4.119. *Maxillaria valenzuelana*

Fig. 4.120. *Maxillaria brunnea*

Fig. 4.121. *Maxillaria cucullata*

**Flowering season:** All year depending on the species.
**Culture**
    **Medium:** Any well-drained epiphytic mix or mounted on plaques.
    **Fertilizers and fertilization:** Monthly, ratio depends on medium.
    **Watering:** Keep medium moist at all times for best growth.
    **Propagation:** Seed or division.
    **Repotting:** Every 2–3 years.

## Mexicoa

**Genus:** *Mexicoa* Garay (mex-ih-KOH-uh)
**Tribe:** Maxillarieae
**Subtribe:** Oncidiinae
**Etymology:** Named in honor of the home of the species, Mexico.
**Native habitat:** Mexico.
**Number of species:** 1
**Commonly grown species:** *ghiesbrechtiana*.
**Hybridizes with:** None recorded.
**Generic description:** The delightful genus *Mexicoa* was separated from *Oncidium* in 1974 by Garay because the floral characteristics differed from *Oncidium*. This monotypic genus of sympodial epiphytic plants is classified as a miniature; most plants are less than 6 inches tall. The tightly arranged, ovoid pseudobulbs are approximately 1 inch tall and slightly ridged. There are 2 or

Fig. 4.122. *Mexicoa ghiesbrechtiana*

3 narrow, lanceolate, leathery leaves atop each pseudobulb. The short, often lax, inflorescence arises as new growth develops and bears up to 6 flowers. The colorful 1-inch flowers are basically yellow with maroon stripes.
**Flowering season:** Spring and summer.
**Culture**
    **Medium:** Mounted on branches or plaques. Use a well-drained, epiphytic medium for potted plants.
    **Fertilizers and fertilization:** Monthly using a 1–1–1.
    **Watering:** Daily for best growth.
    **Propagation:** Seed or division.
    **Repotting:** Only when the mount or medium decomposes.

## Miltonia

**Genus:** *Miltonia* Lindley (mill-TONE-ee-uh)
**Tribe:** Maxillarieae
**Subtribe:** Oncidiinae
**Etymology:** Named in 1838 in honor of Earl Fitz Williams, then Viscount Milton.
**Native habitat:** Brazil.
**Number of species:** 4
**Commonly grown species:** *clowesii, flavescens, regnellii, spectabilis* (color plate 35).
**Hybridizes with:** *Ada, Aspasia, Brassia, Cochlioda, Comparettia, Odontoglossum, Oncidium, Rodriguezia, Trichopilia.*
**Generic description:** It was not till 1979 that taxonomists agreed that the work of Alexandre Godfrey-Lebeuf in 1899, dividing *Miltonia* into two genera (*Miltonia* and *Miltoniopsis*), was valid. Today four valid species are recognized in *Miltonia*. These sympodial

Fig. 4.123. *Miltonia spectabilis*

epiphytes have scaly rhizomes with pseudobulbs spaced as much as 1.5 inches apart. The light green, flattened pseudobulbs, up to 4 inches tall, are topped by two usually light green leaves, which are folded at the base. The erect, bracted inflorescence, bearing one to many flowers, arises from the base of the newest maturing pseudobulb. The basic flower colors are white, purple, and yellow.
**Flowering season:** Spring, summer, and fall.
**Culture**
    **Medium:** Bark mixes or peat and perlite.
    **Fertilizers and fertilization:** Monthly, ratio depends on the medium.
    **Watering:** Water thoroughly and not again until the medium becomes dry to the touch.
    **Propagation:** Seed or division.
    **Repotting:** Every 2–3 years.

## Miltoniopsis

**Genus:** *Miltoniopsis* Godefroy-Lebeuf (mil-toh-nee-OPP-siss)
**Tribe:** Maxillarieae
**Subtribe:** Oncidiinae
**Etymology:** Called *Miltoniopsis* because of their likeness to *Miltonia*.
**Native habitat:** Northern South America and Pannama.
**Number of species:** 7
**Commonly grown species:** *phalaenopsis* (color plate 36), *roezlii, santanae, vexillaria, warscewiczii.*
**Hybridizes with:** *Ada, Aspasia, Brassia, Cochlioda, Comparettia, Odontoglossum, Oncidium, Rodriquezia, Trichopilia.*
**Generic description:** Since 1979, *Miltoniopsis* has been considered a valid genus. It

Fig. 4.124. *Miltoniopsis vexillaria*

has been recognized for its attractive flat flowers that have sired many of the large, spectacular, pansy-like hybrids available today. *Miltoniopsis* is easily separated from *Miltonia* by having only one leaf on the pseudobulb apex. The flattened pseudobulbs of these sympodial epiphytes (sometime lithophytes) are tightly clustered. A long (15-inch) linear leaf tops each pseudobulb. Several deciduous leaf–bearing bracts encase each pseudobulb. The inflorescences arise from the base of the pseudobulb bearing 1–5 very showy, flat flowers. The base color is white, usually with red or pink markings.
**Flowering season:** Spring, summer and fall.
**Culture**
    **Medium:** Any well-drained epiphytic mix.
    **Fertilizers and fertilization:** Monthly, ratio depends on medium.
    **Watering:** Keep medium moist at all times for best growth.
    **Propagation:** Seed, division, or meristems.
    **Repotting:** Every 2–3 years.

## Mormodes

**Genus:** *Mormodes* Lindley (mor-MOH-dees)

**Tribe:** Cymbidieae

**Subtribe:** Catasetinae

**Etymology:** From the Greek words *mormo* (phantom or frightful object) and *eides* (resembling), denoting the unusual twist in the flower.

**Native habitat:** Mexico to southern Brazil.

**Number of species:** 35

**Commonly grown species:** *atropurpureum, colossus, hookeri, maculatum, rolfeanum, sinuata.*

**Hybridizes with:** *Catasetum, Cycnoches.*

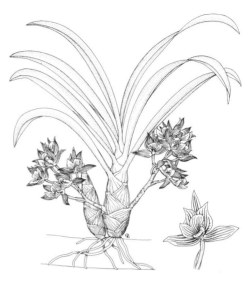

Fig. 4.125. *Mormodes sinuata*

**Generic description:** Looking at *Mormodes* flowers for the first time, it becomes obvious they are unique. When John Lindley identified the genus he noted that the flowers showed "astonishing deviations from ordinary structure." The deciduous, spindle-shaped pseudobulbs of these sympodial epiphytes are tightly clustered. Each pseudobulb, up to 15 inches tall, bears as many as 15 leaves up to 24 inches long. Old pseudobulbs are encased in papery bracts. The usually erect inflorescences, bearing up to 12 fragrant colorful flowers, arise from the midpoint of the pseudobulb. Segments of the flowers, such as the column, are twisted, making the genus easy to recognize. Flower color varies, with pink and deep reds dominant.

**Flowering season:** Fall, winter, and spring.

**Culture**

    **Medium:** Any coarse epiphytic mix.

    **Fertilizers and fertilization:** Monthly during growing season, ratio depends on medium.

    **Watering:** Water sparingly during the dormant season.

    **Propagation:** Seed or division.

    **Repotting:** Every 2–3 years.

## Mormolyca

**Genus:** *Mormolyca* Fenzl (mor-moh-LYE-kuh)
**Tribe:** Maxillarieae
**Subtribe:** Maxillariinae
**Etymology:** From the Greek word *mormolyca* referring to the unusual coloration and bizarre appearance of the flower.
**Native habitat:** Mexico south to northern South America and southern Brazil.
**Number of species:** 6
**Commonly grown species:** *gracilipes*, *peruviana*, *ringens*.
**Hybridizes with:** *Trigonidium*.
**Generic description:** If you are looking for an unusual orchid flower to add to your collection, *Mormolyca* fits the bill. Unfortunately the flowers

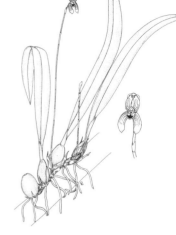

Fig. 4.126. *Mormolyca ringens*

are sometimes described as "odd" or even "grotesque," belying their charm and ease of growth. Vegetatively, these sympodial epiphytes have tightly clustered ellipsoid pseudobulbs, each topped by a single leaf and subtended by several leafy bracts. The lanceolate, leathery leaves are up to 14 inches long. The erect inflorescences arise from the base of the pseudobulbs and bear a single flower. The creamy yellow flowers, up to 0.5 inch and borne above the foliage, are adorned with lavender or maroon, often making them look brown from a distance.
**Flowering season:** Winter, spring, and summer.
**Culture**
    **Medium:** Any epiphytic mix.
    **Fertilizers and fertilization:** Monthly, ratio depending on medium.
    **Watering:** Keep medium moist for best growth.
    **Propagation:** Seed or division.
    **Repotting:** When plants become too large for their containers or the medium decomposes.

## Neobenthamia

**Genus:** *Neobenthamia* Rolfe (nee-oh-ben-THAME-ee-uh)
**Tribe:** Epidendreae
**Subtribe:** Polystachyinae
**Etymology:** In honor of George Bentham. Rolfe added the *Neo-* to distinguish it from *Benthamia*, another genus also named in honor of Bentham.
**Native habitat:** Tanzania and Zanzibar.
**Number of species:** 1
**Commonly grown species:** *gracilis*.
**Hybridizes with:** None recorded.
**Generic description:** These plants form tall canelike clumps topped by clusters of long-lived, white flowers that make them a sight to behold. The tall canes of these sympodial terrestrial orchids attain heights of 6 feet. The clasping, alternate, 10-inch leaves are

Fig. 4.127. *Neobenthamia gracilis*

soft and narrow, almost grasslike. Each cane is topped by a short, bracted inflorescence with a cluster of up to 25 small (0.5-inch) flowers. These durable flowers are basically white; however, the anther cap is rose red and the lip usually has a yellow area in the center with rose-red dots on either side, adding to the attractiveness of the flowers.
**Flowering season:** Spring and summer.
**Culture**
    **Medium:** Any proven terrestrial mix.
    **Fertilizers and fertilization:** Monthly using a 1-1-1.
    **Watering:** Keep medium moist at all times for best growth.
    **Propagation:** Seed, division, or keikis.
    **Repotting:** When plants become too large for their containers.

## Neofinetia

**Genus:** *Neofinetia* Hu (nee-oh-fih-NET-ee-uh)
**Tribe:** Vandeae
**Subtribe:** Aeridinae
**Etymology:** Named in honor of M. A. Finet; *Neo-* designates it as a new Finet genus.
**Native habitat:** China, Korea, Japan and the Ryukyu Islands.
**Number of species:** 1
**Commonly grown species:** *falcata* (color plate 37).
**Hybridizes with:** *Aerides, Angraecum, Ascocentrum, Doritis, Luisia, Phalaenopsis, Renanthera.*

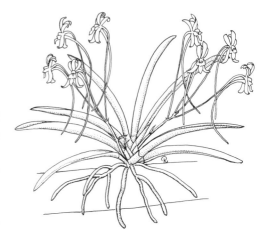

Fig. 4.128. *Neofinetia falcata*

**Generic description:** This monotypic genus is easily recognized by its delightful long-spurred flowers. Vegetatively, this monopodial epiphyte looks like a dense cluster of miniature vandas (see *Vanda*). The 4–8 keeled leaves hide the short stems with clasping leaf bases. The inflorescence arises from the leaf axil and, although short, displays its flowers above the clump of leaves. The pure white, spurred flowers of *Neofinetia* are very fragrant at night. Despite their size, the plants are very showy when in bloom. There are many named varieties in East Asia based on leaf variegations.
**Flowering season:** Summer and fall.
**Culture**
  **Medium:** Sphagnum moss or any epiphytic mix.
  **Fertilizers and fertilization:** Monthly, ratio depending on medium.
  **Watering:** Keep medium moist for best growth.
  **Propagation:** Seed or offsets.
  **Repotting:** When the plant becomes too large for the container or medium decomposes.
**Note:** *Neofinetia* was considered the "orchid of wealth and nobility" and grown by Samurai warriors. Feudal lords in Japan carried *Neofinetia* plants with them on journeys. Many East Asians culture *Neofinetia* plants in ornate ceramic containers and the variegated forms are highly prized.

## Neomoorea

**Genus:** *Neomoorea* Rolfe (nee-oh-MOOR-ee-uh)

**Tribe:** Maxillarieae

**Subtribe:** Lycastinae

**Etymology:** Named by Rolfe in honor of botanist F. W. Moore of Ireland, also previously honored in the name *Moorea*.

**Native habitat:** Panama and Colombia.

**Number of species:** 1

**Commonly grown species:** *wallisii* (color plate 38).

**Hybridizes with:** None recorded.

**Generic description:** At first glance, plants of *Neomoorea* resemble palm seedlings, but once you notice the pseudobulb it is clear that the plant is an orchid. The large, furrowed, almost egg-shaped pseudobulbs, up to 5 inches tall, are topped by two large leaves. The individual leaves, as long as 3

Fig. 4.129. *Neomoorea wallisii*

feet, are soft and pleated. The erect inflorescence arises from the base of the pseudobulb, may be up to 2 feet tall, and bears up to 20 flowers. The tan to brownish red 2-inch flowers fade to white in the center. These sympodial plants may be either epiphytic or terrestrial.

**Flowering season:** Spring.

**Culture**

    **Medium:** Any proven terrestrial or epiphytic mix.

    **Fertilizers and fertilization:** Monthly, ratio depending on medium.

    **Watering:** Water thoroughly and not again until the medium feels dry to the touch.

    **Propagation:** Seed or division.

    **Repotting:** When the plant becomes too large for its container or the medium decomposes.

## Notylia

**Genus:** *Notylia* Lindley (no-TILL-ee-uh)
**Tribe:** Maxillarieae
**Subtribe:** Oncidiinae
**Etymology:** From two Greek words *noton* (back) and *tylon* (hump), denoting the unusual column.
**Native habitat:** Mexico to southern Brazil.
**Number of species:** 40
**Commonly grown species:** *barkeri*, *bicolor*, *carnosiflora*, *cordesii*, *platyglossa*, *punctata*.
**Hybridizes with:** *Comparettia*, *Ionopsis*, *Oncidium*.
**Generic description:** Although notylias are miniature plants, their abundant display of flowers belies their size. There are two distinct vegetative types in this sympodial epiphytic genus. One type has small pseudobulbs

Fig. 4.130. *Notylia barkeri*

and equitant leaves (*N. cordesii*), while the other has pseudobulbs topped by a single, flat leaf (*N. barkeri*). The usually pendent inflorescences arise from the leaf axil and, depending on species, will have up to 100 basically white flowers; some species are spotted with yellow or purple.
**Flowering season:** Spring, summer, and fall.
**Culture**
    **Medium:** Can be mounted or grown in well-drained, epiphytic mix.
    **Fertilizers and fertilization:** Monthly, ratio depends on medium.
    **Watering:** If mounted, water daily.
    **Propagation:** Seed or division.
    **Repotting:** Every 3–5 years.

## Oberonia

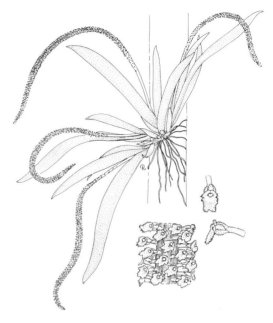

**Genus:** *Oberonia* Lindley (oh-ber-ROW-nee-uh)

**Tribe:** Malaxideae

**Etymology:** Named for Oberon, the mythical King of the Fairies.

**Native habitat:** Tropical Asia and Pacific Islands south to Australia, with 1 species in Madagascar and South Africa.

**Number of species:** 100

**Commonly grown species:** *iridifolia.*

**Hybridizes with:** None recorded.

**Generic description:** Leaves of *Oberonia* species are arranged in fans (iridiform) and terminal inflorescences are densely flowered. The plants may be erect or pendent. Veg-

Fig. 4.131. *Oberonia iridifolia*

etatively, these sympodial epiphytes look like small iris plants at first glance. Each fan comprises 3–4 leaves up to 10 inches long. The small (sometimes minute) non-resupinate flowers may be purple, yellow, green, or white depending on species.

**Flowering season:** Spring and summer.

**Culture**

    **Medium:** Mounted, or any well-drained epiphytic mix.

    **Fertilizers and fertilization:** Monthly, ratio depends on medium.

    **Watering:** Water mounts daily, keep epiphytic medium moist at all times.

    **Propagation:** Seed or division.

    **Repotting:** When mounts decompose, or every 2–3 years for container grown plants.

## Octomeria

**Genus:** *Octomeria* R. Brown (ock-toe-MER-ee-uh)
**Tribe:** Epidendreae
**Subtribe:** Pleurothallidinae
**Etymology:** From two Greek words *octo* (eight) and *meros* (part), denoting the 8 pollinia that are characteristic of this genus.
**Native habitat:** West Indies, Central and South America.
**Number of species:** 50
**Commonly grown species:** *gracilis, grandiflora, sandersiana.*
**Hybridizes with:** None recorded.
**Generic description:** These sympodial epiphytes have creeping rhizomes and erect secondary stems topped by

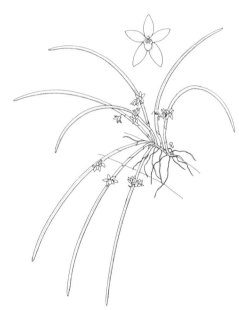

Fig. 4.132. *Octomeria gracilis*

a single leaf. The base of the stems usually has several sheaths. The sessile leaves may be flat or terete and up to 8 inches long. The flowers are borne on axillary inflorescences. Each short inflorescence bears 1 to many small, often dull-colored, slightly scented flowers. The basic flower colors are white, yellow, and straw. The lip may be a different color than the sepals and petals.
**Flowering season:** Spring and summer.
**Culture**
    **Medium:** Any well-drained epiphytic mix.
    **Fertilizers and fertilization:** Monthly, ratio depends on species.
    **Watering:** Keep medium moist at all times.
    **Propagation:** Seed or division.
    **Repotting:** Every 2–3 years.

## Odontoglossum

**Genus:** *Odontoglossum* Humboldt, Bonpland, & Kunth (oh-dont-oh-GLOSS-um)
**Tribe:** Maxillarieae
**Subtribe:** Oncidiinae
**Etymology:** From two Greek words *odonto* (tooth) and *glossa* (tongue), denoting the toothlike projections on the lip.
**Native habitat:** Mexico, northwestern South America south to Ecuador.
**Number of species:** 150
**Commonly grown species:** *constrictum, coronarium* (color plate 39), *crispum, lindenii, odoratum, ramosissimum.*
**Hybridizes with:** *Ada, Aspasia, Brassia, Cochlioda, Comparettia, Gomesa, Miltonia, Miltoniopsis, Oncidium, Trichopilia.*

Fig. 4.133. *Odontoglossum crispum*

**Generic description:** These cool-growing species have long been held in favor by orchidists in cooler climates for their array of very colorful flowers. This was originally a large genus, but the number of species has been greatly reduced by taxonomists removing sections to become new genera (*Lemboglossum*). Vegetatively, these sympodial epiphytic plants grow with their pseudobulbs in tight clusters. As the flattened pseudobulbs develop, they have 4–6 leaves. The lower leaves, which ensheathe the pseudobulb, are short lived, leaving a mature pseudobulb with 1–3 leaves at its apex. The erect inflorescence arises from the base of the pseubobulb and will have up to 24 flowers. The dominant flower colors are white, yellow, and brown.
**Flowering season:** All year depending on species.
**Culture**
    **Medium:** Most well-drained epiphytic mixes.
    **Fertilizers and fertilization:** Monthly, ratio depends on medium.
    **Watering:** Water thoroughly and not again until the medium is dry to the touch.
    **Propagation:** Seed, division, or meristems.
    **Repotting:** Every 2 years or when the plant outgrows its container.

## Oeceoclades

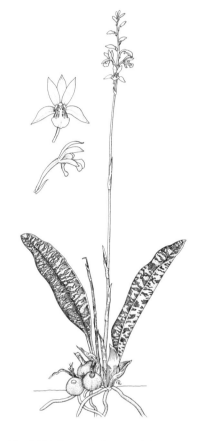

**Genus:** *Oeceoclades* Lindley (oh-ee-see-oh-CLAY-deez)
**Tribe:** Cymbidieae
**Subtribe:** Eulophiinae
**Etymology:** From two Greek words *oikeios* (private) and *klados* (branch). It is believed that when Lindley removed some species from *Angraecum*, he called it a "private branch" to denote their difference.
**Native habitat:** Florida, West Indies, tropical South America, Africa, Madagascar east to the Seychelles.
**Number of species:** 31
**Commonly grown species:** *maculata*.
**Hybridizes with:** *Eulophia*.
**Generic description:** These easy to grow sympodial terrestrial (occasionally epiphytic) plants have small attractive flowers as well as variegated foliage (*O. maculata*). The small, 1-noded pseudobulbs are topped by 1–3 coriaceous leaves up to 10 inches long. Some green leaves are mottled darker green. Each inflorescence, up to 20 inches tall and bearing 12 or

Fig. 4.134. *Oeceoclades maculata*

more flowers, arises from the base of the pseudobulb and is erect to lax. The basic flower colors are white to greenish white with purple spotting.
**Flowering season:** Spring and summer.
**Culture**
    **Medium:** Any well-drained terrestrial mix.
    **Fertilizers and fertilization:** Monthly using a 1-1-1.
    **Watering:** Keep medium moist all year.
    **Propagation:** Seed or division.
    **Repotting:** Every 2–3 years.
**Note:** *Oeceoclades* is naturalizing in Florida and has been reported growing as far north as Gainesville. The plants often arrive in container-grown nursery stock from south Florida.

## Oerstedella

**Genus:** *Oerstedella* Reichenbach f. (er-steh-DELL-uh)
**Tribe:** Epidendreae
**Subtribe:** Laeliinae
**Etymology:** Named in honor of Anders Sandøe Ørsted, who collected the type specimen.
**Native habitat:** Mexico south through the Andes.
**Number of species:** 40
**Commonly grown species:** *centradenia, centropetala, endresii, wallisii.*
**Hybridizes with:** None recorded.
**Generic description:** Although there may be considerable variation in plant size among *Oerstedella* species, they have the same flowering potential. These reed-type,

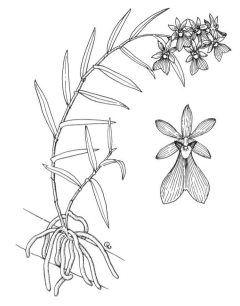

Fig. 4.135. *Oerstedella centradenia*

sympodial epiphytes form tight clusters. The reeds, up to 2 feet tall, are hidden by the clasping leaf bases, which in some species are warty (*O. wallisii*). Each reed will have up to 10 lancelike soft leaves. The inflorescences are borne at the apex of the reed and have 1 or more flowers up to 1 inch in diameter. The base flower colors are lavender and yellow, with some reports of white flowers with purple lips.
**Flowering season:** Fall and winter.
**Culture**
    **Medium:** Most well-drained epiphytic mixes.
    **Fertilizers and fertilization:** Monthly, ratio depends on medium.
    **Watering:** Keep medium moist at all times.
    **Propagation:** Seed or division.
    **Repotting:** Every 2–3 years.

## Oncidium

**Genus:** *Oncidium* Swartz
(on-SID-ee-um)
**Tribe:** Maxillarieae
**Subtribe:** Oncidiinae
**Etymology:** From the Greek word *onkos* (warty), referring to the wartlike growth on the lip.
**Native habitat:** Florida, Mexico, West Indies and south to the northern half of South America.
**Number of species:** 300+
**Commonly grown species:** *ampliatum* (color plate 40), *baueri, cebolleta, concolor, crispum, crista-galli, cucullatum, forbesii, jonesianum, microchilum, ornithorhynchum, sphacelatum* (color plate 41), *tigrinum, triquetrum.*
**Hybridizes with:** *Ada, Aspasia, Brassia, Cochlioda, Comparettia, Gomesa, Miltonia, Miltoniopsis, Odontoglossum, Trichopilia, Trichocentrum.*
**Generic description:** For more than two hundred years, *Oncidium* species have graced the benches of orchid hobbyists' greenhouses. These dainty, delightful flowers, many with large, flaring lips, have been likened to "dancing ladies" in traditional Spanish dress. There are at least five distinct vegetative types in this genus of sympodial epiphytes. They range from small pseudobulbous plants with fanlike leaf

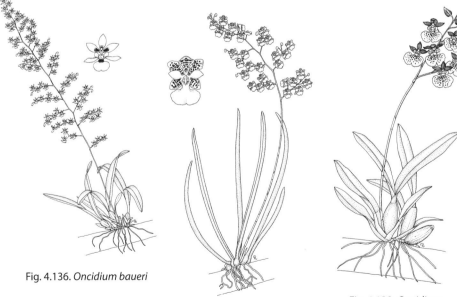

Fig. 4.136. *Oncidium baueri*

Fig. 4.137. *Oncidium cebolleta*

Fig. 4.138. *Oncidium cucullatum*

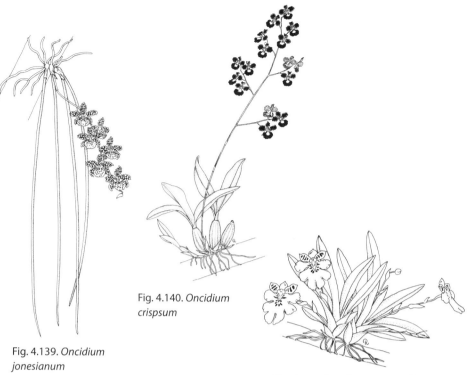

Fig. 4.140. *Oncidium crispsum*

Fig. 4.139. *Oncidium jonesianum*

Fig. 4.141. *Oncidium crista-galli*

arrangements (*O. crista-galli*) to large pseudobulbs topped by long, arching, soft leaves (*O. sphacelatum*). Inflorescences are also variable in size, from a few inches to several feet tall, and bear one to hundreds of flowers. The base flower colors are brown and yellow.

**Flowering season:** All year depending on species.

**Culture**

    **Medium:** Most species grow well either mounted or in an epiphytic mix.

    **Fertilizers and fertilization:** Monthly, ratio depends on medium.

    **Watering:** Mounted species grow best if watered daily.

    **Propagation:** Seed, division, or meristems.

    **Repotting:** When the mount decomposes or plant grows out of its container.

**Note:** Recent taxonomic studies removed the "mule-eared" species (*O. splendidum*) to another genus (*Trichocentrum*).

## Orchis

**Genus:** *Orchis* Linneaus (OR-kiss)
**Tribe:** Orchideae
**Subtribe:** Orchidinae
**Etymology:** From the Greek word *orchis* (testicle), to describe the testiculate shape of the twin tubers.
**Native habitat:** Europe eastward throughout Asia to China.
**Number of species:** 37
**Commonly grown species:** *mascula, militaris, purpurea, simia.*
**Hybridizes with:** *Ophrys, Serapias.*
**Generic description:** These European and Asian species are mostly temperate, sympodial, herbaceous perennials that produce unique flowers (*O. simia*) in spring and summer. An erect stem develops from the small tubers in spring and usually has a basal rosette of glabrous

Fig. 4.142. *Orchis mascula*

leaves. The erect inflorescence, depending on species, may be densely flowered near the apex. The showy flowers are mostly pink and purple, with a few yellow to yellow-green species.
**Flowering season:** Spring and summer.
**Culture**
    **Medium:** Most well-drained terrestrial mixes.
    **Fertilizers and fertilization:** Monthly during the growing season using a 1-1-1.
    **Watering:** Keep medium moist during growing season, reduce watering when dormant.
    **Propagation:** Seed or division.
    **Repotting:** Every 2–3 years.
**Note:** In Turkey, tubers of *Orchis* species are use to make a drink (*salepi*) and a gelatinous desert similar to ice cream (*salepi dondurma*) that comes in thirty flavors.

## Paphinia

**Genus:** *Paphinia* Lindley (pah-FINN-ee-uh)
**Tribe:** Maxillarieae
**Subtribe:** Stanhopeinae
**Etymology:** Named in honor of *Paphia*, the name for Aphrodite (Venus) of Cyprus.
**Native habitat:** West Indies, Central America south to northern South America.
**Number of species:** 4
**Commonly grown species:** *cristata, grandiflora, rugosa*.
**Hybridizes with:** None recorded.
**Generic description:** This small genus is well known for its showy, star-shaped, crisp flowers. These sympodial epiphytes have ovoid compressed pseubobulbs in tight clusters, each topped by 2 or more leaves. Each pseu-

Fig. 4.143. *Paphinia cristata*

dobulb is subtended by small leafy bracts. The lanceolate leaves, up to 10 inches long, are broad and soft. The pendent inflorescence arises from the base of the pseudobulb and bears up to 3 flowers that may be as much as 3 inches in diameter. The base flower colors are white and yellow and, depending on the species, may be heavily marked with reddish brown to maroon stripes or blotches (*P. cristata*).
**Flowering season:** Fall and winter.
**Culture**
   **Medium:** Mounted on plaques or totems. Use a well-drained epiphytic medium for potted plants.
   **Fertilizers and fertilization:** Monthly using a 1-1-1 or other balanced fertilizer.
   **Watering:** Daily for best growth on mounted plants.
   **Propagation:** Seed or division.
   **Repotting:** When the mount or medium decomposes.

## Paphiopedilum

**Genus:** *Paphiopedilum* Pfitzer (paff-ee-oh-PED-ih-lum)
**Subfamily:** Cypripedioideae
**Etymology:** From two Greek words *paphia* (Venus) and *pedilon* (sandal), denoting the slipperlike lip.
**Native habitat:** Southeast Asia, Philippines south to but not including Australia.
**Number of species:** 60 to 65
**Commonly grown species:** *argus, armeniacum, bellatulum, callosum, concolor* (color plate 42), *delenatii* (color plate 43), *emersonii, fairrieanum, glaucophyllum, godefroyae, haynaldianum, insigne, lawrenceanum, lowii, malipoense, micranthum, niveum, philippinense, primulinum, rothschildianum, spicerianum* (color plate 44), *sukhakulii, villosum.*
**Hybridizes with:** *Phragmipedium.*

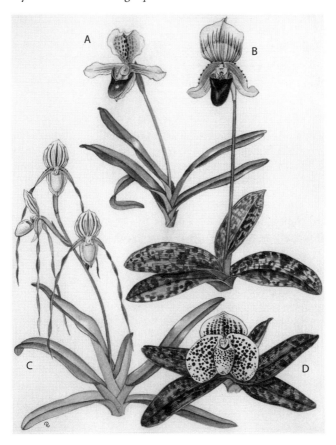

Fig. 4.144. A. *Paphiopedilum insigne;* B. *P. callosum;* C. *P. philippinense;* D. *P. bellatulum*

**Generic description:** Vegetatively, these sympodial terrestrial orchids have fans of conduplicate leaves closely arranged on the rhizome. The fans consist of 6 or more leaves that clasp at the base and, depending on species, may be up to 15 inches long. There are a number of species (e.g., *P. callosum*) that have mottled green leaves, hence the plants are attractive when they are not in flower. The erect inflorescence arises from the center of the leafy fan and will bear one to several long-lived flowers. The inflorescence may be up to 2 feet tall and the flowers range from 2 to 6 inches in diameter. Until the 1980s, most flowers were combinations of browns and greens; however, since the introduction of the *Parvisepalum* group (*P. armeniacum*), from south China and

Fig. 4.145. *Paphiopedilum haynaldianum*

Vietnam, there are now yellow and pink flowers available.

**Flowering season:** All year depending on species.

**Culture**

    **Medium:** Any coarse well-drained terrestrial mix.

    **Fertilizers and fertilization:** Monthly, ratio depends on medium

    **Watering:** Keep medium moist for best growth.

    **Propagation:** Seed or division.

    **Repotting:** Every 2–3 years.

## Papilionanthe

**Genus:** *Papilionanthe* Schlechter (pah-pill-ee-oh-NAN-thee)
**Tribe:** Vandeae
**Subtribe:** Aeridinae
**Etymology:** From two Greek words *papilio* (butterfly) and *anthe* (flower), to describe the flowers in this genus.
**Native habitat:** India east to China and south to Borneo.
**Number of species:** 11
**Commonly grown species:** *hookeriana*, *teres* (color plate 45), *tricuspidata*.
**Hybridizes with:** *Ascocentrum*, *Aerides*, *Vanda*, *Vandopsis*.
**Generic description:** Anyone who has been to Hawaii is familiar with the *Papilionanthe* hybrid named Miss Joaquim (*P. teres* × *P. hookeriana*), the well known lei flower. The genus was first described in 1915, but for many years most taxonomists called it *Vanda*. It was not until 1972 that Garay showed that Schlechter was right and some members should be called *Papilionanthe*. These monopodial

Fig. 4.146. *Papilionanthe tere*

epiphytes or terrestrials have upright stems with alternate, terete leaves up to 8 inches long with clasping leaf bases. Numerous aerial roots are produced and arise from the nodes opposite the leaf blades. The short inflorescence, less than 12 inches long, bears up to 20 flowers and arises from a node opposite the leaf blade. The flowers, which may be as much as 4 inches in diameter, are lavender or white.
**Flowering season:** All year.
**Culture**
    **Medium:** Any epiphytic or terrestrial mix.
    **Fertilizers and fertilization:** Monthly using a balanced fertilizer.
    **Watering:** Keep medium moist at all times for best growth.
    **Propagation:** Seed, cuttings, or keikis.
    **Repotting:** When the medium decomposes or plants become too large for their containers.
**Note:** *Papilionanthe* (= *Vanda*) Miss Joaquim is the national flower of Singapore. This hybrid, the first in the genus to be registered, was the earliest hybrid in Singapore. It was found growing in a clump of bamboo in Agnes Joaquim's garden in 1893.

## Paraphalaenopsis

**Genus:** *Paraphalaenopsis* A. D. Hawkes
(par-uh-fal-en-OPP-siss)
**Tribe:** Vandeae
**Subtribe:** Aeridinae
**Etymology:** From the Greek word *para* (near), denoting that this genus is close to *Phalaenopsis* taxonomically.
**Native habitat:** Borneo.
**Number of species:** 4
**Commonly grown species:** *denevei, laycockii* (color plate 46), *serpentilingua.*
**Hybridizes with:** *Phalaenopsis.*
**Generic description:** This small, interesting, if not somewhat curious genus is endemic to Borneo and sometimes referred to as the Rat-Tailed *Phalaenopsis* because all species have terete leaves. These monopodial epiphytes have short stems usually with about 5 leaves. *Paraphalaenopsis* terete leaves are slightly grooved, with pointed apices, and up to 40 inches long. The short, axillary inflorescence will bear 2–12 or more flowers. When there are multiple flowers, they are borne in dense clusters. The showy flowers vary in color depending on species.
**Flowering season:** Spring and summer.
**Culture**
    **Medium:** Any coarse epiphytic mix or plaques.
    **Fertilizers and fertilization:** Monthly, ratio depending on medium.
    **Watering:** Keep medium moist all year.
    **Propagation:** Seed.
    **Repotting:** Every 2–3 years or when plaques decompose.

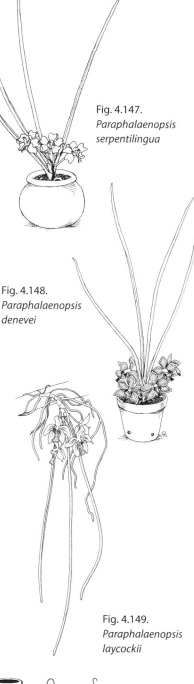

Fig. 4.147.
*Paraphalaenopsis
serpentilingua*

Fig. 4.148.
*Paraphalaenopsis
denevei*

Fig. 4.149.
*Paraphalaenopsis
laycockii*

## Dove Orchid

**Genus:** *Peristeria* Hooker (per-ih-STEER-ee-uh)
**Tribe:** Maxillarieae
**Subtribe:** Stanhopeinae
**Etymology:** From the Greek word *peristerion* (dove), denoting the likeness of a dove in the flower.
**Native habitat:** Costa Rica south to northern South America.
**Number of species:** 6
**Commonly grown species:** *aspersa, cerina, elata, gutata* (color plate 47), *pendula.*
**Hybridizes with:** None recorded.
**Generic description:** Central Americans affectionately refer to *Peristeria elata*, the national flower of Panama, as the Dove Orchid or Holy Ghost Orchid because of the likeness of a dove that appears in the flower. The large pseudobulbs of these sympodial epiphytic or terrestrial orchids are tightly clustered. Each teardrop-shaped, smooth green pseudobulb is topped by 4–5 very large pleated leaves up to 4 feet long (*P. elata*). The inflorescence, pendent or erect, arises from the base of the pseudobulb and, depending on species, is anywhere from 6 inches to 4 feet tall.

Fig. 4.150. *Peristeria elata*

The succulent flowers, 4–20 per inflorescence, open sequentially from base to tips, so the plant is in flower for several weeks. The cup-shaped flowers are basically white to yellowish with some pink or red markings.
**Flowering season:** Winter, spring, and summer.
**Culture**
  **Medium:** Most epiphytic or terrestrial orchid mixes.
  **Fertilizers and fertilization:** Monthly using a balanced fertilizer.
  **Watering:** Keep medium moist for best growth.
  **Propagation:** Seed or division.
  **Repotting:** When plant becomes too large for its container.

## Pescatoria

**Genus:** *Pescatoria* Richenbach f. (pes-kah-TOR-ee-uh)
**Tribe:** Maxillarieae
**Subtribe:** Zygopetalinae
**Etymology:** Named in honor of the French patron of orchids, M. Pescatore.
**Native habitat:** Costa Rica to Equador.
**Number of species:** 16
**Commonly grown species:** *cerina, dayana, lehmannii.*
**Hybridizes with:** *Bollea, Cochleanthes, Kefersteinia, Stenia, Warrea, Zygopetalum.*
**Generic description:** *Pescatoria* species, which lack pseudobulbs, have fans of plicate leaves that are conduplicate at the base. The soft, lanceolate leaves are up to 24 inches long and

Fig. 4.151. *Pescatoria cerina*

acute at the tip. The short inflorescences of these sympodial epiphytes arise from the axil of the basal sheaths. Each short inflorescence bears a single, large (up to 3-inch), showy flower. The base flower color is white often blotched with greenish yellow or reddish brown. In some species (*P. dayana*) the upper half of the petals and sepals are rose purple.
**Flowering season:** Spring and summer.
**Culture**
    **Medium:** Any well-drained epiphytic mix.
    **Fertilizers and fertilization:** Monthly, ratio depends on medium.
    **Watering:** Keep medium moist at all times.
    **Propagation:** Seed or division.
    **Repotting:** Every 2–3 years.
**Note:** If *Pescatoria* plants are tightly packed on the greenhouse bench their flowers may go unnoticed as the flowers are borne close to the rims of their containers.

## Nun's Orchid

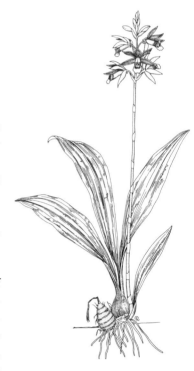

**Genus:** *Phaius* Loureiro (FAY-us)
**Tribe:** Arethuseae
**Subtribe:** Bletiinae
**Etymology:** From the Greek word *phaius* (swarthy), denoting the yellow-brown flower color that dominates the genus.
**Native habitat:** Africa, Madagascar, India east to Japan and south to Australia.
**Number of species:** 20
**Commonly grown species:** *australis, flavus, pictus, tankervilleae.*
**Hybridizes with:** *Calanthe, Cymbidium.*
**Generic description:** *Phaius* is a genus of sympodial, very robust terrestrial and epiphytic plants. The large pseudobulbs are hidden by the clasping bases of the 2–8 ensheathing leaves on each pseudobulb. The large, soft, pleated leaves are up to 4 feet long. The inflorescences, often 4 feet tall, arise between 2

Fig. 4.152. *Phaius tankervilleae*

leaves near the base of the pseudobulb. Each inflorescence bears 15 or more large colorful flowers (up to 4 inches). The base color of the flowers is yellow brown. White varieties are found in some species.
**Flowering season:** Spring, summer, and fall.
**Culture**
  **Medium:** A mixture of equal parts loam, rotted manure, and peat, or any proven terrestrial mix.
  **Fertilizers and fertilization:** Monthly using a 1-1-1.
  **Watering:** Keep medium moist at all times.
  **Propagation:** Seed, division, or flower stalks.
  **Repotting:** Every 2 years.
**Note:** The common name Nun's Orchid arose because the lateral view of the column resembles a statue of the Madonna.

## Phalaenopsis

**Genus:** *Phalaenopsis* Blume (fal-en-OPP-siss)
**Tribe:** Vandeae
**Subtribe:** Aeridinae
**Etymology:** From two Greek words *phalaina* (moth) and *opsis* (appearance), denoting the resemblance of some flowers to moths.
**Native habitat:** Taiwan south to Australia and west to India.
**Number of species:** 36
**Commonly grown species:** *amabilis* (color plate 48), *amboinensis*, *bellina*, *cornu-cervi*, *equestris*, *gigantea*, *lindenii*, *lobbii*, *lueddemanniana* (color plate 49), *mannii*, *mariae*, *pallens*, *pulcherrima*, *pulchra*, *schilleriana*, *stuartiana*.
**Hybridizes with:** *Aërides, Arachnis, Ascocentrum, Neofinetia, Renanthera, Vanda, Vandopsis.*
**Generic description:** These monopodial epiphytes have clasping leaf bases, making the plants appear to be stemless. The wide, leathery leaves are green or variegated and often dark purple beneath. Usually there are 4–8 leaves up to 24 inches long and 8 inches wide. The inflorescence, which arises from the leaf axil, may be erect or lax and is often branched. It ranges from a few inches to 3 feet tall and bears anywhere from one or two flowers to more than 100 flowers up to 3 inches in diameter. The base flower colors are white, pink, and yellow and may have a variety of markings.
**Flowering season:** All season depending on the species.
**Culture**
    **Medium:** Any proven epiphytic mix; some species may be mounted on plaques.
    **Fertilizers and fertilization:** Monthly, ratio depends on medium.
    **Watering:** Keep medium moist for best growth.
    **Propagation:** Seed, keikis, meristems, or flower stalks.
    **Repotting:** When the plant becomes too large for its container or medium decomposes.

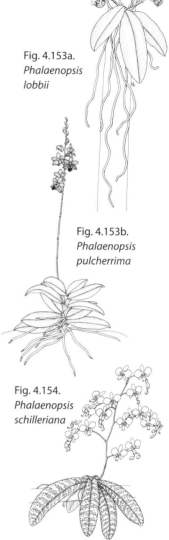

Fig. 4.153a.
*Phalaenopsis
lobbii*

Fig. 4.153b.
*Phalaenopsis
pulcherrima*

Fig. 4.154.
*Phalaenopsis
schilleriana*

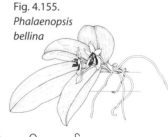

Fig. 4.155.
*Phalaenopsis
bellina*

## Pholidota

**Genus:** *Pholidota* Lindley (pho-lih-DOH-tuh)
**Tribe:** Coelogyneae
**Subtribe:** Coelogyninae
**Etymology:** From the Greek word *pholidotes* (scaly), denoting the bracts on the inflorescences and pseudobulbs.
**Native habitat:** India east to the Philippines and south to northern Australia.
**Number of species:** 40
**Commonly grown species:** *articulate, carnea, gibbosa, longibulba, pallida, ventricosa.*
**Hybridizes with:** None recorded.
**Generic description:** Some orchidologists refer to this interesting but not widely grown orchid as the

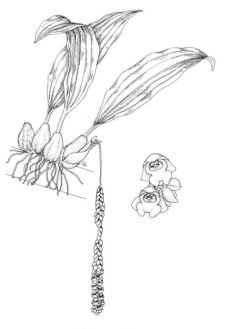

Fig. 4.156. *Pholidota pallida*

Rattle Snake Orchid, alluding to the emerging inflorescences on some species that resemble the buttons on the tail of a rattlesnake. The ribbed, somewhat conical pseudobulbs of these sympodial epiphytes are variously arranged on the rhizome, with some tightly clustered and others spaced 1 inch or more apart. They are subtended by papery bracts as they develop. Occasionally pseudobulbs arise from old bulbs, forming a chainlike growth. One- or 2-stalked, soft, pleated leaves top each pseudobulb. The inflorescence, either pendent or erect, arises from the apex of the newly maturing pseudobulbs and may bear up to 75 flowers. The small scented flowers may be either cream or pinkish.
**Flowering season:** All year depending on the species.
**Culture**
    **Medium:** Any well-drained epiphytic mix or mounted on plaques.
    **Fertilizers and fertilization:** Monthly, ratio depends on medium.
    **Watering:** Keep medium moist; water plaques daily.
    **Propagation:** Seed or division.
    **Repotting:** Every 2 years.

## Phragmipedium

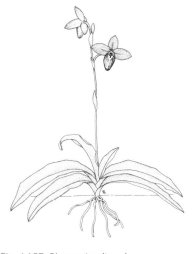

**Genus:** *Phragmipedium* Rolfe
(farg-mih-PEE-dee-um)
**Subfamily:** Cypripedioideae
**Etymology:** From two Greek words *phragma* (fence) and *pedi(l)on* (slipper), denoting the division in the ovary of these slipper orchids.
**Native habitat:** Mexico south to southern Brazil.
**Number of species:** 12
**Commonly grown species:** *besseae, caricinum, caudatum, koveckii, longifolium* (color plate 50), *schlimii.*
**Hybridizes with:** *Paphiopedilum.*

Fig. 4.157. *Phragmipedium besseae*

**Generic description:** This group of sympodial, tropical American slipper orchids may be either epiphytic or terrestrial. The plants have fans of 6–8 tightly arranged leaves. The individual leaves may be up to 3 feet tall (*P. longifolium*). The inflorescence arises from the leaf axil and will bear up to 15 flowers, over time, with some individual flowers having petals up to 15 inches long (*P. caudatum*). In the case of *P. longifolium*, each inflorescence produces one flower at a time and may produce a continuum of flowers for a year or more. The majority of the species have green and brownish flowers, but reddish orange (*P. besseae*) and dark lavender (*P. koveckii*) species have been discovered within the past twenty-five years.

Fig. 4.158. *Phragmipedium longifolium*

**Flowering season:** All year depending on species.
**Culture**
    **Medium:** Most grow well in any well-drained terrestrial or epiphytic mix.
    **Fertilizers and fertilization:** Monthly, ratio depends on medium.
    **Watering:** Keep medium moist at all times for best growth.
    **Propagation:** Seed or division.
    **Repotting:** When plants outgrow their containers or the medium decomposes.
**Note:** In most plants, when flowers go by they usually wilt and then fall off. In *Phragmipedium* the flowers are still turgid when they fall off, and it may appear to the novice as though someone has broken them off.

## Platanthera

**Genus:** *Platanthera* L. C. Richard (pla-TAN-ther-uh)
**Tribe:** Orchideae
**Subtribe:** Orchidinae
**Etymology:** From two Greek words *platys* (broad) and *anthera* (anther), denoting the broad anthers found in this genus.
**Native habitat:** Eastern and south central United States and Canada, Europe, northern Africa and Southeast Asia.
**Number of species:** 200
**Commonly grown species:** *ciliaris, cristata, flava, integra, obtusata.*
**Hybridizes with:** None recorded.
**Generic description:** These colorful, attractive, temperate-zone orchids are often affectionately referred to as Ditch Weeds as they are frequently found growing in roadside ditches. Platantheras are sympodial terrestrials. These plants lack pseudobulbs and are sustained during the dormant season by underground tuberoids. The reedlike stems bear varying numbers and sizes of leaves. There are usually 1 or 2 large (12-inch) basal leaves and all ensuing leaves are

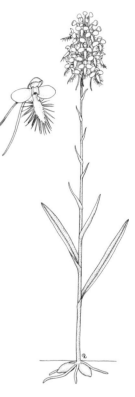

Fig. 4.159. *Platanthera ciliaris*

progressively smaller until they are bractlike under the inflorescence. The flowers are densely clustered at the top of the terminal inflorescences. These attractive flowers (up to 0.75 inch), often with fringed lips, come in orange, white, greenish, and purple.
**Flowering season:** Spring, summer and fall.
**Culture**
    **Medium:** Any proven terrestrial mix.
    **Fertilizers and fertilization:** Monthly during the growing season using a 1-1-1.
    **Watering:** Keep medium moist during growing season and reduce watering during dormant period.
    **Propagation:** Seed.
    **Repotting:** Every 2 years.

## Pleione

**Genus:** *Pleione* D. Don (PLEE-oh-nee)
**Tribe:** Coelogyneae
**Subtribe:** Coelogyninae
**Etymology:** Named in honor of Pleione, the mother of Pleiades.
**Native habitat:** Taiwan west to Nepal, including parts of southeast Asia.
**Number of species:** 16
**Commonly grown species:** *bulbocodioides, formosana, limprichtii, praecox.*
**Hybridizes with:** None recorded.
**Generic description:** These plants have large showy flowers that emerge just as new spring growth commences (*P. formosana*) or in the fall when the leaves are turning brown (*P. praecox*) and remind one of crocuses. Vegetatively, these sympodial terrestrials have small pseudobulbs topped by either 1 or 2 deciduous leaves, depending on species, and may be hidden by green or reddish mottled sheaths. The

Fig. 4.160. *Pleione bulbocodioides*

soft, lanceolate leaves may be up to 10 inches long. The short inflorescence develops at the base of the pseudobulb and bears one or two 3-inch flowers, which are mainly lavender magenta; there are also white and yellow forms.
**Flowering season:** Spring and summer.
**Culture**
    **Medium:** Any proven terrestrial mix.
    **Fertilizers and fertilization:** Monthly during the growing season using 1-1-1.
    **Watering:** Do not allow medium to dry excessively when plants are dormant.
    **Propagation:** Seed or division.
    **Repotting:** Every 2–3 years.

## Pleurothallis

**Genus:** *Pleurothallis* R. Brown
(plu-ruh-THAL-liss)
**Tribe:** Epidendreae
**Subtribe:** Pleurothallidinae
**Etymology:** From two Greek words *pleuron* (rib) and *thallos* (shoot), denoting the thin stems, or ramicauls, on these plants.
**Native habitat:** Tropical America.
**Number of species:** 900–1,000
**Commonly grown species:** *acuminate, brighamii, endotrachys, flexuosa, grobyi* (color plate 51), *loranthophylla, nossax* (color plate 52), *prolaticollaris, racemiflora, ruscifolia, secunda, viduata.*
**Hybridizes with:** None recorded.
**Generic description:** *Pleurothallis* is one of the largest genera in the Orchidaceae. This highly variable genus has been divided into as many as 27 subgenera, but over time taxonomists have elevated some of the subgenera to genus level, thus removing them from *Pleurothallis*. These sympodial epiphytes (sometimes terrestrial) form dense clumps of thin, wiry stems topped by a single leaf. The ramicauls may be erect or pendent. The inflorescence arises from the leaf axil bearing one to many flowers that are often prone on the upper surface of the leaf blades. Some flowers are borne on erect inflorescences (*P. grobyi*). The small flowers, many measured in millimeters, come in a variety of colors.
**Flowering season:** All year depending on species.

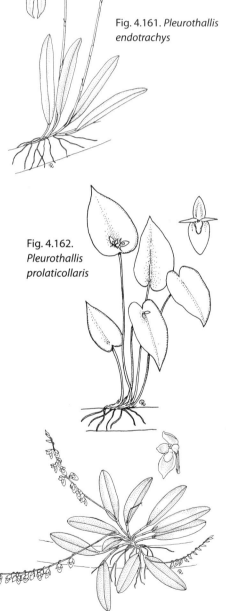

Fig. 4.161. *Pleurothallis endotrachys*

Fig. 4.162. *Pleurothallis prolaticollaris*

Fig. 4.163. *Pleurothallis racemiflora*

Fig. 4.164. *Pleurothallis viduata*

Fig. 4.165. *Pleurothallis brighamii*

## Culture

**Medium:** Most species are best mounted on plaques, but can be potted in epiphytic mixes.

**Fertilizers and fertilization:** Monthly, ratio depends on medium.

**Watering:** Water plaques daily for best growth.

**Propagation:** Seed or division.

**Repotting:** Only when the plaques decompose or every 2 or 3 years if potted.

## Polystachya

**Genus:** *Polystachya* Hooker
(pol-ee-STAKE-ee-uh)
**Tribe:** Epidendreae
**Subtribe:** Polystachyinae
**Etymology:** From two Greek words
*polys* (many) and *stachys* (ear of grain),
referring to the many branched inflo-
rescences with small seed pods.
**Native habitat:** Central and South
America, southern Africa, India and
southeast Asia.
**Number of species:** 100
**Commonly grown species:** *affinis,
bella, flavescens, odorata, pubescens.*
**Hybridizes with:** None recorded.
**Generic description:** This easy to
grow genus does not enjoy the popu-
larity it deserves. The flowers are small,

Fig. 4.166. *Polystachya bella*

but they are usually borne in sufficient numbers to make the plants attractive. The
small pseudobulbs of these sympodial epiphytes, up to 2 inches depending on
species, may be in tight clusters or chainlike. Two to four leathery leaves with
clasping leaf bases often completely hide the pseudobulbs. The inflorescence arises
from the apex of the pseudobulb and, depending on species, may be branched.
The flowers, up to 2 inches in diameter but usually smaller, come in white, green,
yellow orange, and pink.
**Flowering season:** All year depending on species.
**Culture**
  **Medium:** Any proven epiphytic mix.
  **Fertilizers and fertilization:** Monthly using a balanced fertilizer.
  **Watering:** Keep medium moist for best growth.
  **Propagation:** Seed or division.
  **Repotting:** When plant becomes too large for the container or medium
  decomposes.

## Promenaea

**Genus:** *Promenaea* Lindley
(prom-en-EE-uh)
**Tribe:** Maxillarieae
**Subtribe:** Zygopetalinae
**Etymology:** Named in honor of Promeneia, a priestess at Dodona.
**Native habitat:** Southeastern Brazil.
**Number of species:** 15
**Commonly grown species:** *microptera, rolinsoni, stapelioides, xanthina.*
**Hybridizes with:** *Aganisia, Anguloa, Ansellia, Chondrorhyncha, Cochleanthes, Colax, Zygopetalum.*
**Generic description:** These attractive min-

Fig. 4.167. *Promenaea xanthina*

iatures deserve a place in every collection, not because they are miniatures, but because of the brightly colored flowers they bear. Vegetatively, these sympodial epiphytes are occasionally found growing on rocks (lithophytes). The slightly furrowed, 1-inch pseudobulbs grow tightly clustered, subtended by 2 or 3 leaf-bearing bracts and topped by 2 sharp-pointed lanceolate leaves. The short, arching inflorescences arise from the base of the pseudobulbs and bear up to 3 flowers. The colorful, showy, mostly yellow flowers, may be up to 2 inches in diameter.
**Flowering season:** Summer and fall.
**Culture**
    **Medium:** Mounted, or grow in any epiphytic mix.
    **Fertilizers and fertilization:** Monthly, ratio depends on the medium.
    **Watering:** If mounted, water daily, keep medium moist.
    **Propagation:** Seed or division.
    **Repotting:** When it becomes too large for its container or when medium or plaque decomposes.

## Prosthechea

**Genus:** *Prosthechea* Knowles & Westcott (pros-THEE-key-uh)
**Tribe:** Epidendreae
**Subtribe:** Laeliinae
**Etymology:** From the Greek word *prostheke* (appendage), denoting the tissue on the back of the column of *P. glauca*.
**Native habitat:** Florida, West Indies and Tropical America.
**Number of species:** Approximately 100
**Commonly grown species:** *cochleata, fragrans, radiata, vespa*.
**Hybridizes with:** *Brassavola, Broughtonia, Cattleya, Encyclia, Epidendrum, Laelia, Rhyncholaelia, Sophronitis*.
**Generic description:** *Prosthechea* is closely related to *Encyclia*, but is easily separated by having mostly nonresupinate flowers, many with lips like clamshells, and often flattened pseudobulbs. Each pseudobulb of these sympodial epiphytes is topped by one or more soft lanceolate leaves. The terminal inflorescences will bear from a few to many flowers up to 2 inches in diameter. The base flower color is creamy white with many flowers having purple lines on their lips (*P. cochleata*), or the entire flower may be spotted (*P. vespa*).
**Flowering season:** Spring and summer.
**Culture**
  **Medium:** Any proven epiphytic mix, or mounted.
  **Fertilizer and fertilization:** Monthly using a balanced fertilizer.
  **Water:** Water medium thoroughly and not again until the surface is dry to the touch. Mounts are best watered daily.
  **Propagation:** Seed, division, or meristems.
  **Repotting:** Only when the medium or mount decomposes.
**Note:** This genus was identified in 1838 by Knowles and Westcott; however, taxonomists continued to categorize the plants as *Epidendrum* and later as *Encyclia*. Studies by Higgins indicated that *Prosthechea* was a valid genus and reestablished it in 1997, hence many species are still being sold as *Encyclia*.

Fig. 4.168a. *Prosthechea vespa*

Fig. 4.168b. *Prosthechea cochleata*

## Psychopsis

**Genus:** *Psychopsis* Raf. (sye-COP-siss)
**Tribe:** Maxillarieae
**Subtribe:** Oncidiinae
**Etymology:** From two Greek words *psyche* (butterfly) and *opsis* (like), alluding to the appearance of the flower.
**Native habitat:** West Indies and Costa Rica to Peru.
**Number of species:** 4
**Commonly grown species:** *kramerianum, papilio* (color plate 53).
**Hybridizes with:** *Aspasia, Brassia, Miltonia, Trichopilia, Trichocentrum.*
**Generic description:** The charming flowers of *Psychopsis* have been conversation pieces since they were first discovered in 1823. The large butterfly-like flowers atop long wiry stems are always a sight to behold. Vegetatively, these sympodial epiphytes have very small, slightly flattened pseudobulbs that form tight clusters and are topped by a single leathery leaf. The 12-inch flat leaves are medium to dark green with reddish purple mottling. The erect inflorescence, up to 40 inches tall, bears a single flower as large as 7 inches in diameter. The inflorescence will continue to produce flowers sequentially for months. The base flower color is yellow, overlaid with various reddish purple markings.

Fig. 4.169. *Psychopsis papilio*

**Flowering season:** All year depending on species.
**Culture**
  **Medium:** Any proven epiphytic mix.
  **Fertilizers and fertilization:** Monthly using a balanced fertilizer.
  **Watering:** Keep medium moist at all times for best growth.
  **Propagation:** Seed, division, or meristem.
  **Repotting:** When plant outgrows container or medium decomposes.

## Psygmorchis

**Genus:** *Psygmorchis* Dodson & Dressler
(sig-MORE-kiss)
**Tribe:** Maxillarieae
**Subtribe:** Oncidiinae
**Etymology:** From two Greek words *psygma*
(fan) and *orchis* (orchid), describing the
characteristic leaf arrangement of this ge-
nus.
**Native habitat:** Mexico south to southern
Brazil.
**Number of species:** 4
**Commonly grown species:** *glossomystax,*
*gnoma, pumilio, pusilla.*

Fig. 4.170. *Psygmorchis pusilla*

**Hybridizes with:** *Ada, Aspasia, Brassia, Cochlioda, Comparettia, Gomesa, Milto-*
*nia, Odontoglossum, Rodriguezia, Trichopilia.*
**Generic description:** It is not uncommon in the tropics to come upon a citrus
grove with trees that appear to be bearing bright yellow flowers. It's not a new
variety, only trees adorned with *P. pusilla*, considered a weed in some areas. In
nature and in the greenhouse, *Psygmorchis* is short lived, but it deserves a place
in collections. Vegetatively, these miniature sympodial epiphytes produce a small
fan of up to 10 leaves that are soft and seldom more than 2.5 inches long. The short
inflorescence arises from the leaf axils and will bear up to 3 flowers that open sequentially, usually with one opening at a time. Because it is such a small plant, the
large flowers can hide the fan of leaves. The base flower color is yellow or greenish
yellow, with reddish brown markings.
**Flowering season:** All year depending on species.
**Culture**
    **Medium:** Mounted on branches or tree fern totems.
    **Fertilizers and fertilization:** Monthly using a balanced fertilizer.
    **Watering:** Should be watered daily for best growth. Growers often use only
    rainwater for these plants.
    **Propagation:** Seed or division.
    **Repotting:** Only when mount decomposes.
**Note:** These precocious plant seedlings have been known to flower while still in
the seedling flask.

## Rangaeris

**Genus:** *Rangaeris* (Schlechter) Summerhayes (ran-GEER-iss)
**Tribe:** Vandeae
**Subtribe:** Aerangidinae
**Etymology:** *Rangaeris* is closely related to *Aerangis*, hence the name is a near anagram.
**Native habitat:** Tropical Africa and South Africa
**Number of species:** 6
**Commonly grown species:** *amaniensis*, *muscicola*, *rhipsalisocia*.
**Hybridizes with:** *Aerangis*.
**Generic description:** *Rangaeris* species, like many of their angraecoid relatives, are cherished for their usually stellate flowers often with long spurs. These small, monopodial, epiphytic species have short stems (3 inches) with distichous,

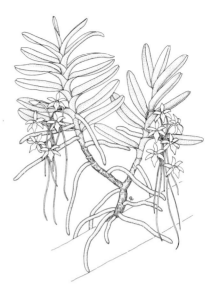

Fig. 4.171. *Rangaeris amaniensis*

loosely 2-ranked leaves (up to 8) that have 2 lobes at the apex. The multiflowered inflorescences, approximately 8 inches long, arise from the leaf axils and are often lax. The white spurred flowers are borne alternately on the inflorescence. The base color is white, but some flowers fade to orange as they age (*R. muscicola*).
**Flowering season:** Spring and summer.
**Culture**
   **Medium:** Mount on plaques or limbs, or grow in pots.
   **Fertilizers and fertilization:** Monthly using a weak 1-1-1.
   **Watering:** Water daily for best growth.
   **Propagation:** Seed or keikis.
   **Repotting:** Only when the mount or medium decomposes.

## Renanthera

**Genus:** *Renanthera* Loureiro
(reh-NANN-ther-uh)
**Tribe:** Vandeae
**Subtribe:** Aeridinae
**Etymology:** From two Greek words *renes* (kidney) and *anthera* (anther), denoting some of the kidney-shaped pollinia found in this genus.
**Native habitat:** Southeast Asia and the Philippines south to New Guinea.
**Number of species:** 15
**Commonly grown species:** *coccinea, imschootiana* (color plate 54), *monachica, philippinensis, storiei.*
**Hybridizes with:** *Aerides, Arachnis, Ascocentrum, Doritis, Neofinetia, Phalaenopsis, Rhynchostylis, Vanda, Vandopsis.*

Fig. 4.172. *Renanthera monachica*

**Generic description:** Renantheras are among the tallest (up to 15 feet) monopodial epiphytic orchids. The erect, thick stems often become almost woody with age. The alternate, stiff, leathery leaves, up to 12 inches long, have clasping leaf bases that hide the stem. After the leaf blades fall the clasping bases appear as papery bracts enclosing the stem. *Renanthera* produces many large aerial roots that emerge from the side opposite the leaf blade. The axillary inflorescences are often branched and up to 4 feet long, bearing from 10 to 150 flowers depending on species. The 2–3-inch basically red or yellow flowers are long lived.
**Flowering season:** All year depending on species.
**Culture**
    **Medium:** Any coarse well-drained epiphytic mix.
    **Fertilizers and fertilization:** Monthly, ratio depends on medium.
    **Watering:** Water thoroughly and not again until the medium becomes dry to the touch.
    **Propagation:** Seed, tip cuttings, or keikis.
    **Repotting:** When plants become too large for containers.

## *Restrepia*

**Genus:** *Restrepia* Humboldt, Bonpland, & Kunth (reh-STREP-ee-uh)
**Tribe:** Epidendreae
**Subtribe:** Pleurothallidinae
**Etymology:** Named in honor of the explorer José E. Restrepo, an early investigator of the Colombian Andes.
**Native habitat:** Mexico south to Argentina.
**Number of species:** 30
**Commonly grown species:** *antennifera, elegans, maculata, striata.*
**Hybridizes with:** None recorded.

Fig. 4.173. *Restrepia striata*

**Generic description:** These attractive, miniature plants are easy to grow and take up minimal space in the greenhouse. These sympodial epiphytic orchids are sometimes lithophytic. *Restrepia* species form clumps of short, almost wiry stems (ramicauls), each topped by a single leaf. The leathery leaves, up to 2 inches long, may be erect or suberect with revolute margins. One to three short, slender, sometimes terete inflorescences arise from the axil of the leaf and may be erect or prone on the leaf blade. In some species (*R. maculate*), the flowers are hidden beneath the leaf blade. Flower color varies among the species; some have brownish purple flowers.

**Flowering season:** All year depending on species.

**Culture**
    **Medium:** Most well-drained epiphytic mixes, or mounted.
    **Fertilizers and fertilization:** Monthly, ratio depends on medium.
    **Watering:** Keep medium moist at all times; water mounts daily.
    **Propagation:** Seed or division.
    **Repotting:** Every 3–5 years or when mount or medium decomposes.

## Restrepiella

**Genus:** *Restrepiella* Garay & Dunsterville
(reh-strep-ee-ELL-uh)
**Tribe:** Epidendreae
**Subtribe:** Pleurothallidinae
**Etymology:** Named for its close resemblance to *Restrepia*.
**Native habitat:** Mexico south to Costa Rica.
**Number of species:** 1
**Commonly grown species:** *ophiocephala*.
**Hybridizes with:** None recorded.
**Generic description:** *Restrepiella*, a monotypic genus, was placed in its own genus because it has 4 pollinia whereas the other close relatives in the Pleurothallidinae have 2. These sympodial epiphytic plants form very tight clumps of erect, lateral branches (ramicauls) up to 8 inches tall. Each ramicaul is composed of 3 nodes, each with a large papery bract and topped by a 7-inch petioled leaf. Small flowers

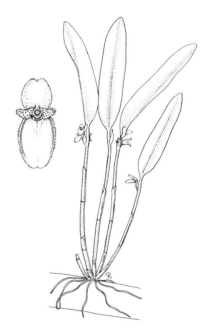

Fig. 4.174. *Restrepiella ophiocephala*

measuring up to 1.5 inches are borne in the leaf axils; usually one flower opens at a time. The dorsal sepal forms a hood and the lateral sepals are fused, almost hiding the very small petals from view. The basic flower color is creamy yellow with varying degrees of reddish spots.
**Flowering season:** Flowers when the new growth matures.
**Culture**
    **Medium:** Any proven epiphytic mix.
    **Fertilizers and fertilization:** Monthly, ratio depends on medium.
    **Watering:** Keep medium moist at all times for best growth.
    **Propagation:** Seed or division.
    **Repotting:** Every 3–5 years or when the medium decomposes.

## Rhyncholaelia

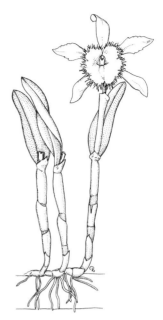

**Genus:** *Rhyncholaelia* Schlechter (rink-oh-LAY-lee-uh)
**Tribe:** Epidendreae
**Subtribe:** Laeliinae
**Etymology:** From the Greek word *rhynchos* (snout), referring to the unusual seed capsule, and the genus name *Laelia*.
**Native habitat:** Southern Mexico and northern Central America.
**Number of species:** 2
**Commonly grown species:** *digbyana* (color plate 55), *glauca*.
**Hybridizes with:** *Barkeria, Broughtonia, Cattleya, Encyclia, Epidendrum, Laelia, Schomburgkia, Sophronitis.*
**Generic description:** Although first described by Schlechter in 1918 as a valid genus, other taxonomists have placed it in *Laelia* or *Brassavola* over time. Today most taxonomists consider *Rhyncholaelia* a valid genus. These sympodial epiphytes are easy to identify. The often tightly clustered, spindle-shaped pseudobulbs have off-white sheaths

Fig. 4.175. *Rhyncholaelia digbyana*

that hide the pseudobulbs. A single, glaucous, stiff, leathery leaf (up to 8 inches) tops each pseudobulb. Each pseudobulb bears a single, terminal flower subtended by a fleshy sheath which may be green or purplish. The base flower color is white to light green and some flowers may have a light purplish tint.
**Flowering season:** Spring and summer.
**Culture**
    **Medium:** Any proven epiphytic mix, or mounted on plaques.
    **Fertilizers and fertilization:** Monthly, ratio depends on medium.
    **Watering:** Keep medium and plaques moist at all times.
    **Propagation:** Seed, division, or meristems.
    **Repotting:** When plants outgrow their containers or plaques decompose.
**Note:** Both *Rhyncholaelia* species play an important role in orchid breeding, especially *R. digbyana* with its large, fringed lip, which is dominant in its offspring.

## Rhynchostylis

**Genus:** *Rhynchostylis* Blume
(rink-oh-STY-liss)
**Tribe:** Vandeae
**Subtribe:** Aeridinae
**Etymology:** From two Greek words *rhynchos* (beak) and *stylis* (pillared), a reference to the beaked column.
**Native habitat:** India east to the Philippines and south to Indonesia.
**Number of species:** 4

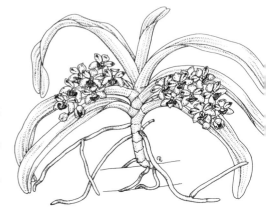

Fig. 4.176. *Rhynchostylis gigantea*

**Commonly grown species:** *coelestis*, *gigantea* (color plate 56), *retusa*.
**Hybridizes with:** *Aerides*, *Arachnis*, *Ascocentrum*, *Doritis*, *Neofinetia*, *Phalaenopsis*, *Renanthera*, *Vanda*.
**Generic description:** *Rhynchostylis* is often called the Foxtail Orchid because of the large bushy inflorescences found in some species. These monopodial epiphytes are stout plants and range up to 4 feet in height. The leaves, with bilobed tips and prominent keels, are thick and leathery and up to 12 inches long. The clasping leaf bases hide the stem and become papery after the blades fall. Thick aerial roots are produced along the erect stem. The axillary inflorescences may be erect or pendent and bear numerous colorful flowers. The base flower color is white with a variety of red, magenta, or lavender spots. Completely dark reddish flowers are found in the cultivar 'Sagarik's Wine.'
**Flowering season:** All year depending on species.
**Culture**
    **Medium:** Any coarse, epiphytic mix.
    **Fertilizers and fertilization:** Monthly, ratio depends on medium.
    **Watering:** Keep medium moist at all times.
    **Propagation:** Tip cuttings or keikis.
    **Repotting:** When plants become too large for their containers.

## Rodriguezia

**Genus:** *Rodriguezia* Ruiz & Pavón (rod-rih-GEEZ-ee-uh)
**Tribe:** Maxillarieae
**Subtribe:** Oncidiinae
**Etymology:** Named in honor of Emanuel Rodriguez, an early Spanish botanist.
**Native habitat:** Costa Rica south to southern Brazil.
**Number of species:** 20
**Commonly grown species:** *batemannii, candida, lanceolata, venusta.*
**Hybridizes with:** *Aspasia, Brassia, Comparettia, Ionopsis, Miltonia, Odontoglossum, Oncidium.*

Fig. 4.177. *Rodriguezia lanceolata*

**Generic description:** These small plants with their colorful flowers have been cherished greenhouse plants for well over 100 years. Vegetatively, these sympodial epiphytes have small pseudobulbs that become furrowed with age. They may be topped by one leaf (*R. batemannii*) or many leaves (*R. lanceolata*). The 9-inch leaves are leathery and folded near the base. The usually arching inflorescences, each bearing up to 30 flowers, are about the same length as the leaves. The base colors are white and rose.
**Flowering season:** Winter, spring, and summer.
**Culture**
  **Medium:** Best grown on plaques.
  **Fertilizers and fertilization:** Monthly using a 1-1-1.
  **Watering:** Plaques should be watered daily for best growth.
  **Propagation:** Seed or division.
  **Repotting:** Only when plaques decompose.

## Rodrigueziella

**Genus:** *Rodrigueziella* Kuntze
(rod-rih-GEEZ-ee-ELL-uh)
**Tribe:** Maxillarieae
**Subtribe:** Oncidiinae
**Etymology:** Named in honor of
João Barbosa-Rodrigues, an avid
plant collector in Brazil.
**Native habitat:** Southern Brazil.
**Number of species:** 6
**Commonly grown species:** *gomezoides, handroi.*
**Hybridizes with:** *Oncidium.*
**Generic description:** Although
these plants are diminutive and

Fig. 4.178. *Rodrigueziella gomezoides*

their small flowers are not brightly colored, you know when they are in flower as their pleasing fragrance emanates throughout the greenhouse. Vegetatively, these sympodial epiphytes have small, smooth pseudobulbs, usually tightly clustered, each topped by 2 soft leaves and ensheathed by 2 or more leafy bracts. The erect to lax inflorescence, about the same size as the leaves, arises from the base of the pseudobulb and bears 10 flowers. The base flower color is pale yellow green; occasionally there is yellow on the lip and reddish brown at the base of the petals.
**Flowering season:** Spring and summer.
**Culture**
    **Medium:** Best grown mounted on a plaque.
    **Fertilizers and fertilization:** Monthly using a 1-1-1.
    **Watering:** Plaques should be watered daily for best growth.
    **Propagation:** Seed or division.
    **Repotting:** When plaque decomposes.

## Rossioglossum

**Genus:** *Rossioglossum* (Schlechter) Garay & Kennedy (ross-ee-oh-GLOSS-um)
**Tribe:** Maxillarieae
**Subtribe:** Oncidiinae
**Etymology:** Named in honor of John Ross, who collected orchids in Mexico.
**Native habitat:** Mexico and Central America.
**Number of species:** 6
**Commonly grown species:** *grande, insleayi, schlieperianum, williamsianum.*
**Hybridizes with:** *Ada, Aspasia, Brassia, Cochlioda, Gomesa, Miltonia, Odontoglossum, Oncidium, Rodriguezia, Trichopilia.*
**Generic description:** In 1976, Garay and Kennedy transferred six species of *Odontoglossum* into a new genus, *Rossioglossum*, because of lip and column differences. These latter species also had large col-

Fig. 4.179. *Rossioglossum insleayi*

orful flowers. *Rossioglossum* species are sympodial epiphytes with tight clusters of ovoid pseudobulbs. Two petiolate, lanceolate leaves top each pseudobulb. The almost leathery leaves may be up to 8 inches long. The short inflorescence arises from the base of the pseudobulb and is subtended by a large bract. Each inflorescence bears up to 8 colorful flowers measuring 3.5 inches across. The base color of the flowers is yellow with variable blotches of reddish brown.
**Flowering season:** Fall, winter, and spring.
**Culture**
  **Medium:** Any proven epiphytic mix.
  **Fertilizers and fertilization:** Monthly, ratio depends on medium.
  **Watering:** Water thoroughly and not again until the medium is dry to the touch.
  **Propagation:** Seed or division.
  **Repotting:** Every 2–3 years.

## Sarcochilus

**Genus:** *Sarcochilus* R. Brown
(sar-koh-KYE-luss)
**Tribe:** Vandeae
**Subtribe:** Aeridinae
**Etymology:** From two Greek words *sarx* (flesh) and *cheilos* (lip), to describe the fleshy lips in this genus.
**Native habitat:** East coast of Australia and eastern New Guinea.
**Number of species:** 50
**Commonly grown species:** *australis, falcatus, fitzgeraldii, hartmannii, pallidus, stenoglottis, virescens.*
**Hybridizes with:** *Stenorrhynchus.*

Fig. 4.180. *Sarcochilus hartmannii*

**Generic description:** Although *Sarcochilus* and its interesting hybrids are widely grown in Australia, they are not as widely grown elsewhere, though they justly deserve it. These monopodial epiphytes or lithophytes have two distinct vegetative growth habits. One resembles *Phalaenopsis* species (*S. stenoglottis*) while others look more like miniature vandas (*S. hartmannii*). Most plants have usually 5 leathery leaves up to 12 inches long with clasping leaf bases. The lax inflorescence arises from the leaf axil and bears 5 or more colorful 2-inch flowers. The base flower colors are white and yellow, often with red spotting on the lip and basal one-third of the petals and sepals.
**Flowering season:** All year depending on species.
**Culture**
  **Medium:** Any proven epiphytic mix, or on plaques.
  **Fertilizers and fertilization:** Monthly, ratio depends on medium.
  **Watering:** Keep medium moist at all times, water plaques daily.
  **Propagation:** Seed, division, or meristems.
  **Repotting:** Every 2–3 years or when the plaque decomposes.

## Sarcoglottis

**Genus:** *Sarcoglottis* Presl (sar-koh-GLOTT-iss)
**Tribe:** Cranichideae
**Subtribe:** Spiranthinae
**Etymology:** From two Greek words *sarx* (fleshy) and *glotta* (tongue), denoting the fleshy lip on these flowers.
**Native habitat:** Mexico south to Brazil.
**Number of species:** 35
**Commonly grown species:** *acaulis*, *grandiflora*, *metallica*, *sceptrodes*.
**Hybridizes with:** *Stenorrhynchus*.
**Generic description:** These are delightful plants despite their one major drawback: during four months of the year they are deciduous and the pot appears to be empty; however, they do rebound every spring. *Sarcoglottis* species are sympodial terrestrial plants that lack pseudobulbs. Each plant produces a rosette of large

Fig. 4.181. *Sarcoglottis sceptrodes*

soft leaves up to 14 inches long and variegated with white stripes. The erect green inflorescences arise from the center of the rosette and bear 12 or more flowers. Each node and flower is subtended by a leafy bract. Some plants bear greenish cream flowers, but color varies depending on species.
**Flowering season:** Spring, summer, and fall.
**Culture**
    **Medium:** Any well-drained terrestrial mix.
    **Fertilizers and fertilization:** Monthly during the growing season using a 1-1-1.
    **Watering:** Keep medium moist during growing season and water sparingly during dormant period.
    **Propagation:** Seed.
    **Repotting:** Every 2–3 years.

## Schomburgkia

**Genus:** *Schomburgkia* Lindley (shom-BURG-kee-uh)
**Tribe:** Epidendreae
**Subtribe:** Laeliinae
**Etymology:** Named in honor of the German botanist Richard Schomburgk, who collected the first plant.
**Native habitat:** Mexico to southern Brazil.
**Number of species:** 12
**Commonly grown species:** *gloriosa, superbiens, undulata.*
**Hybridizes with:** *Brassavola, Broughtonia, Cattleya, Encyclia, Epidendrum, Laelia, Rhyncholaelia, Sophronitis.*
**Generic description:** The sympodial epiphytic genus *Schomburgkia* has been a controversial one among taxonomists. Some feel it belongs in *Laelia* but, for the time being, most consider it to be a valid genus; however, some species, those with hollow pseudobulbs (e.g., *tibicinis*), have been transferred to *Myrmecophila*, leaving 12 valid species in the genus. The name *Myrmecophila* denotes that ants live in the hollow pseudobulbs. *Schomburgkia* species develop into massive plants. The large, spindle-like pseudobulbs are stalked and have 2 or 3 leathery apical leaves. The long terminal inflorescence can reach 5 feet and bears up to 15 flowers.

Fig. 4.182. *Schomburgkia undulata*

The individual flowers, 1.5–3.5 inches in diameter, vary in color from cream to red brown to reddish purple to wine purple.
**Flowering season:** All year depending on species.
**Culture**
    **Medium:** Any coarse, well-drained epiphytic mix or plaques.
    **Fertilizers and fertilization:** Monthly, ratio depends on medium.
    **Watering:** Keep medium moist at all times for best growth.
    **Propagation:** Seed or division.
    **Repotting:** When plants become too large for their containers or plaques decompose.

## Scuticaria

**Genus:** *Scuticaria* Lindley (skoo-tih-CARE-ee-uh)
**Tribe:** Maxillarieae
**Subtribe:** Zygopetalinae
**Etymology:** From the Greek word *scuta* (lash), referring to the long, whiplike, terete leaves.
**Native habitat:** Eastern South America.
**Number of species:** 4
**Commonly grown species:** *hadwenii*, *steelii*.
**Hybridizes with:** None recorded.
**Generic description:** This is a small genus of two or possibly four species that are most interesting for their long terete leaves and large almost fleshy flowers. *Scuticaria* species are sympodial epiphytes. The pendent, grooved, terete leaves are generally 2–3 feet long, but may reach as much as 4 feet. They are about as thick as a pencil and borne in tight clusters on short, knotty stems often swollen at the base. The very short inflorescence arises near the base of the leaves and bears two to three 3-inch flowers. The flowers are basically yellow with reddish brown markings.
**Flowering season:** Spring, summer and fall.
**Culture**
  Medium: Mount on plaques.
  **Fertilizers and fertilization:** Monthly using a 1–1–1.
  **Watering:** Daily for best growth.
  **Propagation:** Seed or division.
  **Repotting:** When plaque decomposes.

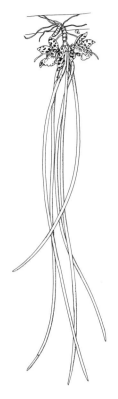

Fig. 4.183. *Scuticaria steelii*

## Sievekingia

**Genus:** *Sievekingia* Reichenbach f.
(seeve-KING-ee-uh)
**Tribe:** Maxillarieae
**Subtribe:** Stanhopeinae
**Etymology:** Named in honor of Dr. Sieveking, Burgomeister of Hamburg, Germany.
**Native habitat:** Costa Rica south to Bolivia.
**Number of species:** 10–15
**Commonly grown species:** *herrenhusana, peruviana, reichenbachiana, suavis.*
**Hybridizes with:** None recorded.
**Generic description:** Although *Sievekingia* species resemble *Stanhopea* plants vegetatively, they are easy to separate by the distinctly different flowers. These sympodial epiphytic (sometimes lithohytic) species can be divided into two sections, those having fringed lips (*S. reichenbachiana*) and those with entire lips (*S. herrenhusana*). The ovoid, ribbed, single-noded pseudobulbs form tight clusters and are topped by a single leaf. The sheaths subtending the

Fig. 4.184. *Sievekingia herrenhusana*

pseudobulbs are not persistent. The petioled leaves, up to 12 inches long, are soft and heavily ribbed. The short, pendent inflorescence arises from the base of the pseudobulb. The attractive flowers, up to 2 inches across, are clustered near the apex of the inflorescence and open rapidly. The basic flower color is white, creamy white, or yellow; some species also have purple markings.
**Flowering season:** Spring and summer.
**Culture**
    Medium: Mount on plaques, or use a well-drained epiphytic medium.
    **Fertilizers and fertilization:** Monthly using a 1-1-1.
    **Watering:** Daily for best growth on plaques.
    **Propagation:** Seed or division.
    **Repotting:** Only when plaques or medium decomposes.

1. *Acanthephippium mantinianum*

2. *Aerides lawrenciae*

3. *Ansellia africana*

4. *Ascocentrum garayi*

5. *Bollea coelestis*

6. *Brassavola cordata*

7. *Brassia pumila*

8. *Bulbophyllum medusae*

9. *Bulbophyllum polystictum*

10. *Catasetum pileatum*

11. *Cattleya harrisoniana*

12. *Cattleya percivaliana*

13. *Caularthron bicornutum*

14. *Chysis bractescens*

15. *Cochleanthes marginata*

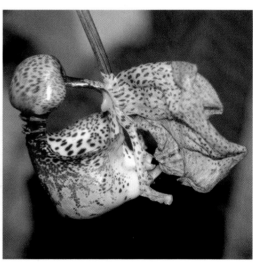

16. *Coryanthes macrantha*

17. *Cymbidium ensifolium*

18. *Cypripedium acaule*

19. *Dendrobium formosum*

20. *Dendrobium victoriae-reginae*

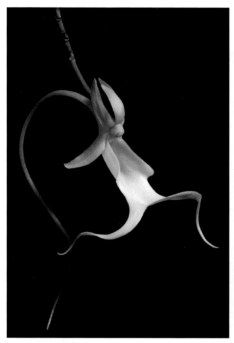

21. *Dendrophylax lindenii*

22. *Dracula marsupialis*

23. *Encyclia alata*

24. *Epidendrum pseudepidendrum*

25. *Gongora fulva*

26. *Grammatophyllum scriptum*

27. *Huntleya meleagris*

28. *Ionopsis utricularioides*

29. *Isochilus linearis*

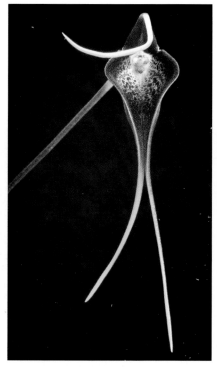

30. *Laelia purpurata*

31. *Lycaste dowiana*

32. *Masdevallia princeps*

33. *Maxillaria sophronitis*

34. *Maxillaria tenuifolia*

35. *Miltonia spectabilis*

36. *Miltoniopsis phalaenopsis*

37. *Neofinetia falcata*

38. *Neomoorea wallisii*

39. *Odontoglossum coronarium*

40. *Oncidium ampliatum*

41. *Oncidium sphacelatum*

42. *Paphiopedilum concolor*

43. *Paphiopedilum delenatii*

44. *Paphiopedilum spicerianum*

45. *Papilionanthe teres*

46. *Paraphalaenopsis laycockii*

47. *Peristeria gutata*

48. *Phalaenopsis amabilis*

49. *Phalaenopsis lueddemanniana*

50. *Phragmipedium longifolium*

51. *Pleurothallis grobyi*

52. *Pleurothallis nossax*

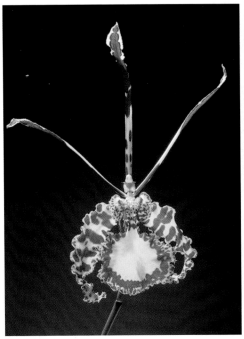

53. *Psychopsis papilio*

54. *Renanthera imschootiana*

55. *Rhyncholaelia digbyana*

56. *Rhynchostylis gigantea*

57. *Sobralia virginalis*

58. *Sophronitis cernua*

59. *Stanhopea wardii*

60. *Tolumnia bahamensis*

61. *Vanda coerulea*

62. *Vanda testacea*

63. *Vanilla planifolia*

64. *Zygosepalum lindeniae*

## Sobralia

**Genus:** *Sobralia* Ruiz & Pavón
(soh-BRAIL- ee-uh)
**Tribe:** Epidendreae
**Subtribe:** Sobraliinae
**Etymology:** Named in honor of Francisco So-
bral, a Spanish physician and botanist.
**Native habitat:** Mexico to southern Brazil.
**Number of species:** 35
**Commonly grown species:** *decora, fimbriata,
leucoxantha, macrantha, rosea, virginalis* (color
plate 57), *yauaperyensis.*
**Hybridizes with:** None recorded.
**Generic description:** The large, *Cattleya*-like
flowers of *Sobralia* are very showy and colorful, but have one serious drawback: the flowers
last but a day. Depending on species, however,
an inflorescence may have up to 10 flowers that
bloom sequentially. Vegetatively, these sympo-

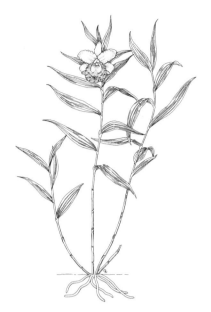

Fig. 4.185. *Sobralia macrantha*

dial terrestrials have reedlike stems and form dense clumps. Leaves are leathery
or almost papery, and the number per reed varies among species. The reeds are
usually 3–6 feet tall, but in some species they can approach 20 feet or more (*S.
dichotoma*). The short terminal inflorescence, usually subtended by a large leafy
bract, bears one flower at a time. The base flower colors are white, yellow, magenta,
pink, and lavender.
**Flowering season:** All year depending on species.
**Culture**
    **Medium:** Any well-drained, terrestrial mix.
    **Fertilizers and fertilization:** Monthly using a 1-1-1.
    **Watering:** Keep medium moist at all times for best growth.
    **Propagation:** Seed or division.
    **Repotting:** When plants become too large for their containers.

## Sophronitis

**Genus:** *Sophronitis* Lindley (sof-roh-NYE-tiss)
**Tribe:** Epidendreae
**Subtribe:** Laeliinae
**Etymology:** From the Greek word *sophros* (modest), a descriptive word for these miniature species.
**Native habitat:** Southeastern Brazil.
**Number of species:** 3
**Commonly grown species:** *cernua* (color plate 58), *coccinea, pterocarpa.*
**Hybridizes with:** *Barkeria, Brassavola, Broughtonia, Cattleya, Encyclia, Epidendrum, Laelia, Schomburgkia.*

Fig. 4.186. *Sophronitis pterocarpa*

**Generic description:** A small miniature genus with colorful flowers, *Sophronitis* plays a very important role in hybridization as it is the source of the red flowers of *Cattleya* and *Laelia* bigeneric hybrids. Vegetatively, these sympodial epiphytes have small pseudobulbs forming dense clusters, each topped by a single leaf. The leathery leaves, up to 3 inches long, may be shiny dark green or gray green. The flowers arise from the tip of the pseudobulbs. Depending on species, each pseudobulb will have a solitary flower or 2–5 flowers. The flowers, ranging from 1 to 3 inches, may be scarlet, orange red, or yellow.
**Flowering season:** Fall and winter.
**Culture**
    **Medium:** Mounted on plaques, or any epiphytic mix.
    **Fertilizers and fertilization:** Monthly, ratio depends on medium.
    **Watering:** Keep medium moist and water plaques daily for best growth.
    **Propagation:** Seed, division, or meristems.
    **Repotting:** Every 2–3 years or when plaques decompose.

## Spathoglottis

**Genus:** *Spathoglottis* Blume
(spah-tho-GLOT-tiss)
**Tribe:** Arethuseae
**Subtribe:** Bletiinae
**Etymology:** From two Greek words *spathe* (spathe) and *glotta* (tongue), a reference to the tongue-like midlobe of the lip.
**Native habitat:** Widespread from India to China to Australia and the Pacific Islands.
**Number of species:** 40
**Commonly grown species:** *aurea, ixioides, plicata, ×powelii, pubescens, unguiculata.*
**Hybridizes with:** *Bletia.*
**Generic description:** *Spathoglottis* species are not only fine greenhouse subjects, but also excellent landscape plants for tropical and warmer subtropical areas. The small pseudobulbs of these sympodial terrestrial plants are sheathed

Fig. 4.187. *Spathoglottis plicata*

by the leaf bases. These plants can form large, dense clumps . The long, sometimes arching leaves are soft and plicate. The erect, up to 2.5-foot inflorescences arise from the base of the pseubobulbs and bear from a few to many showy, colorful flowers near the apex. The base flower colors are purple or yellow.
**Flowering season:** All year for some species.
**Culture**
    **Medium:** Any well-drained terrestrial mix.
    **Fertilizers and fertilization:** Monthly using a 1-1-1.
    **Watering:** Keep medium moist all year.
    **Propagation:** Seed or division.
    **Repotting:** Every 2–3 years.

## Spiranthes

**Genus:** *Spiranthes* Reichenbach (spy-RAN-theez)
**Tribe:** Cranichideae
**Subtribe:** Spiranthinae
**Etymology:** From two Greek words *speira* (coil) and *anthos* (flower), denoting the spiral inflorescences of this genus.
**Native habitat:** The majority of species are in the Americas; some are in Europe and Asia, one species is found in Australia, and some are on Pacific Islands.
**Number of species:** 40–50
**Commonly grown species:** *cernua, romanzoffiana, sinensis, spiralis.*
**Hybridizes with:** None recorded.
**Generic description:** When *Spiranthes* are in flower, they are easy to spot along roadsides and fields, despite the fact that their flowers, arranged spirally on the erect inflorescences, are almost minute in some species. These sympodial terrestrial species have tuberous roots

Fig. 4.188. *Spiranthes cernua*

and several leaves in basal rosettes. The soft to sometimes fleshy leaves vary in shape among the species. The terminal, erect inflorescences, up to 20 inches long, bear from a few to 35 flowers in 2 or 3 tight spiral rows. The small flowers, some only about an eighth of an inch across, are mostly white, but some pink (*S. sinensis*) flowers do occur.
**Flowering season:** Spring and summer.
**Culture**
  **Medium:** Most well-drained terrestrial mixes.
  **Fertilizers and fertilization:** Monthly during growing season using a 1-1-1.
  **Watering:** Keep medium moist during growing season, reduce water when dormant.
  **Propagation:** Seed.
  **Repotting:** Every 3–5 years.

## Stanhopea

**Genus:** *Stanhopea* Frost *ex* Hooker
(stan-HOPE-ee-uh)
**Tribe:** Maxillarieae
**Subtribe:** Stanhopeinae
**Etymology:** In honor of the Fourth Earl of Stanhope, president of the Medica-Botanical Society of London.
**Native habitat:** Mexico south to southern Brazil.
**Number of species:** 25
**Commonly grown species:** *ecornuta, grandiflora, insignis, oculata, tigrina, wardii* (color plate 59).
**Hybridizes with:** *Cirrhaea, Coryanthes, Gongora, Polycycnis.*

Fig. 4.189. *Stanhopea wardii*

**Generic description:** The unique, large, fragrant and colorful flowers of *Stanhopea* are definitely conversation pieces and deserve a place in every collection, though the flowers are short lived. These sympodial epiphytes have short, deeply ribbed pseudobulbs that form tight clusters. A single, large, stalked, soft, distinctly veined leaf tops each pseudobulb and can be up to 15 inches long. The inflorescence arises from the base of the pseudobulb, grows downward, and bears 3 to 7 unusual flowers up to 7 inches in diameter. The 3-sectioned lip is the most interesting part of the flower. The midsection has two hornlike projections and the basal third may have two large eye spots. The base colors are white to light creamy yellow with varying amounts of red, yellow, and brownish spotting.
**Flowering season:** Spring and summer.
**Culture**
 **Medium:** Any proven well-drained epiphytic mix.
 **Fertilizers and fertilization:** Monthly, ratio depends on medium.
 **Watering:** Keep medium moist at all times for best growth.
 **Propagation:** Seed or division.
 **Repotting:** When plant outgrows container or medium decomposes.
**Note:** To ensure flowering, never grow *Stanhopea* in pots. In Mexico, these flowers are called Toritos (literally, small bulls) because of the horns and eye spots on the flowers.

## Stenia

**Genus:** *Stenia* Lindley (STEN-ee-uh)
**Tribe:** Maxillarieae
**Subtribe:** Zygopetalinae
**Etymology:** From the Greek word *stenos* (narrow), describing the narrow pollinia in this genus.
**Native habitat:** Northern South America.
**Number of species:** 5
**Commonly grown species:** *guttata*, *pallida*.
**Hybridizes with:** *Chaubardiella*, *Cochleanthes*, *Pescatoria*.
**Generic description:** Although *Stenia* resembles a number of other genera (*Bollea*) vegetatively, it is readily distinguished when

Fig. 4.190. *Stenia pallida*

in flower by its long narrow pollinia. These sympodial epiphytic species have very small pseudobulbs. One to 3 leaves, up to 5 inches long, with clasping leaf bases, encase each pseudobulb, completely hiding them. The short inflorescence arises from a leaf axil and may be recurved or prostrate. A single 2.5-inch flower is borne on each inflorescence. The beautiful light yellow flowers, often borne close to the rim of the pot, may go unnoticed.
**Flowering season:** Summer and fall.
**Culture**
    **Medium:** Plaques, or any proven epiphytic mix.
    **Fertilizers and fertilization:** Monthly, ratio depends on medium.
    **Watering:** Water plaques daily for best growth.
    **Propagation:** Seed or division.
    **Repotting:** Every 2–3 years or when the plaque decomposes.

## Stenoglottis

Fig. 4.191. *Stenoglottis longifolia*

**Genus:** *Stenoglottis* Lindley (sten-oh-GLOT-tiss)
**Tribe:** Orchideae
**Subtribe:** Habenariinae
**Etymology:** From two Greek words *stenos* (narrow) and *glotta* (tongue), referring to the narrow lip in this genus.
**Native habitat:** Eastern part of Central and South Africa.
**Number of species:** 3
**Commonly grown species:** *fimbriata, longifolia.*
**Hybridizes with:** None recorded.
**Generic description:** Like most perennials, *Stenoglottis* is deciduous for 4–5 months of the year, but when the tall spikes of dainty flowers appear in the fall, the wait has been well worth it. These sympodial terrestrials have basal rosettes of soft green leaves that vary among species. *Stenoglottis fimbriata* leaves are dark green with reddish brown spots, while *S. longifolia* has lighter, bright green, spotless leaves. The thin, erect inflorescence arises from the center of the rosette. The inflorescence may bear up to 50 small flowers measuring only about a third of an inch and has a minute bract at each node. The pale flowers range from rose to purple.
**Flowering season:** Summer and fall.
**Culture**
  **Medium:** Any well-drained terrestrial mix.
  **Fertilizers and fertilization:** Monthly during the growing season using a 1-1-1.
  **Watering:** Reduce water during the dormant season.
  **Propagation:** Seed.
  **Repotting:** Every 2–3 years.

## Telipogon

**Genus:** *Telipogon* Humboldt, Bonpland, & Kunth
(tel-ee-POE-gon)
**Tribe:** Maxillarieae
**Subtribe:** Telipogoninae
**Etymology:** From two Greek words *telos* (end) and *pogos* (beard), denoting the hairy tip of the column.
**Native habitat:** Costa Rica and northern South America south to Bolivia.
**Number of species:** 60
**Commonly grown species:** *nervosus, panamanensis, pulcher.*
**Hybridizes with:** None recorded.
**Generic description:** The hairy area around the column and callus in *Telipogon* flowers resembles a tachinid fly that looks so real it dupes the flies into pollinating the flowers. Vegetatively, these sympodial plants may be either epiphytic or terrestrial. The creeping rhizome has lateral stems that vary in length depending on species, each topped by one or more leaves. The erect, terminal inflorescence bears one or more large, colorful, almost

Fig. 4.192. *Telipogon panamanensis*

triangular flowers that may almost hide the plant when open. The base flower colors are creamy white or yellowish, many with strong reddish purple stripes or tessellation.
**Flowering season:** Spring and summer.
**Culture**
    **Medium:** An epiphytic or terrestrial mix, depending on species.
    **Fertilizers and fertilization:** Monthly, ratio depends on medium.
    **Watering:** Keep medium moist all year.
    **Propagation:** Seed or division.
    **Repotting:** Every 2–3 years.

## Tetramicra

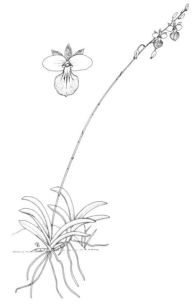

**Genus:** *Tetramicra* Lindley (teh-truh-MIKE-kruh)
**Tribe:** Epidendreae
**Subtribe:** Laeliinae
**Etymology:** From two Greek words *tetra* (four) and *mikros* (small), probably a reference to the four small pollinia found in this genus.
**Native habitat:** West Indies.
**Number of species:** 12
**Commonly grown species:** *canaliculata, elegans, parviflora.*
**Hybridizes with:** *Barkeria, Brassavola, Broughtonia, Cattleya, Diacrium, Epidendrum, Laeliopsis.*
**Generic description:** Plants of *Tetramicra* form chains, with each fan of leaves spaced as much as 6 inches apart on a thin rhizome and often appearing as individual plants among the rocks. In their native

Fig. 4.193. *Tetramicra canaliculata*

habitat these sympodial plants are lithophytes and sometime become epiphytic on shrubs. The leaves, approximately 5 on each fan and up to 7 inches long, are stiff, leathery, recurved and sometimes almost terete. The 2-foot-tall, erect, almost wiry terminal inflorescence bears its flowers near the apex. The few to many 1-inch flowers often have purple lips and greenish purple sepals and petals.
**Flowering season:** All seasons, depending on species.
**Culture**
    **Medium:** River gravel or well-drained epiphytic mix.
    **Fertilizers and fertilization:** Monthly, ratio depends on medium.
    **Watering:** Keep medium moist at all times for best growth.
    **Propagation:** Seed or division.
    **Repotting:** When plants outgrow their containers.

## Thrixspermum

**Genus:** *Thrixspermum* Loureiro (thrix-SPERM-um)
**Tribe:** Vandeae
**Subtribe:** Aeridinae
**Etymology:** From two Greek words *thrix* (hair) and *sperma* (seed), denoting the hairlike seeds.
**Native habitat:** India east to the Philippines and the tropical Pacific Islands.
**Number of species:** 100
**Commonly grown species:** *arachnitiforme, centipeda*.
**Hybridizes with:** None recorded.
**Generic description:** The spidery flowers of *Thrixspermum* are most attractive but unfortunately seldom last more than a day or two. These epiphytic or lithophytic monopodial plants have distichous leaves. The stem, hidden by the clasping leaf bases, may be short or climbing and anchored by aerial roots. The 5-inch leaves are bilobed at the apex. The axillary inflorescences, up to 10 inches long, may be flattened or terete. Flowers, produced in two rows, usually open one at a time. The base flower colors are white and yellow. Some white flowers turn pale pink on their second, last day.

Fig. 4.194. *Thrixspermum centipeda*

**Flowering season:** All year depending on species.
**Culture**
    **Medium:** Any well-drained epiphytic mix.
    **Fertilizers and fertilization:** Monthly, ratio depending on medium.
    **Watering:** Keep medium moist at all times.
    **Propagation:** Seed or tip cuttings.
    **Repotting:** When plant becomes too large for the container.

## Thunia

**Genus:** *Thunia* Reichenbach f. (THOON-ee-uh)
**Tribe:** Coelogyneae
**Subtribe:** Thuniinae
**Etymology:** Named in honor of Count Thun Hohenstein of Tetschin, Bohemia.
**Native habitat:** India east to China and Indochina.
**Number of species:** 6
**Commonly grown species:** *alba, bensoniae, marshalliana.*
**Hybridizes with:** None recorded.
**Generic description:** *Thunia* is very interesting because the plants have biennial stems, growing one year and flowering the next. Vegetatively, these sympodial terrestrial or semiepiphytic plants have reedlike stems, up to 50 inches tall, covered with lance-shaped leaves whose bases ensheathe the stem. When the leaf blades

Fig. 4.195. *Thunia marshalliana*

fall, the bases become papery and white. The short, slightly pendent, terminal inflorescence bears up to 9 short-lived spurred flowers. The base flower colors are white and purple; some flowers have showy orange-red lips.
**Flowering season:** Spring and summer.
**Culture**
  **Medium:** Any proven epiphytic or terrestrial mix.
  **Fertilizers and fertilization:** Monthly, ratio depends on medium.
  **Watering:** Water thoroughly and not again until the surface of the medium is dry.
  **Propagation:** Seed or division.
  **Repotting:** Every 2–3 years.

## Tolumnia

**Genus:** *Tolumnia* Rafinesque (toh-LUM-nee-uh)
**Tribe:** Maxillarieae
**Subtribe:** Oncidiinae
**Etymology:** Believed to be named for Tolumnius, a Rutulian.
**Native habitat:** West Indies and south Florida.
**Number of species:** 31
**Commonly grown species:** *bahamensis* (color plate 60), *pulchella*, *triquetrum*, *variegata*.
**Hybridizes with:** *Oncidium.*

**Generic description:** These delightful, colorful epiphytes can grow on twigs and require little space in the greenhouse, yet produce copious amounts of showy flowers. *Tolumnia* plants are truly miniature, seldom reaching 6 inches, but may have inflorescences as tall as 3.5 feet. The flattened, equitant leaves of these sympodial plants have a groove on top and are borne in fans. The usually erect inflorescence may

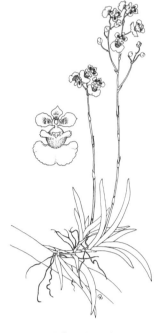

Fig. 4.196. *Tolumnia variegata*

be branched, and arises from the axil of one of the lower leaves. Each thin inflorescence bears from a few to many yellow, pink, or white flowers with varying degrees of reddish brown markings.
**Flowering season:** All year depending on species.
**Culture**
   **Medium:** Plaques, twigs, or a coarse well-drained epiphytic mix.
   **Fertilizers and fertilization:** Weekly with a dilute 1-1-1 for best growth.
   **Watering:** Daily for plaques and twigs; keep epiphytic medium moist.
   **Propagation:** Seed or division.
   **Repotting:** Only when too large for container or when plaques decompose.

## Trichocentrum

**Genus:** *Trichocentrum* Poeppig & Endlicher
(trick-oh-SEN-trum)
**Tribe:** Maxillarieae
**Subtribe:** Oncidiinae
**Etymology:** From two Greek words *tricho* (hair) and
*kentron* (spur), denoting the long spurs on the flowers
of some species.
**Native habitat:** Mexico to southern Brazil.
**Number of species:** About 20

Fig. 4.197a. *Trichocentrum tigrinum*

**Commonly grown species:** *albococcineum, carthagenense, fuscum, lanceanum, leucochilum, panduratum, pfavii, splendidum, tigrinum.*
**Hybridizes with:** *Miltonia, Odontoglossum, Oncidium.*
**Generic description:** These delightful plants are truly spectacular when in flower, as some flowers are so large (*T. tigrinum*) they almost obscure the plant. Vegetatively, these sympodial epiphytes have small tightly clustered pseudobulbs each topped by a single, erect, stiff, leathery leaf. The individual leaves may be up to 24 inches long (*T. leucochilum*). Because of the unusual size and shape of the leaves, these orchids are affectionately referred to as the Mule-Eared Orchids. The green leaves are often speckled purple on the upper surface and completely purple on the undersides. The inflorescence, arising from the base of the pseudobulb, bears one to many flowers up to 2 inches across. The basic flower color is yellow green with various degrees of purplish spotting.
**Flowering season:** All year depending on species.

**Culture**
    **Medium:** Any epiphytic mix or mounted on plaques.
    **Fertilizers and fertilization:** Monthly, ratio depends on medium.
    **Watering:** Water plaques daily for best growth.
    **Propagation:** Seed.
    **Repotting:** Every 2 years or when the plaque decomposes.

Fig. 4.197b. *Trichocentrum splendidum*

## Trichoglottis

**Genus:** *Trichoglottis* Blume (trick-oh-GLOT-tiss)
**Tribe:** Vandeae
**Subtribe:** Aeridinae
**Etymology:** From two Greek words *tricho* (hairy) and *glotta* (tongue), denoting the hairs found on lips of these species.
**Native habitat:** India through Southeast Asia to New Guinea and tropical Pacific Islands.
**Number of species:** 30
**Commonly grown species:** *brachiata, luzonensis, philippinensis, rosea, sagarikii.*
**Hybridizes with:** *Aerides, Arachnis, Ascocentrum, Phalaenopsis, Renanthera, Vanda, Vandopsis.*
**Generic description:** Vegetatively, *Trichoglottis* resembles *Vanda*, but the leaves are much shorter and the flowers are borne in small axillary clusters, often close to the stem. These monopodial epiphytes have erect (*T. luzonensis*) or pendent (*T. rosea*) stems with alternate, short, 2–6-inch leaves with clasping leaf bases. Numerous aerial roots are produced and emerge opposite the leaf blade. The short inflorescences bear from one to a few flowers

Fig. 4.198. *Trichoglottis brachiata*

0.5–2 inches wide, depending on species. Flower colors vary from yellow to pink to very dark maroon. The yellow flowers are often spotted dark brown.
**Flowering season:** All year depending on species.
**Culture**
 **Medium:** Any coarse well-drained epiphytic mix.
 **Fertilizers and fertilization:** Monthly, ratio depends on medium.
 **Watering:** Keep medium moist for best growth.
 **Propagation:** Seed, cuttings or keikis
 **Repotting:** When plants become too large for their containers.

## Trichopilia

**Genus:** *Trichopilia* Lindley
(trick-oh-PILL-ee-uh)
**Tribe:** Maxillarieae
**Subtribe:** Oncidiinae
**Etymology:** From two Greek words *tricho* (hair) and *pilos* (cap), a reference to the hairy anther cap found in this genus.
**Native habitat:** Mexico to southern Brazil.
**Number of species:** 25
**Commonly grown species:** *brevis, fragrans, maculata, marginata, suavis, tortilis.*
**Hybridizes with:** *Helcia, Lockhartia, Miltonia, Odontoglossum, Oncidium.*

Fig. 4.199. *Trichopilia marginata*

**Generic description:** Although the flowers of *Trichopilia* are large and very showy, they often go unnoticed in a greenhouse as they are often resting on the rim of the container and hidden by the leaves of surrounding plants. The pseudobulbs of these sympodial epiphytes, up to 6 inches tall, are flattened and tightly clustered. One or more leathery, lanceolate leaves up to 12 inches long top each pseudobulb. The short, pendent inflorescences arise from the base of the pseudobulbs. Depending on species there may be anywhere from a few to ten 6-inch flowers on an inflorescence. The basic flower colors are white, creamy white, greenish, and reddish brown; flowers often have darker lips or spotting.
**Flowering season:** All year depending on species.
**Culture**
    **Medium:** Any well-drained epiphytic mix, or mounted on plaques.
    **Fertilizers and fertilization:** Monthly, ratio depends on medium.
    **Watering:** Water plaques daily for best growth.
    **Propagation:** Seed or division.
    **Repotting:** Every 2–3 years.

## Tridactyle

**Genus:** *Tridactyle* Schlecter (try-DAK-till-ee)
**Tribe:** Vandeae
**Subtribe:** Aerangidinae
**Etymology:** From two Greek words *tri* (three) and *daktylos* (finger), denoting the distinctive three-lobed lips in this genus.
**Native habitat:** Tropical and South Africa.
**Number of species:** 42
**Commonly grown species:** *bicaudata*, *gentilii*.
**Hybridizes with:** None recorded.
**Generic description:** *Tridactyle* species may be monopodial epiphytes or lithophytes but all are tied together by their pronounced 3-lobed lips. Vegetatively, these plants are variable. The stems may be erect or pendulous, branched or not branched, and short or long. The distichous leaves are very narrow. The inflorescences rise

Fig. 4.200. *Tridactyle bicaudata*

from the leaf axils, may be short or long, and bear up to 16 flowers. The 1-inch flowers may be white, yellowish, pale green, or a buff that often turns orange with age.
**Flowering season:** All year depending on species.
**Culture**
    **Medium:** Any well-drained epiphytic mix.
    **Fertilizers and fertilization:** Monthly, ratio depends on medium.
    **Watering:** Thoroughly and not again until the medium becomes dry to the touch.
    **Propagation:** Seed or tip cuttings.
    **Repotting:** When plants become too large for container or medium decomposes.

## Trigonidium

**Genus:** *Trigonidium* Lindley (trig-oh-NID-ee-um)
**Tribe:** Maxillarieae
**Subtribe:** Maxillariinae
**Etymology:** From the diminutive of the Greek word *trigonos* (three-cornered), denoting the unique arrangement of the three sepals.
**Native habitat:** Mexico south to Brazil and Peru.
**Number of species:** 12
**Commonly grown species:** *egertonianum.*
**Hybridizes with:** *Mormolyca.*
**Generic description:** The three sepals, with rolled-back tips forming a triangle, comprise the showiest portion of the *Trigonidium* flower. The remaining floral segments are enclosed in the sepaline tube. Vegetatively, these sympodial epiphytes have short

Fig. 4.201. *Trigonidium egertonianum*

pseudobulbs topped by 1 or 2 leaves and subtended by several sheaths. The leaves are very narrow and may be erect or suberect and up to 25 inches long. The basal, erect, 1-flowered inflorescences hold the flowers above the leaves. The base flower colors are yellow green to greenish, usually with distinct reddish brown veins. The small lips are often green with purple markings.
**Flowering season:** Spring and summer.
**Culture**
   **Medium:** Any well-drained epiphytic mix.
   **Fertilizers and fertilization:** Monthly, ratio depends on medium.
   **Watering:** Water thoroughly and not again until the medium feels dry to the touch.
   **Propagation:** Seed or division.
   **Repotting:** Every 3–5 years.

## Vanda

**Genus:** *Vanda* R. Brown (VAN-duh)
**Tribe:** Vandeae
**Subtribe:** Aeridinae
**Etymology:** From the Sanskrit word describing orchid plants of vandaceous growth.
**Native habitat:** India east to southern China and southeast to New Guinea and northern Australia.
**Number of species:** 60
**Commonly grown species:** *coerulea* (color plate 61), *coerulescens, cristata, dearei, denisoniana, insignis, lamellata, luzonica, merrillii, testacea* (color plate 62), *tricolor.*
**Hybridizes with:** *Acampe, Aeranthes, Aerides, Arachnis, Ascocentrum, Doritis, Neofinetia, Phalaenopsis, Renanthera, Rhynchostylis, Trichoglottis, Vandopsis.*

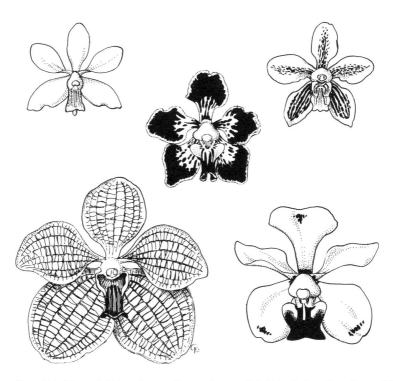

Fig. 4.202. (Upper left) *Vanda coerulescens;* (upper right) *Vanda lamellata;* (center) *Vanda merrillii;* (lower left) *Vanda coerulea;* (lower right) *Vanda luzonica*

Fig. 4.203. *Vanda cristata*

Fig. 4.204. *Vanda tricolor*

**Generic description:** *Vanda* species and hybrids have long been cherished, especially in the tropical and subtropical areas around the world, as both garden and greenhouse plants. These monopodial epiphytes have conduplicate, strap-shaped, 2-ranked leaves with clasping leaf bases. Vandas are easy to identify, as each leaf looks like someone tore off its tip. Large aerial roots emerge from the stem on the side opposite the leaf blade. The axillary inflorescence may be erect to somewhat pendent. Each inflorescence bears from a few to many colorful flowers. Vandas have two types of flowers: one type is flat (*V. coerulea*), and in the other, the margins of the floral segments are rolled back (*V. tricolor*). The flower color covers a wide range, including a very nice lavender blue (*V. coerulea*).

**Flowering season:** All year depending on species.

**Culture**

    **Medium:** Can be grown without medium, or use any coarse epiphytic medium.

    **Fertilizers and fertilization:** Monthly using a balanced fertilize.

    **Watering:** Daily for best growth.

    **Propagation:** Seed, tip cuttings, keikis, or meristems.

    **Repotting:** When plants become too large for their containers.

## Vanilla

**Genus:** *Vanilla* Miller (vah-NILL-uh)
**Tribe:** Vanilleae
**Subtribe:** Vanillinae
**Etymology:** Derived from the Spanish *vainilla* (pod or small sheath), a reference to the seed pods on these plants.
**Native habitat:** Pantropical.
**Number of species:** 60
**Commonly grown species:** *africana, aphylla, barbellata, phaeantha, planifolia* (color plate 63), *pompona*.
**Hybridizes with:** None recorded.
**Generic description:** Vanilla ice cream is known and cherished the world over, but it is always amazing how few people know that the flavoring, vanillin, comes from the seed pods of *Vanilla* orchids. The plants are vines, with aerial roots that attach to tree trunks and limbs as the plants scamper all over their host. The alternate leaves are borne on soft, green stems. Most have large, leathery leaves up to

Fig. 4.205. *Vanilla planifolia*

9 inches (*V. planifolia*) while on other species the leaves are reduced to small bracts (*V. aphylla*). The axillary inflorescences bear a few to many flowers that are open for only a day. The large fleshy flowers, up to 3 inches across, are yellow, greenish, or white; the more colorful lips have yellow or lavender markings.
**Flowering season:** Spring, summer, and fall.
**Culture**
    **Medium:** Best grown on totems or small trees.
    **Fertilizers and fertilization:** Monthly using a 1-1-1.
    **Watering:** Water daily for best growth
    **Propagation:** Seed or cuttings.
    **Repotting:** When plants overgrow their mount.
**Note:** Discovered by the Aztecs more than a thousand years ago, vanilla flavoring is now used in ice cream, air fresheners, soft drinks, and more than five hundred other products. The United States imports more than two million pounds of dried and processed *Vanilla* seed pods annually.

## Warrea

**Genus:** *Warrea* Lindley (WAR-ee-uh)
**Tribe:** Maxillarieae
**Subtribe:** Zygopetalinae
**Etymology:** Named in honor of Frederick Warre, who collected orchids for John Lindley in the early 1800s.
**Native habitat:** Mexico south to Brazil.
**Number of species:** 4–7
**Commonly grown species:** *warreana*.
**Hybridizes with:** *Pescatoria, Zygopetalum.*
**Generic description:** *Warrea* species have ovoid, several-noded pseudobulbs that are completely hidden by the sheathing leaf bases. These sympodial terrestrial plants have approximately 5 leaves per pseudobulb. The soft, large leaves, up to 2 feet long, are heavily veined and usually lanceolate. The erect, tall inflorescence arises from the base of the developing growth to as tall as 3 feet. Each inflorescence bears up to 10 flowers on the upper quarter of the stem. The large fleshy flowers are white to yellowish white and have a prominent lavender spot on the lip.
**Flowering season:** Spring and summer.
**Culture**
    **Medium:** Any proven well-drained terrestrial mix.
    **Fertilizers and fertilization:** Monthly using a 1-1-1.
    **Watering:** Keep medium moist at all times.
    **Propagation:** Seed or division.
    **Repotting:** When plants become too large for their containers.

Fig. 4.206. *Warrea warreana*

## Zeuxine

**Genus:** *Zeuxine* Lindley (ZOYX-een).
**Tribe:** Cranichideae
**Subtribe:** Goodyerinae
**Etymology:** From the Greek word *zeuxis* (yoking), to denote the partial fusion of the lip and column.
**Native habitat:** Tropical and subtropical Africa and Asia. Common from Afghanistan east to Japan.
**Number of species:** 50
**Commonly grown species:** *strateumatica*.
**Hybridizes with:** None recorded.
**Generic description:** This is a very interesting group of sympodial terrestrial plants. Some often act as if they are annuals, appearing in different locations each year (*Z. strateumatica*). Vegetatively, these plants have a fleshy rhizome that produces erect lateral branches. The almost fleshy, often gray green leaves have clasping leaf bases. As the stem elongates the upper leaves diminish in size until they are almost bractlike below the flowers. The terminal inflorescence may have anywhere from a few to many small white or greenish white flowers measuring only a quarter of an inch across.
**Flowering season:** Fall and winter.
**Culture**
 **Medium:** Any proven terrestrial mix.
 **Fertilizers and fertilization:** Monthly during growing season using a 1-1-1.
 **Watering:** Keep medium moist during growing season.
 **Propagation:** Seed.
 **Repotting:** Every 2–3 years.

Fig. 4.207. *Zeuxine strateumatica*

**Note:** *Zeuxine strateumatica* has become naturalized in a large part of the Florida peninsula, where it is often seen in large numbers in lawns. It is believed the seed came in a shipment of centipede grass from China in 1927. As early as 1940, plants were being reported from Jacksonville to Miami.

## Zootrophion

**Genus:** *Zootrophion* Luer (zoo-TRO-fee-on)
**Tribe:** Epidendreae
**Subtribe:** Pleurothallidinae
**Etymology:** From the Greek word *zootrophion* (menagerie), as Luer thought that some flowers resembled the heads of animals.
**Native habitat:** Central Caribbean Islands and Central and South America.
**Number of species:** 11
**Commonly grown species:** *atropurpureum*, *dayanum*, *hypodiscus*.
**Hybridizes with:** None recorded.
**Generic description:** This genus was established by Luer in 1982, when he removed them from *Crytophoranthus*, as they were unrelated to the original type specimen. Vegetatively,

Fig. 4.208. *Zootrophion hypodiscus*

*Zootrophion* species are very similar to pleurothallids but differ in floral characters. These sympodial epiphytes have short, reedlike stems (ramicauls) covered by papery bracts and topped by a single leaf. One or two flowers are borne on a very short inflorescence arising from the leaf axil. Sepals of the often fenestrate flowers are only partially split, thus hiding the petals, lip and column from view. The base flower colors are maroon and yellow, the latter often spotted maroon.
**Flowering season:** Spring, summer and fall.
**Culture**
    **Medium:** Any well-drained epiphytic mix.
    **Fertilizers and fertilization:** Monthly, ratio depends on medium.
    **Watering:** Keep medium moist at all times.
    **Propagation:** Seed or division.
    **Repotting:** Every 2–3 years.

## Zygopetalum

**Genus:** *Zygopetalum* Hooker
(zye-goh-PET-uh-lum)
**Tribe:** Maxillarieae
**Subtribe:** Zygopetalinae
**Etymology:** From two Greek words *zygon* (yoke)
and *petalon* (petal), denoting the callus tissue that
appears on the lip and unites the sepals and petals.
**Native habitat:** Venezuela south to Brazil.
**Number of species:** 50
**Commonly grown species:** *brachypetalum,
burkei, intermedium, mackayi.*
**Hybridizes with:** *Aganisia, Bollea, Chondrorhyncha, Cochleanthes, Colax, Lycaste, Pescatoria, Zygosepalum.*
**Generic description:** The large white lips of *Zygopetalum* with pronounced purplish spots and
stripes are the hallmark of the genus. These sympodial epiphytes have pseudobulbs, 2–3 inches
inches tall, that are heavily ensheathed. The

Fig. 4.209. *Zygopetalum mackayi*

sheathes deteriorate into fibers with age. The tightly clustered pseudobulbs bear
up to 6 fairly stiff lanceolate leaves with folded bases. The strong, erect inflorescence arises from the axil of a sheath and will bear up to 10 flowers 2–3 inches in
diameter. The flowers have greenish sepals and petals heavily overlaid with reddish brown markings, while the lips are white heavily adorned with lavender to
lavender brown lines and spots.
**Flowering season:** All year depending on species.
**Culture**
    **Medium:** Any well-drained epiphytic mix.
    **Fertilizers and fertilization:** Monthly, ratio depends on medium.
    **Watering:** Keep medium moist at all times for best growth.
    **Propagation:** Seed, division, or meristems.
    **Repotting:** Every 2–3 years.

## *Zygosepalum*

**Genus:** *Zygosepalum* Reichenbach f.
(zye-goh-SEEP-uh-lum)
**Tribe:** Maxillarieae
**Subtribe:** Zygopetalinae
**Etymology:** From two Greek words *zygon*
(yoke) and *sepalum* (sepal), denoting the
connate nature of the sepals.
**Native habitat:** Venezuela to northern Bra-
zil.
**Number of species:** 5
**Commonly grown species:** *labiosum, linde-
niae* (color plate 64), *tatei*.
**Hybridizes with:** *Aganisia, Cochleanthes,
Colax, Promenaea, Zygopetalum*.
**Generic description:** This small genus with
attractive 2 to 3-inch flowers is not widely

Fig. 4.210. *Zygosepalum labiosum*

grown, but is worthy of a place in any orchid collection. *Zygosepalum* species
have small, 1-noded pseudobulbs often spaced as much as 2 inches apart on the
rhizome. Each pseudobulb on these sympodial epiphytic plants is subtended by
one or more leafy bracts, which may be as long as the leaves and are topped by 2
lanceolate, 5-nerved leaves up to 12 inches long. The lax, usually single-flowered
inflorescence arises from the base of the pseudobulb. Flower color is white with
peachy brown and greenish markings.
**Flowering season:** Winter, spring, and summer.
**Culture**
    **Medium:** Mount on plaques, or grow in any epiphytic mix.
    **Fertilizers and fertilization:** Monthly, ratio depends on medium.
    **Watering:** Keep medium moist at all times and water plaques daily.
    **Propagation:** Seed or division.
    **Repotting:** Every 2–3 years or when plaques decompose.

## 5

## Buying and Showing Orchids

### Where to Buy Orchids

In the past, orchid plants could be purchased only at orchid nurseries and occasionally at a flower shop, orchid show, or garden supply store. During the past decade, the marketing of orchid plants has changed drastically; in addition to the traditional orchid retailers, many chain garden centers and supermarkets now offer orchids, and now that they are readily available and generally reasonably priced, more and more people are becoming interested in growing orchids as a hobby.

Hobbyists usually begin by buying their first plants at major retail garden centers. As they become more sophisticated growers, they begin shopping at orchid nurseries to enhance their collection with additional genera and species.

### Available Orchids

The national marketplace now usually offers a good selection of *Phalaenopsis* and *Dendrobium* hybrids. Depending on the area of the country and season of the year, additional genera will appear on the market, such as *Phaius, Cymbidium, Cattleya,* and a host of complex *Oncidium*-type hybrids. *Phalaenopsis* and *Dendrobium* are good genera for the novice grower because they are easy to grow and have long-lasting flowers.

Orchids are available as flowering pot plants and as bare-root plants in plastic packages at major garden centers. Bare-root plants are usually less expensive, but offer a greater challenge to the hobbyist as they require potting and may need to be grown for a year or more before they flower. Orchid nurseries offer flowering plants as well as seedlings in a variety of pot sizes, community pots, and flasks. Depending on the size, seedlings may take three to five years to flower. Beginning hobbyists should start out with flowering plants, or seedlings that will flower in the next growth, before advancing to community pots and flasks.

## Selecting a Good Plant

*Flowers*

When plants have flowers in spikes (*Phalaenopis*), it is best to select specimens with at least half the flower buds not yet open to ensure a longer blooming period in the home. Buy plants having a few large flowers (*Cattleya*) just as the buds are opening or when the flowers are turgid and crisp.

*Leaves*

All the leaves of most orchid plants should be light to medium green with no blemishes or insects present. Plants having brown leaf tips, brown or yellow spotting on the leaf blades, or yellow leaves should be avoided because these symptoms are usually an indication of cultural or disease problems.

*Roots*

All visible roots on healthy plants should be plump or firm, whitish, and usually with green tips. Soft and mushy or dried and shriveled roots are indications of poor culture and the plants should be avoided. While checking the roots, look at the medium to observe whether the particles are identifiable. If they are decomposed beyond recognition, the medium will be soggy. Plants growing in this medium should not be purchased as root damage is often associated with soggy media.

## Preparing Orchids for Exhibition

Sooner or later, every orchid hobbyist will want to enter a prized plant in a local orchid show. Here are some tips that may prove helpful in making your plant a winner. As soon as the inflorescences appear, they should be supported on galvanized wire or bamboo stakes (fig. 5.1) to present the flowers in their best arrangement. The inflorescence should be tied to the support with an inconspicuous wire, twist tie, or butterfly clip (fig. 5.2). As the buds develop, do not move the plant as it can change the arrangement of some of the buds and thus disrupt a typical arrangement of flowers, lessening the value of the plant for judging. Temporary stakes will prevent damage to the flowers during transportation. Prior to the showing, all dead and dying leaves should be removed and the remaining leaves and container should be cleaned. The leaves can be cleaned using a piece of soft cotton cloth moistened with low fat milk or a weak acetic acid solution. Commercial plant shines, although great for foliage plants, should not be used on orchids as they make the normal matte-finished leaves too shiny. Carefully rub the leaves to remove the debris that has accumulated over time. Just before taking the plant to the exhibition, water it thoroughly as it will likely be exposed to a very dry atmosphere.

Fig. 5.1. Staking an orchid plant

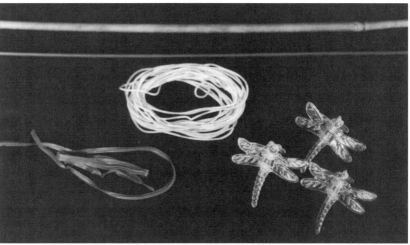

Fig. 5.2. Materials used to stake orchids include bamboo and wire stakes (top) and (from left to right) twist ties, soft wire, and plastic clips

# 6

# Orchids in Use and as Collectibles

## Orchids in Use

When the word "orchid" is mentioned most people envision one or more of a wide array of spectacular flowers. Few are aware of the myriad of other uses of orchids.

The hollow pseudobulbs of *Myrmecophila*, named from the Greek *myrmeko* (ants) because ants nest in them, are used as horns in Mexico and Central America to call the cattle home. Salep, the powder obtained from the tuberoids of some European orchids, has been used medicinally for its nutritive value in cases of malnutrition. Native North American Indians boiled the roots of *Cypripedium* plants, added a sweetener, such as maple sugar, and drank the solution as a cure for headaches. Malayan natives not only used the flowers of *Cymbidium finlaysonianum* as talismans to ward off evil spirits, but also chewed the roots and then sprinkled the roots over sick elephants to heal them. Moluccan natives considered the seeds of *Grammatophyllum scriptum* to be a love potion.

In addition to their use as medicinals, orchids are valuable in crafts and as food. Tribes in New Guinea, Philippines, and Indonesia have used the pliable needlelike canes of *Dendrobium utile* and other dendrobiums to weave bracelets and baskets. Natives in the Philippines obtain a glue from *Geodorum nutans*, while in Brazil, *Cyrtopodium* is a source of glue used in the manufacture of musical instruments.

Orchids have found their way into the human food chain. Southeast Asians cook *Dendrobium salaccense* leaves with rice for a delicate and exotic flavor. During the Victorian era, leaves of Madagascar orchid (*Jumellea fragrans*) were used widely for "faham tea." Leaves and pseudobulbs of *Cattleya*, *Bletia*, and *Renanthera* have also reportedly been used for tea. When they were plentiful in the wild, the succulent leaves of *Anoectochilus* species were sold as vegetables in native markets in Indonesia and Malaysia. As recently as the early 1980s *Paphiopedilum purpuratum* was sold by green grocers in Hong Kong as a salad green.

Fig. 6.1. *Vanilla* plant

Probably the most widely used orchid food product is seldom recognized as being a product of orchids. It is vanilla, a favorite flavoring in many parts of the world, yet the average individual is not aware that its source is the *Vanilla* orchid (fig. 6.1). The United States is the world's largest consumer of vanilla flavoring and imports two million pounds of dried *Vanilla* seed pods annually.

Vanillin, the compound that produces vanilla flavor, comes from the seed pods of *Vanilla planifolia* and other *Vanilla* species. *Vanilla* flowers open in the morning and close in late afternoon, hence they must be pollinated soon after they open in the morning. All the flowers must be hand pollinated because the insect pollinator is not found in the islands where the majority of *Vanilla* plants are grown. It takes several months for the pods, which resemble string beans, to mature, then they must be cured for several months. The entire process takes about one year.

The majority of *Vanilla* seed pods are produced in Reunion, Madagascar, Comoros, Seychelles, and Indonesia. Tahiti and Mexico also produce vanilla.

There are five recognized grades of vanilla:

1. Bourbon vanilla: The finest grade comes from Madagascar, Comoros, and Reunion Islands and accounts for about 60% of the world's production.
2. Java vanilla: Comes from the island of Java, contains less vanillin than bourbon vanilla and accounts for 30% of the total production.
3. Bourbon-like vanilla: Because of improved growing conditions on the island of Bali, they have been able to produce a vanilla very similar to bourbon vanilla.
4. Tahitian vanilla (*Vanilla tahitiensis*): Considered a lower grade, but the bean produces a sweet coumarinic flavor not found in the other vanillas. Most of Tahiti's production goes to Europe.
5. Mexican vanilla: Mexico produces a good product, but it is lower in vanillin content. Although Mexico was the original source of vanilla, dating back to the Aztec era before the voyages of Cortez, production is dwindling today.

Seed pods of *Vanilla griffithii* were eaten in their native Indo-Malayan habitat as a delicacy for their sweet flavor. Most individuals know its use in vanilla ice cream, but vanilla is used in a myriad of other products. Literally hundreds of foods contain vanilla, including yogurt, candies, liqueurs, soft drinks, flans, and even meat stews. When vanilla was added to vodka, sales rose by 37%. In addition to its food role, many other products use vanilla, including scented candles and other oil-based air fresheners.

Another interesting use of orchids occurs in Turkey, where tons of roots of *Orchis* species are used annually to produce not only a drink but also a gelatinous ice cream. A cold weather hot toddy is made using salep (the processed dried tuberoids of *Orchis*), flour, sugar, milk, and cinnamon. It is believed by some Turkish men that this drink strengthens their bodies.

The gelatinous ice cream, which comes in more than thirty flavors, is called *salepi dondurma*, freely translated from the original Arabic as "fox testicle ice cream." The origin of this delicacy is continually debated but it is believed to be the city of Maras, where reputedly it was developed more than three hundred years ago. Unlike most ice creams, *salepi dondurma* does not melt rapidly and reportedly was rolled out to form a long rope that was used for a jump rope. It should be noted that the species collected changes from year to year, depending on weather, and also to prevent over-collection in any given area. This is important as 2,600 tubers are used to obtain 1 kilogram of dried tubers and it has been reported that one ice cream factory uses up to three tons of salep or twelve million plants a year.

It is obvious that orchids play a very active role in our lives. Potted orchids in flower are the number two flowering potted plant sold in the United States and sales are increasing annually. Also, *Vanilla* is a very important economic crop not only in the United States, but also worldwide. One would have to conclude that *Vanilla* is the most widely used orchid today.

## Collectibles

There is no doubt that orchid collectibles or memorabilia are as important to some individuals as orchid growing is to others, and many orchid growers collect not only plants but also memorabilia. A wide variety of orchid collectibles cover a wide range of interests.

Postage stamps depicting orchids have been issued by countries worldwide (fig. 6.2). In many cases multiple stamps depicting different flowers are issued

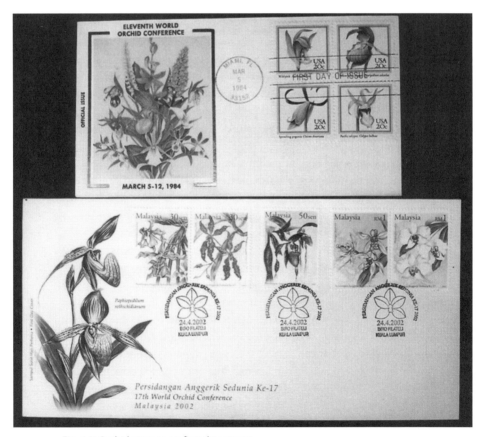

Fig. 6.2. Orchid stamps on first day covers

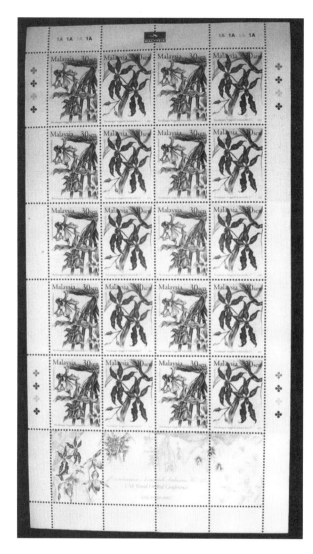

Fig. 6.3. Plate of commemorative orchid stamps

at the same time (fig. 6.3), and there are collectors who specialize in orchid stamps.

Today, Heisey orchid etched glass (fig. 6.4) is very popular among collectors as is the more elusive Paden City Glass Company orchid 1 and 2 etched glass in 7 colors, both manufactured around 1930–1950. Many china companies, including Lenox, Royal Copenhagen, and Limoges, have offered orchid patterns that are very collectible (fig. 6.5). There are also a number of silver flatware patterns (fig. 6.6) featuring orchids and, of course, lots of jewelry featuring orchids.

Fig. 6.4. Heisey dish etched with orchids

Fig. 6.5. Ceramic china decorated with orchids

Fig. 6.6. Orchids displayed on (from left to right) glassware, pewter, and table flatware

Fig. 6.7. Orchids are used to adorn currency

Fig. 6.8. Commemorative orchid pins

Orchids have adorned foreign currency (Singapore, fig. 6.7), whiskey bottles (Old Forester), candy boxes, and greeting cards, to name a few of the myriad places where orchids have turned up. Orchids, mostly flowering plants, are very popular in advertising, especially in home decor magazines. Commemorative orchid pins are also popular and inexpensive collectables (fig. 6.8).

Collecting orchid memorabilia is just like growing orchids—once smitten by the bug, there is no cure and you are smitten for life.

# 7

## Culture

Jo-an Matsuoka, whose pen name was Ignansai, is credited with writing the first Japanese orchid book in 1772. He is well known for his four-step method for *Cymbidium* orchid culture: "1. In spring don't put them out-of-doors; 2. In summer don't expose to too much sun; 3. In autumn don't keep too dry; and 4. In winter don't keep too wet."

When it comes to orchid culture it is obvious that things have changed. The proper culture of orchid plants to ensure healthy growth and flowering involves a number of environmental factors, including light, water, temperature, humidity, fertilizer, and medium. Depending on the genus and species there is considerable variation in these factors, and each group of plants requires a certain blend of them to promote best growth and flowering. Any deviation in the level of any of these factors can spell disaster in some cases (e.g., moving a *Phalaenopsis* plant from low light to very bright light can cause severe leaf burn in a very short time). Hence, it behooves orchidologists to know as much as possible about these cultural factors.

It should be pointed out that the cultural levels recommended are those at which the orchid plants grow best. For example, when a temperature is given (e.g., 65°F for *Phalaenopsis*), it is the minimum night temperature for best growth. Most orchid plants will thrive over a range of conditions so being slightly above or below the recommended levels will not be disastrous.

### Light

In terms of both quality and quantity, light is the most important cultural factor as far as plant growth is concerned. No matter how much fertilizer or water you give a plant it will not grow without light. Plants combine water and carbon dioxide in the presence of sunlight and convert them to carbohydrates and proteins. The more light plants receives, within their given limits, all other factors being equal, the better they grow. Unfortunately, not all orchid genera or species require the same light levels, hence orchids are usually divided into low, medium, and high light levels, depending on their requirements. A good rule of thumb is to give plants all the light they can stand without getting burned.

*Quality*

Most orchid hobbyists whose plants grow in greenhouses or lath houses or on window sills do not need to worry about light quality. The sun's rays have all the wavelengths of the color spectrum necessary to enhance the growth of orchid plants. Plants growing in a basement or other similar dark situation need to be illuminated to provide light that is as close as possible to sunlight in quality. There are a variety of lamps on the market designed specifically for growing plants that will provide adequate light for good orchid growth.

*Quantity*

The quantity of light supplied by the sun is far in excess of the needs of most orchid plants. In Florida, the amount of sunlight ranges from around 8,000 foot-candles (fc) in December to as high as 15,000 fc in June and July. In the snow belt, light intensities are much lower in winter. Therefore, depending on location, most orchid greenhouses need to be shaded all year in southern climates and only in the summer months in northern climates. Over the years, growers have classified orchids into four groups according to light levels required for best growth:

1. Heavy shade: 1,500–2,000 fc (*Phalaenopsis, Paphiopedilum*).
2. Moderate shade: 2,000–3,000 fc (*Cattleya, Epidendrum, Laelia, Maxillaria, Oncidium*).
3. Partial shade: 3,000–3,500 fc (*Vanda, Cymbidium, Ascocentrum*).
4. Full sun: more than 3,500 fc (*Arundina*).

In tropical areas, some books cite vandas as growing in full sun. These areas are blessed with trade winds and are also partially clouded most of the time, so the plants are not continually in full sun, but in alternate sun and shade with the cooling effects of trade winds. Hence, it behooves orchidists to compare ideal conditions for a particular type of orchid with their own local climatic conditions. Without clouds and trade winds, for example, vandas could burn.

Plants can indicate whether they are receiving the correct amount of light. If an orchid plant is growing well but is dark green and not flowering, it may be receiving too little light. Plants that are light green and blooming are receiving adequate light. If the plants are receiving too much light, they will have large brown areas on their leaves.

The amount of light entering a greenhouse can be easily measured with a light

Fig. 7.1. Light entering a greenhouse can be easily measured by using a light meter

meter (fig. 7.1). The best time to check light levels in a greenhouse is at noon on a clear day as close to June 21st (December 21st in the Southern Hemisphere) as possible, because that is the date when the maximum amount of sunlight reaches Earth. During the rest of the year the greenhouse will receive less sunlight, with a minimum level on December 21st (June 21st in the Southern Hemisphere).

If you do not have a light meter, there are two easy ways to tell whether your low- and intermediate-level plants are receiving too much light. On a bright, sunny day place your open hand 12 inches above the plant. If you see a distinct shadow of your hand, there is too much light for most orchids. The other way is to feel the leaves; if they are warm there is too much light.

*Duration*

Day length (photoperiod) can be a very important factor in the flowering of many plants (e.g., poinsettias, chrysanthemums). Knowing the photoperiodic response enables a grower, by manipulating the day length, to make some plants flower on any day of the year. There are only a few orchids (e.g., *Cattleya labiata, C. trianaei*) that flower under short days and can be manipulated to flower twice a year or for any desired holiday. Most other orchid plants flower during their annual cycle and cannot be manipulated.

## Water

Most of the plant's weight is water, sometimes as much as 90%; water is thus a very essential part of orchid culture. Water within the plant is necessary as it is the major transport system. It brings the nutrients from the roots to the leaves, where the leaves in the presence of sunlight produce food, which the water then transports to the growing regions to help support growth. Water pressure also supports the plant; when lacking, plants wilt and sometimes collapse. Water also evaporates (transpires) through leaf pores (stomata), thus cooling the leaves.

It is unfortunate, but true, that improper watering kills more orchid plants than all other factors combined. Hence, it is extremely important that orchidists get watering right. For cultural purposes when discussing water both quality and quantity need to be considered.

### Quality

In general, and especially in the United States, orchid growers using municipal water have little to worry about. Federal law in the United States governs the quality of drinking water and it is safe to use on orchids. When using water from other sources (wells and lakes) it is very important to check the pH (acidity or alkalinity) and soluble salt levels of the water before using it.

### pH

Most orchids do well over a wide pH range. However, a pH in the range of 5.0–6.5 is ideal because in this range nutrient availability is at its maximum and most plants thrive at these levels. (There are reports of orchids growing well when water with pH of 8.5 was used.)

### Soluble Salts

The amount of dissolved salts is very important for plant growth as very high salt levels can be detrimental. Salinity is reported in either parts per million (ppm) or decisiemens per meter (dS/m). There is a direct relation between these ratios of dS/m and ppm. Each individual salt solution varies from 550 to 700 ppm for every 1 dS/m. The following salt levels can be used as a guide to determine whether water is suitable for orchids.

1. 0–125 ppm (0–0.20 dS/m): Excellent for orchids.
2. 125–525 ppm (0.20–0.80 dS/m): Very good for orchids.
3. 525–800 ppm (0.80–1.25 dS/m): Use with caution, do not let plants dry out excessively.
4. > 800 ppm (> 1.25 dS/m): It is best to find another water source.

In some areas water may have copious amounts of calcium or iron. This water can be used if applied properly. When the calcium and iron are high the water should be applied directly to the medium. If water is applied from overhead sprinklers, calcium and iron deposits will build up on the leaves. Calcium forms a salt-like crust whereas iron causes the leaves to become rusty. As these elements build up on the leaves, they reduce the amount of light reaching the leaf surface and can become detrimental to plant growth. When the calcium is greater than 150 ppm (0.25 dS/m) the water is said to be "hard"; water with less calcium is called "soft." Soap produces less lather in hard water and this is a good indication of water type. Hard water is more apt to leave deposits on orchid leaves.

*Quantity*

When it comes to quantity of water to apply to orchids there is no rule of thumb. In the average greenhouse, there are plants in various types and sizes of containers, in hanging baskets, and mounted on plaques or tree branches, and each of these dries out at a different rate. If the plants were all the same size, in the same size container, and in the same medium, overhead irrigation would be ideal. Unfortunately, the latter is the exception rather than the rule in orchid hobbyist greenhouses. The best rule of thumb is to water thoroughly; that is, apply water in sufficient quantity that it starts running out of the bottom of the pot. This not only assures that the medium is thoroughly wet, but also helps to leach out some of the excess soluble salts. Do not water again until the top half-inch layer of the medium is dry to the touch. Allowing the plants to dry out a little between waterings allows for additional aeration for the roots, which helps promote growth. Depending on weather conditions, but especially in dry weather, orchids on plaques or tree limbs need to be watered daily.

## Temperature

There is a great misconception when it comes to temperature and orchids. For some unknown reason when orchids are mentioned, individuals envision a plant growing in a hot, steamy, tropical jungle. It is true that some orchids come from tropical jungles, but these are not always steamy and can even be very cool at night, especially at higher elevations. However, many orchids come from temperate zones and are found even as far north as Alaska. Therefore, orchids grow, depending on genus and species, over a wide range of temperatures. Temperature is very important as it governs the rate of metabolic activities within the plant. For the majority of garden plants, activity is minimal below 40°F. Activity increases with increasing temperature, reaching a maximum at 85°F, then declines with increasing temperature until the thermal death point is reached at approximately

120°F for some orchids. A good rule of thumb is that if the temperature feels comfortable to humans, that is also the best temperature for plants.

Orchids can be divided into three groups on the basis of night temperatures at which the plants grow best, with day temperatures 15–20°F higher preferred. Keeping the temperatures as close to these ranges as possible will produce excellent growth and flowering. The following temperature ranges have been established for orchids:

1. Low temperature, 50–55°F: *Cymbidium, Masdevallia, Odontoglossum*.
2. Intermediate temperature, 55–60°F: *Bulbophyllum, Cattleya, Encyclia*.
3. High temperature, 65°F: *Phalaenopsis, Vanda*.

## Humidity

Relative humidity is a measure of the amount of moisture in the air. The higher the percentage the more moisture in the air; above 90%, chances are good it will be raining or foggy. When humidity is high, many refer to the atmosphere as "muggy."

Many humidistats have an area listed as the comfort zone, which is usually 40–60% and is the range where humans feel most comfortable. Plants thrive in the same range. The best way to ensure that the humidity is well within the range is to install a humidistat. Wetting down greenhouse walkways raises the humidity, but 20–30 minutes later, it will return to its previous level.

## Air Movement

It is essential that there is good air movement in the greenhouse at all times. The moving air prevents cold or hot temperature pockets from forming, thus ensuring uniform temperatures throughout the greenhouse. In addition, it prevents water

Fig. 7.2. Good air circulation in a greenhouse can be obtained by using fans

droplets from forming at night, thus reducing the chances of *Botrytis* or other fungal pathogens attacking the flowers. Another beneficial effect is that moving air reduces leaf temperature, especially during the summer months. Even if the greenhouse has an evaporative cooler, it behooves the hobbyist to install additional fans to ensure 24-hour air circulation (fig. 7.2).

## Fertilizers and Fertilization

In orchid culture, fertilizers and fertilization are the most widely discussed topics, as there is a diversity of opinion among orchid hobbyists as to what is the proper fertilizer and the correct amount to apply. Ask 25 orchidists and you are apt to come up with 25 different recommendations. This problem is not easy to solve when you see the myriad of products available to growers. The following are three major types of fertilizers used in orchid culture.

1. Organic: These are derived from cottonseed meal, tankage, and many other organic substances. Organic fertilizers are more user friendly than inorganic since they require microorganisms in the medium to break them down slowly and make nutrients available to plants; hence, applying a little extra is usually not a problem. Unfortunately, when the medium temperature drops below 50°F, most microbial activities cease and the nutrients in the fertilizer are no longer available to the plants. This is usually not a problem in most orchid greenhouses, since night temperatures rarely go below 50°F.

2. Inorganic: These are derived from chemicals such as potassium nitrate, ammonium nitrate, and magnesium sulfate. Inorganic fertilizers are more readily available to the plants so care must be taken that the right amount of fertilizer is applied. Excessive amounts of inorganic fertilizers are more apt to burn plant roots than the same amount of organic fertilizer.

3. Controlled-release: These have chemicals encapsulated in synthetic resins that allow for the slow release of the nutrients. There are many controlled-release fertilizers on the market, including Osmocote®, Nutricote®, and Dynamite®. They are more user friendly than water-soluble fertilizers because they have extended nutrient release periods compared to water soluble fertilizers, described below. However, at high temperature and humidity levels these fertilizers tend to release nutrients at a faster rate than stated by the manufacturer.

Some fertilizers come in both dry and liquid forms. Both forms produce excellent plant growth when properly applied. Soluble (i.e., liquid) fertilizers dissolve readily in water and can be easily applied using either a sprayer or a hose-on injector. The advantage of using soluble fertilizer is that it is applied while watering and the nutrients are spread throughout the medium at once, whereas the dry fertilizer remains on the surface and gradually releases the nutrients to the roots.

Numbers on a fertilizer label describe the ratio of nitrogen to phosphorus to potassium, or the element symbols N-P-K, in the mix. The majority of orchids in most media grow very well when a 1-1-1 (balanced fertilizer) is used as recommended on the container. Orchids growing in mixes where the predominant ingredient is bark should be fertilized with a 3-1-1 fertilizer. The higher level of nitrogen is required because the myriad of microorganisms breaking down the bark are utilizing the nitrogen at the expense of the plant, therefore, enough nitrogen is needed to satisfy both the plant and the microorganisms.

Foliar fertilization, i.e., applying directly to leaves, is another method. This is most often referred to as "foliar feeding," but this is a misnomer as we do not "feed" plants. We apply the nutrients through fertilization and watering and the plant in turn takes these raw materials and manufactures its own food. Nevertheless, foliar fertilization is a very valid method of supplying nutrients to plants as orchid plants are very capable of taking up nutrients through their leaves. To avoid problems with algae, the plants should be washed off with water 24 hours after applying a foliar fertilizer. Most of the nutrients applied to the leaves are assimilated in a matter of 24 hours; any excess not washed off can become the medium for growth of an apple green algae that, if allowed to build up on the leaf, can reduce the light reaching the leaf, eventually becoming detrimental. Algae will also build up on wooden benches or any other place excess nutrients are allowed to remain. Despite this precaution, foliar fertilization is practical and it works.

## Growing Media

Orchids grow in a wide array of media and vandas can be grown successfully in wooden baskets without any medium. The medium used for growing orchids will depend on whether the species and/or hybrids are terrestrial or epiphytic.

1. Terrestrial: Most terrestrial orchids grow in soils rich in organic matter, often in litter on the forest floor. Most media suggested for terrestrial orchids are thus rich in organic matter, yet well drained. Most good terrestrial mixes are combinations of peat moss, bark, soil, and/or sand and contain 40% or more organic matter. When selecting ingredients for a terrestrial medium, pick materials that are readily available in your area, as there is nothing more frustrating than to develop a fine terrestrial medium and find a year or so later that one or more of the ingredients are no longer available. Many species also grow in field soils with less organic matter content, but when grown in a greenhouse a terrestrial medium can be used. There are four basic factors to consider when choosing or

producing a terrestrial mix for orchids. A good terrestrial mix must have the following characteristics:

a. Contains organic matter (at least 40%).

b. Supplies some nutrients.

c. Holds moisture but drains well.

d. Supports the plant.

2. Epiphytic: Epiphytes can be grown in a wide variety of materials and/or mixes. It has often been stated that "epiphytic orchids can be grown in any medium, except soil, as long as watering and fertilization are adjusted to fit the medium." Some of the proven media for epiphytic orchids are:

a. Bark and bark mixes (figs. 7.3 and 7.4): Bark alone or bark mixes, which are usually composed of varying amounts of bark (fir bark), charcoal (fig. 7.5) and perlite. Bark and its mixes require high levels of nitrogen for the plants to thrive. Bark mixes last at least two years and when properly handled produce excellent plants.

Fig. 7.3. Fir bark

Fig. 7.4. Fir bark mix

Fig. 7.5. Charcoal

Fig. 7.6. Peat moss                    Fig. 7.7. Perlite

b. Peat and perlite (figs. 7.6 and 7.7): Usually Canadian or European peat mixed with perlite in a 1:1 ratio by volume. This mix has excellent water-holding capacity yet drains well. This mix is good for two or more years, as acidic peat is slow to break down.

c. Tree fern fiber: This material is equally good when used alone or mixed with other materials. Tree fern provides excellent aeration and drainage, yet has good moisture-holding capability. Tree fern fiber supplies some nutrients as it decomposes and can last for seven years.

d. Sphagnum moss (fig. 7.8): This is an excellent medium for orchids. It has very good water-holding capacity, yet drains well. Unfortunately, it does not last as long as other media and may need to be replaced every six to twelve months.

e. Coconut husk chunks or fiber (coir): Both of these materials serve equally well as potting mixes. They drain well and have excellent aeration. They should be replaced when they begin to decompose.

f. Aggregates: There are a variety of aggregates that can be used (e.g., Aliflor®, fig. 7.9). These materials are inert and have no nutrient buffer

Fig. 7.8. Sphagnum moss                    Fig. 7.9. Aliflor®

capacity, therefore, when first using them care must be taken to ensure that plants are not over fertilized. Most aggregates can be reused if sterilized before reusing.

In addition to the mixes above, epiphytic orchids can be easily grown on plaques of tree fern or cork and many can be readily mounted on small tree branches. These materials are usually good for five or more years.

Using one acceptable medium is the best thing for an orchid hobbyist because it makes watering and fertilizing much easier.

## Containers

A wide variety of containers can be used to grow orchids (fig. 7.10). The main consideration when selecting a container is that it have sufficient holes in the bottom to ensure the rapid drainage of any water supplied. This is especially important to those hobbyists who place their plants outside and expose them to drenching summer showers. Choose from the following containers.

1. Clay pots: These come in an array of sizes, from 1.5-inch-diameter thumb pots to pots as large as 2 feet in diameter. Most orchids are grown in pots smaller than 12 inches in diameter. Clay pots are very user friendly. Water evaporates as it comes through the wall of the pot, helping to keep the medium a little cooler. Also, as water goes down into the medium, moisture seeps through the wall of the pot, making it darker and indicating where the moisture is; thus a hobbyist can readily see if the water is getting to the bottom of the pot. Clay pots can be used over and over again as long as they are sterilized before they are reused. Although

Fig. 7.10. Containers are made from many kinds of materials (from left to right): clay, plastic, ceramic, and plastic mesh

clay pots are the containers of choice for many hobbyists, there are some minor problems associated with them. Unfortunately, clay pots break easily and large pots are very heavy. Depending on the amount of soluble salts in the medium, these are often deposited on the outside or rim of the pot as water evaporates. If this builds up, it will look like a chalky white layer and can eventually harm any roots that come in contact with it. In many greenhouses where the pots are kept continuously moist and the plants are adequately fertilized, green algae will grow on the walls of the pot. Although this does not harm the plant it is unsightly and the pots become slippery and hard to handle.

2. Plastic pots: Solid plastic pots, like those of clay, come in a huge array of sizes, up to 3 feet in diameter. They come in several colors as well as clear and can be round or square. Plastic pots have the advantage of being inexpensive and lightweight, and, since they are not porous, the medium does not dry out as quickly. Clear pots have the advantage that the roots are visible, making it easy to determine if there are any problems.

There are also black plastic mesh pots, either round or square, that come in a variety of sizes. These are very suitable for orchids as they provide better aeration and drainage than either clay or plastic pots. The only disadvantage is that they dry out more rapidly.

Unfortunately, plastic pots become brittle with age. The rate of becoming brittle is governed by their exposure to sunlight. After using a pot once or twice, it may become brittle and when the hobbyist tries to lift the pot a piece may break off and the plant can go crashing to the floor. Hence, it is wise to put a little pressure on an old plastic pot before picking it up to determine if it is brittle. Nevertheless, plastic pots are excellent containers for orchids.

3. Ceramic pots: These are the most expensive containers; nevertheless, orchids can be grown in them. When selecting a ceramic container, whether it be to complement a setting in the home or to show off a prize orchid, it is important that there is a hole in the bottom to ensure adequate drainage. The container should not be so elaborate that it takes the focus away from the orchid.

4. Hanging baskets (fig. 7.11): Baskets may be made of galvanized wire, wood (cypress, teak, or red wood), plastic, or tree fern. All serve equally well and it may get down to cost as to which one a hobbyist would select. Many epiphytic orchids grow very well in baskets. Indeed, it behooves hobbyists to grow some of their orchids in baskets, especially those with large drooping

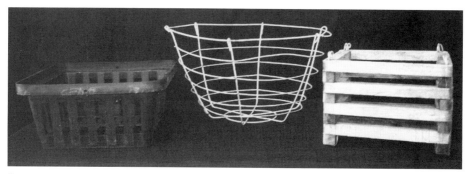

Fig. 7.11. Hanging baskets (from left to right): plastic, wire, and wood

Fig. 7.12. Plaques (from left to right): cork, tree limbs, and tree fern

leaves (*Bulbophyllum phalaenopsis*), pendent growth (*Dendrobium superbum*), or pendent inflorescences (*Gongora, Stanhopea*).

5. Plaques and tree limbs (fig. 7.12): Plaques and tree limbs can be considered containers when they have epiphytic orchids mounted on them. Tree fern and cork are the most popular plaques as they have a long shelf life. However, slabs of wood, or plaques of cypress and palm have also proven to be good containers. Tree limbs are also very popular and in some areas are easing out tree fern and cork plaques. The longevity of a tree limb will depend on the tree species and condition of the wood.

## Potting and Repotting

Repotting orchids is probably one of the most tedious and neglected aspects of orchid culture. However, to encourage good growth, the repotting of orchids is an essential part of good orchid culture. The major questions posed by hob-

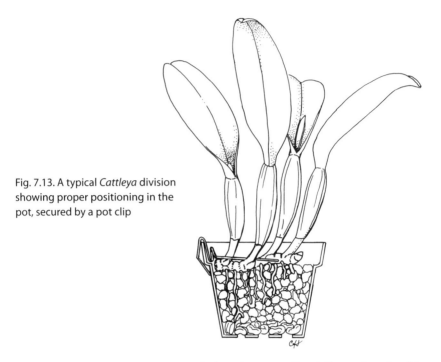

Fig. 7.13. A typical *Cattleya* division showing proper positioning in the pot, secured by a pot clip

byists with respect to repotting are, "when do I repot?" and "how often should I repot?"

Sympodial orchids should be repotted immediately after flowering or just as new roots emerge from the newly developing growth. It is best to repot sympodial orchids every two years. Monopodial orchids can be repotted any time they are in active growth. Usually they do not require repotting until they become too tall for the container or the medium decomposes.

When repotting sympodial orchids, select a container large enough to accommodate at least two years' growth (fig. 7.13), but not too large. A pot that is too large wastes potting mix and also takes up additional greenhouse space. When preparing the plant for repotting, you will usually see numerous roots attached to the inside of the container. In general, these can be separated by inserting a **sterile**, **dull** knife between the roots and the container. If this method does not work, the container may have to be destroyed to remove the plant. Once the plant is out of the pot, remove all the medium, or as much as possible. Also, remove any dead or damaged roots using **sterilized tools**. If the pseudobulbs have dry sheaths (*Cattleya*) they should be removed as they present potential areas for unseen buildup of scale insects. Place the plant in the new pot with the back of the rhizome against the side of the pot to leave maximum space for new growth. The rhizome should be positioned as horizontally as possible about 0.5–0.75 inch below the rim of the pot; when the pot is filled with medium it should end up resting on the surface.

The plant should be staked and tied to hold it steady until new roots develop. There are a wide variety of stakes and pot clips available to assist in this process. Now it should be good for two more years.

Monopodial orchid plants are usually repotted in the same manner, except that they are usually placed in the center of a container that is only slightly larger than their previous one.

Orchid plants mounted on plaques or tree limbs are usually not repotted until the plaque or limb decomposes. In the case of tree fern or cork it may be seven to ten years before plants require remounting. When repotting plants on plaques or tree limbs all that may be necessary is to attach it to a new mount. The plants may be attached using twine, wire (do not use exposed copper wire), solder wire, or so-called liquid nails.

Plants in hanging baskets need to be repotted when the medium decomposes or the basket breaks down, following the procedure described above. Remove the plant from the basket gently in order to damage as few roots as possible, and remove old medium and dead or injured roots from the plant. Monopodials can usually be repotted in the same size basket whereas sympodials may require a larger basket.

## Propagation

Orchids, like many other members of the plant kingdom, are readily propagated both asexually (vegetatively) and sexually (by seed). The standard method is asexual, by division of plants, as well as some other interesting methods.

*Asexual*

1. Division (fig. 7.14A,B,C). This propagation method is used for many horticultural plants, including daylilies, irises, and sympodial orchids (e.g., *Cattleya*, *Dendrobium*, *Paphiopedilum*). These plants have a horizontal rhizome with determinant lateral branches. Remove the plant from the pot, and remove all old medium and any dead or damaged roots, using a **sterile** knife or clipper. All dry sheaths should be removed from pseudobulbs as they are excellent hiding places for scale insects and mealybugs, which can build up rapidly when they go undetected. The *Cattleya* plant (fig. 7.14) has eight pseudobulbs and can be readily divided into two four-bulb divisions. The front division is called the "lead" (fig. 7.13) and will usually flower on the next growth. The rear division is called the "backbulb" and, depending on the condition of the pseudobulbs and leaves, may take one to three years to flower. Generally, in most genera, a three-bulb division is the minimum. However, in some genera (*Cymbidium*, *Calanthe*,

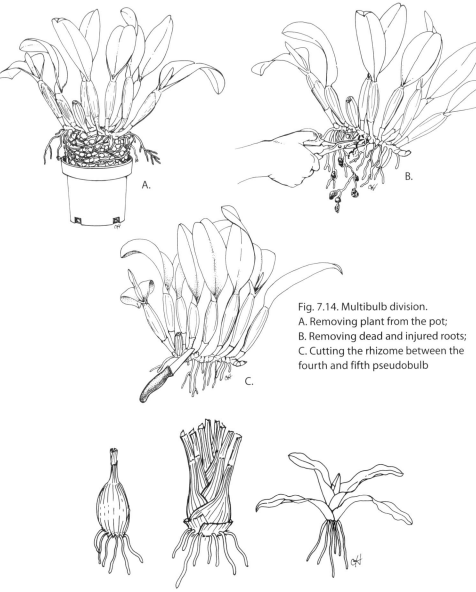

Fig. 7.14. Multibulb division.
A. Removing plant from the pot;
B. Removing dead and injured roots;
C. Cutting the rhizome between the fourth and fifth pseudobulb

Fig. 7.15. Single bulb division can be used to propagate *Calanthe* (left), *Cymbidium* (center), and *Paphiopedilum* (right)

*Paphiopedilum*), a division comprising a single pseudobulb or fan of leaves (fig. 7.15) will produce a flowering plant on the next growth. After the divisions have been made they are potted (fig. 7.13).

2. Keikis. Keiki, the Hawaiian word for "little child," refers to "offsets" in orchids that develop, produce roots, and sometimes flower while still

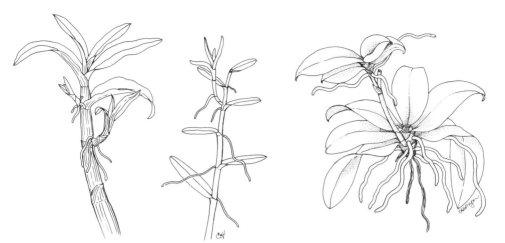

Fig. 7.16. Keikis are commonly produced on dendrobiums (left) and epidendrums (right)

Fig. 7.17. *Phaleanopsis* keikis are often produced on the inflorescence

attached to the parent plant. *Dendrobium* and *Epidendrum* produce keikis (fig. 7.16) in the axils of the upper leaves on the canes. When the keiki is large enough it will usually have three or more roots, 1–2 inches long; this can be snapped off the cane by pulling it sharply downward. After removal it can be potted. Even if the keiki is in bloom when removed, it will continue to bloom when potted if it has sufficient roots and is properly cultured. *Phalaenopsis* plants produce their keikis on the tips of the inflorescences (fig. 7.17). These keikis are handled in the same manner as those of *Dendrobium* and *Epidendrum*.

3. Flower stalks. Spent inflorescences of *Phaius* and *Phalaenopsis* can be used to increase the number of plants.

a. *Phaius* inflorescences (fig. 7.18A,B,C) can be removed when the last flower fades. Cut the inflorescence off at its base and then cut off the portion on the top where the flowers were (easily recognized by the small black ovate spot on the upper stem not covered by a bract). The remaining segment of cane will contain a number of nodes (usually 5–7), each subtended by a triangular light green bract. There is a latent bud under each bract that under the right conditions will produce a new growth. Lay the cane segments in a flat containing a layer of damp sphagnum moss. If the canes are too long for the flat they can be cut in half. Cover the ends of the canes with damp moss to keep them from drying out and place the flat under a greenhouse bench. Keep the moss damp and in six to eight weeks growths should have formed at the nodes. Once the young plants have three or more roots that are more than 1 inch long they can be snapped off and planted in small

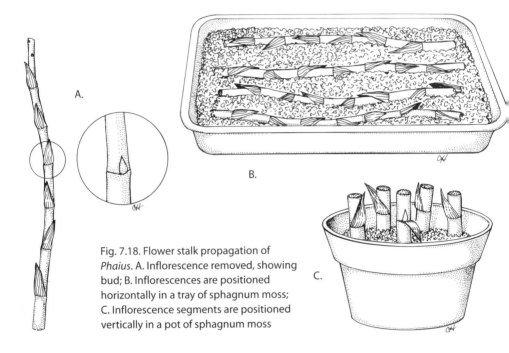

Fig. 7.18. Flower stalk propagation of *Phaius*. A. Inflorescence removed, showing bud; B. Inflorescences are positioned horizontally in a tray of sphagnum moss; C. Inflorescence segments are positioned vertically in a pot of sphagnum moss

pots. Do not expect 100% of the buds to produce plantlets. Some growers prefer to cut the cane into 4–6-inch segments, each containing a bracted node in the center of the segment. These segments are then stood upright in a pot of damp sphagnum moss (fig. 7.18C). Once plantlets develop they are handled in the same manner as above.

b. Propagation of *Phalaenopsis* (fig. 7.19A,B) from flower stalks requires growing under aseptic conditions and is best performed in a laboratory. In this case, after the last flower has faded, the inflorescence is removed. Like *Phaius,* the inflorescence has a number of nodes, each subtended by a small triangular bract. The top portion, where the flowers were, is removed, leaving usually 5–7 nodes. The inflorescence is then cut, removing 3-inch segments that each have a bracted node in the middle. The bracts are surgically removed to expose the latent bud. These are then surface sterilized and placed in a sterile container with a nutrient medium. Once a plantlet forms in the container and has three or more roots it can be removed from the container and potted. Not all nodes will produce plantlets.

4. Tip cuttings. Tip cuttings (fig. 7.20A,B,C) are commonly used to increase the numbers of many plants, including chrysanthemums and coleus. In these cases the cuttings are usually 4–6 inches long; however, tip cuttings in orchids are usually much larger. *Vanda, Papilionanthe, Arachnis,* and

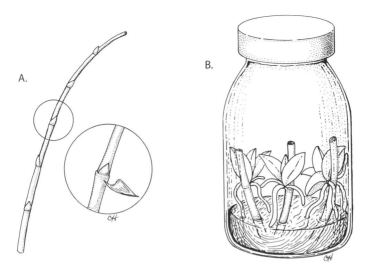

Fig. 7.19. Flower stalk propagation of *Phaleanopsis*. A. Inflorescence removed, showing bud; B. Plantlets developing in an enclosed container under aseptic conditions

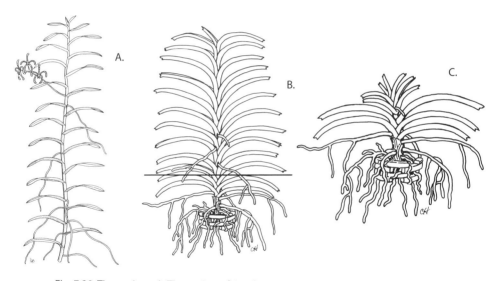

Fig. 7.20. Tip cuttings. A. Tip cutting of *Arachnis*; B. Tip cutting of *Vanda*; C. The base of the same *Vanda* plant 6 months later showing a developing keiki

*Mokara* are among the monopodial genera easily propagated by tip cuttings. *Arachnis* tip cuttings are usually 24–30 inches long and have several aerial roots and may even have an inflorescence or two. *Vanda* and *Mokara* cuttings are usually 18–20 inches long and have several aerial roots. *Papilionanthe* cuttings are often sold by the foot. Once the tip cuttings are removed they can be potted and grown on. After tip cuttings are removed from monopodial plants, the base of the plant can be left in the pot. The basal portion will usually produce one or more keikis in six to eight weeks. Once the keikis have produced roots, as noted above, they too can be removed and potted.

5. Meristeming. In the 1960s a major breakthrough occurred in orchid asexual propagation. Drs. George Morel and Don Wimber, working independently of one another, were instrumental in developing a rapid multiplication process now known as meristeming (also known as mericloning), where a small cube of tissue is removed from the apical meristem and grown aseptically to produce multiple clones of the same plant. More recent studies have shown that orchid leaves can also be used for meristeming. Theoretically, one could produce a million divisions in one year from a tiny cube of tissue, which could be grown into mature plants. However, in practice, usually fewer than 1,000 divisions are made before going back to the mother plant for new tissue. These divisions are handled in the same manner as seeds, and flower in about the same time as a seedling. Meristeming is best conducted in a laboratory where it is easy to maintain aseptic conditions.

*Sexual*

1. Seed. Orchid seed (fig. 1.6) is unique in several aspects. First of all, it is produced in copious amounts, with the average seed pod containing between five hundred thousand and one million seeds. In addition, orchid seeds do not contain endosperm to help them germinate. In edible peas and beans, the majority of the material ingested is endosperm, nutritive tissue that sustains the seed during germination until it has leaves to produce its own food. Since orchid seeds have no endosperm, in the wild they require the association of a specific fungus that plays a role comparable to that of endosperm. Fortunately, a number of years ago, a scientist at Cornell University, L. Knudson, discovered a method of germinating orchid seed aseptically on nutrient agar. Literally millions of orchid plants are now produced annually by this method. Although seeds can be sown in the kitchen at home, most amateur growers prefer to purchase flasks of already germinated seeds.

# 8

# Diseases, Insects, and Cultural Problems

Every orchid hobbyist, no matter how good or how careful, find sooner or later that some pesky little insect, obnoxious leaf spot, or even a virus has invaded the greenhouse. In many cases these will never become serious pests; however, it is always wise to take the appropriate control measures to ensure that a severe infection does not occur. It behooves the hobbyist to be constantly vigilant so any potential problem can be nipped in the bud.

The incidence of pests or diseases invading an orchid collection is greatly minimized by good sanitation. Always use sterilized tools for cutting flowers or dividing plants and do not use them on more than one plant before sterilizing them again. Keep the greenhouse free of weeds, which are often alternate hosts for insects and disease organisms. Try not to crowd your plants, as good air circulation is vital to keeping plants healthy. Water plants early in the day so the foliage and flowers are dry before night fall; flowers going into the dark with droplets of water on them, especially on a cool night, will be highly susceptible to invasion by fungi (*Botrytis*). Having constant air circulation is also helpful in reducing disease incidence. Improve sanitation as much as possible to minimize disease problems and always be sure you are purchasing pest-free plants.

Pest problems of orchids can be divided into three categories: diseases, viruses, and insects. The following are some of the more commonly occurring maladies.

1. Bacterial and Fungal Diseases
   a. Bacterial root and stem rots
   i. Soft rot: *Erwinia* species attack a wide variety of orchid genera, usually in warm weather with an abundance of moisture. They form dark grayish green lesions that appear water soaked and spread very rapidly through leaves and roots. Since the lesions usually have a watery exudate in their centers that contains copious amounts of the bacteria, overhead watering should be discontinued as splashing water rapidly spreads the infection to other plants.
   ii. Brown spot: *Pseudomonas cattleya* (= *Acidovorax cattleya*) also attacks

a wide range of orchid genera. The first symptoms are water-soaked lesions with exudates in the center. The water-soaked area will turn brown or black as it ages. This disease spreads very rapidly and can easily kill a plant if not controlled. At first sight, sanitize the plant and stop overhead irrigation to deter further spread of this potent disease.

b.  *Fungus diseases*

i.  Leaf spots: A variety of fungi, including *Anthracnose, Cercospora, Guignardia* and *Phylosticta*, cause leaf spotting on a wide variety of orchid genera. In many cases the spotting caused by these fungi is not life threatening but simply makes the leaves unsightly. Good sanitation helps reduce the incidence of many leaf spots.

ii. Flower blight (*Botrytis* petal blight): *Botrytis* is an ever-present fungus as it attacks not only living flowers but also dead flowers and foliage. Hence, it is extremely hard to keep the greenhouse free of *Botryis*. Immediate removal of dead flowers and leaves will cut down on the source of inoculum. *Botryis* spores require moisture to germinate; once germinated, they can quickly penetrate the tissue. The first signs are small, circular brown lesions on the sepals and petals, which enlarge slightly over time, but usually do not coalesce. Unfortunately, once the spots appear the flowers are marred for life. Keeping flowers dry with good air circulation will greatly reduce or sometimes prevent an infestation.

iii. Root rots: *Rhizoctonia* and *Fusarium* are two of the more prevalent root rotting organisms of orchids. The first visual symptoms are loss of vigor and a yellowing of the foliage due to death of the roots. Roots infected with *Rhizoctonia* are usually dry, whereas those infected with *Fusarium* are often soft or even watery. If no control is attempted, it may take up to a year for the fungus to destroy a plant.

iv. Black rot: These fungi, *Pythium* and *Phytophora*, can spread rapidly; once they reach the crown they will kill the plant. They usually first appear as black lesions on roots, pseudobulbs, or leaves. The leaf lesions often appear on one side of the leaf and may be soft. Black rot can be spread using unsterile pots or media. It can also be introduced via irrigation water or by splashing water. At first sight, sanitize the leaves with a fungicide and keep them as dry as possible.

v.  Rusts: *Uredo* species are the prime cause of rust in orchids. It is easily recognized by the raised brown pustules on the undersides of the leaves. These will rupture when mature and expose the spores. There is no cure for rust; therefore, it is wise to destroy the plants. Rusts will attack one or two species in *Encyclia, Epidendrum, Ionopsis, Oncidium, Rodriguezia,* and *Trigonidium.*

2. Viruses

Viruses may be considered essentially silent diseases of orchids because, in some cases, virus-infected plants have no outward symptoms and usually go undetected in a collection. If good sanitation is not practiced, then the hobbyist may have a "Typhoid Mary" in the greenhouse. A hobbyist cannot label a plant as being infected by a virus by looking at symptoms alone, as the symptoms often mimic other diseases. Only a laboratory test can establish whether or not a plant has a virus.

The first orchid virus was detected in 1943 and since then more than twenty different viruses have been found in orchids. *Cymbidium* mosaic and tobacco mosaic viruses are the most prevalent.

Unfortunately, there are no known cures for orchid viruses. The most common vectors of these viruses are cutting tools, which, if unsterilized, transfer virus-containing sap from an infected plant to disease-free plants. Since orchid hobbyists are indirectly the most common vectors of viruses, it behooves them to maintain greenhouse sanitation at the highest level. Isolate suspect plants, use only sterilized tools, and sterilize pots as well, because old roots adhering to a pot may contain inoculum. The isolated plants should be tested by a laboratory and if positive for a virus should be destroyed. However, there is one exception: if the virus-infected plant is a very good stud plant, it can be isolated and used for breeding, since the virus is not transmitted by seeds. The two major viruses hobbyists may encounter are:

a. *Cymbidium* Mosaic Virus (CyMV): This is by far the most widespread virus of orchids and is know to attack a wide array of orchid genera. The typical symptoms are black spots and/or streaks on the foliage; the patterning is usually different on each side of the leaf (*Cymbidium*) or appears as sunken streaks on the leaves (*Phalaenopsis*). Unfortunately, in many genera (e.g., *Cattleya* and *Dendrobium*) the plants usually lack symptoms. CyMV can also show up as necrotic color streaking in mature flowers but the streaks may not appear until a week or more after the flowers have opened. This can be a serious problem when cut flowers are given away or sold before the virus symptoms appear.

b. Tobacco Mosaic Virus (TMV): TMV was at one time called *Odontoglossum* Ring Spot Virus when originally isolated from *Odontoglossum grande,* where it formed ring spots on the leaves. *Odontoglossum* Ring Spot Virus was later recognized as TMV and called the TMV-O strain. In addition to ring spots, infected plants may have chlorotic spots and streaks. The symptoms vary among genera. Purple-flowered cattleyas may have purple pigment associated with the symptoms, whereas in *Epidendrum,* only chlorotic spotting symptoms are evident. TMV is also associated with "color break" in flowers. The breaks are not uniform and vary among the floral segments of each flower. Novices sometime confuse "color splash" on the petals with color break, but color splash that is uniform on the petals it is due to genetic factors.

3. Insects

   No orchid greenhouse is immune to insects and sooner or later some insect will gain entrance. Over the years, a wide variety of insects has been reported to attack orchids. Fortunately, only a few ever become serious problems. Most of the more commonly encountered insects are illustrated in the text. Among those depicted, the following are the most prevalent and destructive.

   a. Cockroaches (figs. 8.1J, 8.3G): These nocturnal insects feed especially on young root tips, buds, and flowers and can destroy an inflorescence overnight. They often hide in the bottom of the containers or under the bench in the daytime.

   b. Snails and slugs (figs. 8.1G,H, 8.3E,F): Like cockroaches, snails and slugs are more apt to eat root tips and flowers, thus at first glance it is difficult to determine which critter caused the damage. This problem can

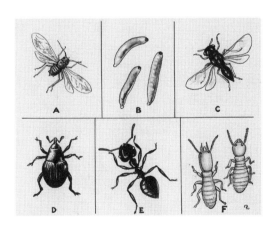
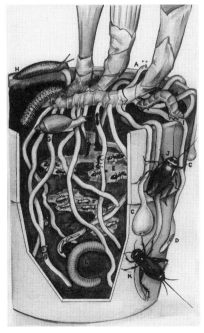

Fig. 8.1. Pests of roots and their damage. A. Woodlice or slaters; B. Fungus gnats; C. Root flies; D. Orchid weevil; E. Ants; F. Termites; G. Snail; H. Slug; I. Caterpillar; J. Cockroach; K. Cricket; L. Millipede

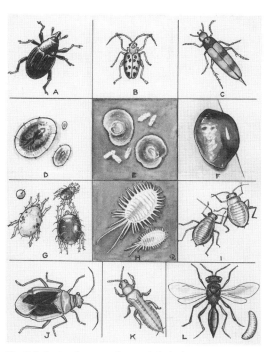
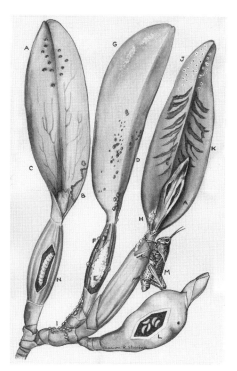

Fig. 8.2. Pests of vegetation and their damage. A. Weevil; B. Beetle; C. Leaf miner; D. Brown scale; E. Boisduval scale; F. Hemispherical scale; G. Mites (Red spiders); H. Mealybugs; I. Aphids; J. Orchid plant bug; K. Thrips; L. *Cattleya* wasp (fly); M. Grasshopper; N. Caterpillar

easily be solved by going into the greenhouse at first light. If the plants have slime trails on them, snails or slugs are the problem. If the trails are lacking, then cockroaches become suspect.

c. Scale insects (fig. 8.2D,E,F): A number of scale insects attack orchids, including boisduval, hemispherical, and soft brown (or brown soft scale). Boisduval is by far the most common and widespread scale insect that attacks orchids. It commonly attacks the underside of leaves or crawls in under the dry pseudobulb sheaths (*Cattleya*) where it they multiplies very rapidly. The first symptom is a small yellow spot appearing on the leaf surface. Under the spot will be a mass of scale insects. The females are almost round and lack wings and legs. They attach themselves to the leaves, become sedentary, and lay eggs under a scalelike covering. When the eggs hatch, the crawlers (immature scale), which look like cotton masses, move about and attach themselves to the leaves where they lay more eggs. When orchid plants are crammed on a greenhouse bench, scale insects tend to spread more readily. Close inspection of all plants, especially the undersides of the leaves, will allow for early detection and easy control.

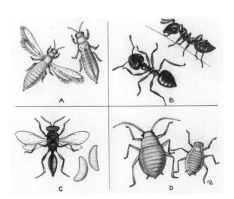

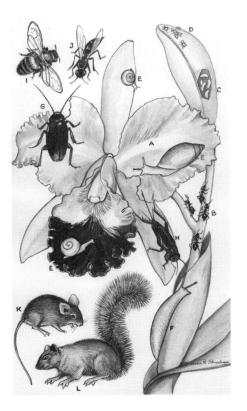

Fig. 8.3. Flower pests and their damage. A. Thrips; B. Ants; C. *Cattleya* wasp (fly); D. Aphids; E. Snail; F. Slug; G. Cockroach; H. Cricket; I. Bee; J. Wasp; K. Mouse; L. Squirrel

d. Ants (figs. 8.1E, 8.3B): Whenever possible ants should be kept out of the greenhouse. Ants may appear to be very innocent visitors crawling up inflorescences and eating the sugary exudates (honeydew) from the buds and flowers but, unfortunately, this is not true of all ants. Many ant colonies pasture both aphids and scale insects. They introduce them into the greenhouse and leave them on orchid plants. The ants then collect the honeydew produced by both insects to feed their colony. Unfortunately, ant colonies move on and when they do, they leave plenty of aphids and scale insects behind. Therefore, keeping ants out of the greenhouse is very important.

e. Thrips (figs. 8.2K, 8.3A): Flower thrips are 1/16–3/8 inch long and can become a very serious problem in warm dry weather. Counts of fifty or more thrips per flower are not uncommon when thrips are swarming. They usually arrive on a gentle breeze. Once on the flowers, thrips use their rasping mouthparts to tear the tissue so they can devour the cell contents, leaving behind numerous small brown spots on the flowers. Their damage is most evident on white flowers, which ruins their aesthetic value. Thrips also damage leaves, but lesions are less conspicuous. When thrips are prevalent almost daily spraying is necessary to control them.

f. Spider mites (fig. 8.2G): Spider mites are only about 1/50 of an inch long when mature and may be greenish, yellowish, reddish, or virtually colorless. They are commonly found on the undersides of leaves. When plants are heavily infested, fine webbing will be noticed. Mites suck juices from plants through their needlelike mouthparts. A 10 or 15 power magnifying glass is very helpful in detecting infestations before severe damage occurs. The first signs of mite damage on orchids is the appearance of silvery spots on the upper leaf surface.

g. Aphids (figs. 8.2I, 8.3D): Aphids may be green, pink, black, brown, yellow, or blue in color. They vary from 1/25 to 1/8 inch in length and may or may not have wings. They are pear shaped and have long antennae and two short cornicles or tubes extending from the rear end of the body. Aphids suck plant juices. They are usually found on young orchid inflorescences and if not controlled can cause bud malformation.

## Controlling Diseases and Insects

Carefully examine any purchased or donated orchid plants to be sure they are free of pests. After bringing a plant home, isolate it for at least a month before placing it with other plants. Always use sterilized potting mixes and clean containers to help prevent infestations of pests.

If sanitation fails and a hobbyist is faced with a disease or insect problem, then the immediate area around the infected plant should be treated. If the hobbyist is vigilant and spots the problem early there is no need to spray the entire green-house. Minimal use of chemicals should always be the goal of every orchid hobbyist.

Since the rules for the use and handling of chemical pesticides are constantly changing and also vary within the United States and between and among countries, no chemical controls are included in these pages. It should also be noted that pesticides are constantly being withdrawn from the market and new ones introduced.

## Cultural and Physiological Problems

In addition to a variety of pest occurrences, occasionally the hobbyist may experience additional problems that are culture related. The most widely reported cultural problems are probably caused by improper watering. One of the first signs of improper watering in sympodial orchids is shriveled pseudobulbs. When there is a lack of water, the roots will look normal; with excess moisture, in addition to shriveled pseudobulbs, roots will exhibit signs of rotting. Overwatered plants should be repotted after all damaged roots and old medium have been removed. When a new leaf on soft-leaf plants (i.e., *Miltonia, Lycaste, Stanhopea*) emerges in a pleated condition, this too is an indication of inadequate watering. When the plant is properly watered, the next new leaf should be normal.

## Bud Drop

Bud drop can often be a problem under certain environmental conditions. For example, when a *Dendrobium* plant with flower spikes growing under ideal conditions in a greenhouse is moved into a home with central heating and air conditioning, it will often lose some or maybe all of its flower buds. This condition can also occur in the greenhouse when there are sudden fluctuations in temperature of 20°F or more. In selecting plants from the greenhouse for display in the home, it is wise to pick those with open flowers, thus avoiding bud drop.

## Weeds

Weeds have the potential of becoming a serious problem and, unfortunately, there is no easy solution. It is wise to pull the weeds by hand as early as possible. This is especially true of some fern seedlings, as they can be very detrimental and if not removed will eventually kill the orchid. *Oxalis* and artillery plants are two very problematic weeds as their exploding seed pods rapidly disseminate seeds throughout the greenhouse.

## Salt Deposits

When a white, crustlike material forms on the rims or sides of clay pots, this is a good indication of either excessive salts in the water or overfertilization. When water evaporates through the sides of a pot, mineral salts are deposited on the surface. As these salt deposits build up, they can become detrimental to new roots and, if not leached, can weaken the plant. In addition to root damage, excess salts can cause browning of leaf margins and tips. Check the salt level in the water supply and be sure fertilization applications are normal; if they are out of line make the necessary adjustments to prevent further problems.

## Oedema

Oedema is a malady that occurs occasionally that is never serious, but simply a cosmetic problem. Under certain atmospheric conditions, the roots take up water faster than the leaves are transpiring, causing small watery blisters to appear. They usually form on the underside of the leaf, but in some cases they will appear on both leaf surfaces. Over time a corky layer will cover the blister and remain there until the leaf falls. Aside from the slight disfigurement of the leaves oedema does little to harm the plant.

## Mesophyll Cell Collapse

During the winter months, *Phalaenopsis* plants with newly developing leaves exposed to low temperatures for two hours at 45°F will develop mesophyll cell collapse. The first signs are small, yellow, slightly depressed streaks on the developing leaves very similar to virus symptoms; with time the streaks eventually turn black. Mesophyll cell collapse is most evident in winter and early spring. Unfortunately, the symptoms do not appear until about six weeks after the drop in temperature. Aside from disfiguring one or two leaves there is no major damage to the plants as the next leaves to develop will be normal. Most *Phalaenopsis* plants with mature leaves can stand up to eight hours at 45°F with no damage to the leaves.

## Ethylene

Ethylene can damage orchid flowers. The damage is more apt to occur during the winter months when overcast skies prevent industrial gases from escaping and allow ethylene to build up in the atmosphere. Dr. Wes Davidson showed that as little as 2 parts per billion (ppb) of ethylene in the air could cause sepals of *Cattleya* orchid flowers to dry. The dorsal sepal becomes papery and turns brown at the tip. *Phalaenopsis* flower buds are also susceptible to ethylene. Young buds are the most sensitive. The buds become grayish white a day after exposure and usually abort about ten days later. If the amount of ethylene in the atmosphere exceeds 75 ppb even some newly opened *Phalaenopsis* flowers will abort.

## Indicators of Cultural Problems

If a hobbyist watches plants closely, orchids will indicate whether or not cultural practices are adequate or if pest problems may be occurring. The growth of the plant is a good indicator. In sympodial (*Cattleya*) seedlings, each ensuing growth should be larger than the previous growth. When the plant reaches maturity and is flowering, each new growth should be equal to or larger than the last mature growth. If the new growth is smaller, it is an indicator of either a cultural or pest problem and it is time to check both. Similarly, monopodial plants (*Vanda*) can also indicate problems. As the plants grow to maturity each new leaf is longer than the previous one. When the plants mature and flower the leaves should all be the same size. A hobbyist can easily check by placing a ruler upright next to the plant's leaf tips. If all the leaf tips touch the ruler everything is normal. However, if the uppermost mature leaves are smaller, this too is an indicator of a cultural problem.

When a problem is noted and the hobbyist is not sure of the cause, a sample should be taken to an Agriculture Extension Agent or Farm Advisor for identification of the problem and how to control it. The best information with good pictures on orchid pests and diseases can be found in the American Orchid Society's *Handbook on Orchid Pests and Diseases*.

# 9

## Greenhouses and Shade Houses

### Greenhouses

A small greenhouse can be very useful to an orchid hobbyist. It can be used to grow orchids, germinate seeds, root cuttings for the outdoor garden, and grow vegetables out of season. A carefully designed and constructed greenhouse can be enjoyed year-round. The first step is to decide whether a homemade or a ready-made greenhouse best suits your needs. Ready-made greenhouses are precisely built so they are usually more attractive and expensive than homemade types.

Homemade greenhouses can be made from leftover building materials, but pressure-treated wood is preferred. They are much cheaper to build than factory made greenhouses and can be built to any size that best fits the hobbyist's particular needs.

Fig. 9.1. Freestanding greenhouse

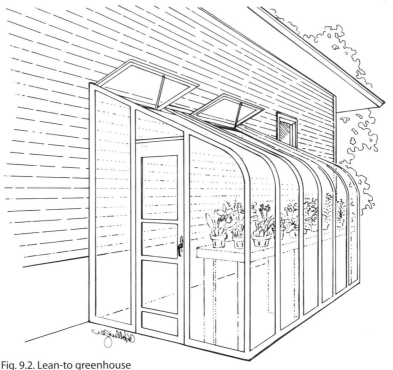
Fig. 9.2. Lean-to greenhouse

The next decision will be what type of greenhouse would best fit your location. There are two basic types of greenhouses: freestanding (fig. 9.1) and attached (lean-to, fig. 9.2). The freestanding greenhouse is a complete independent structure. The attached greenhouse is built against a building, using the existing structure for one or more of its sides. It has the advantage that you can usually get into it easily in bad weather. Some lean-tos can be completely open on the attached wall with sliding glass doors, making the greenhouse an integral part of the living area. It also costs less to heat because it shares one wall with the house.

The size of a greenhouse is influenced by available space, location, intended use, and cost. Many orchid hobbyists find their greenhouse is too small the day they move in. Therefore, it should be large enough to house not only the plant collection, but also a workbench and a small storage area. Larger greenhouses are easier to manage because the temperature fluctuates more slowly.

*Structures*

Wood, steel, or aluminum are used for the supporting framework of greenhouses. The type of structural materials used will depend on a number of factors including cost, longevity, and availability of materials.

Fig. 9.3. Typical orchid hobbyist greenhouse with an aluminum frame and covered with polycarbonate

Wood: Seasoned, construction-grade lumber should be used when building a wood-framed greenhouse. When possible, rot-resistant woods such as redwood or cypress should be used. If lumber is not rot resistant, it should be pressure treated, especially if coming in contact with the ground. Do not use creosote or pentachlorophenol wood preservatives because they release vapors harmful to plants and also may discolor plastic films.

Steel: Greenhouses built with steel require higher maintenance to prevent the steel from rusting. The potential for rusting can be reduced by using galvanized steel. If bowed members are used, then the steel should be bent and holes drilled before galvanizing.

Aluminum: Aluminum is the best material to use for the supporting framework of a greenhouse. It is lightweight, strong, and rust resistant, requires little maintenance, and will last many years. It comes in a variety of shapes, which helps simplify construction (fig. 9.3).

*Greenhouse Coverings*

A wide variety of materials are available and, depending on cost, may have a life span of less than one year to well in excess of twenty years. The greenhouse design and structural material will often determine the covering that can be used.

Glass: Clear glass is one of the most durable greenhouse coverings and has very high light transmission. When glazing, use double-strength glass panes, which are the most durable and resist thermal stress better. Current manufacturing technology can produce panes up to 6 feet wide; however, wider panes require stronger support. Most hobby greenhouse are constructed with smaller panes (e.g., 16–24 inches wide). In colder climates, double-pane glass can be used to help reduce heat loss and moisture condensation. Glass is more vulnerable to hail or vandalism damage and double-pane glass tends to slow snow melt, which can significantly reduce light transmission.

Fiberglass: Fiberglass is an excellent greenhouse covering and is available in corrugated or flat sheets. It is lightweight, strong, and practically hail proof. It has good light transmission, and requires only a simple superstructure for support. There are poor grades of fiberglass that will soon discolor, reducing light penetration. Use a good grade that is guaranteed for ten to twenty years. For best light transmission, reseal the fiberglass every four to five years with an acrylic liquid sealer. When selecting fiberglass, choose the clearest grade as it is much easier to reduce light than to increase it once the greenhouse is constructed. Do not use colored fiberglass (e.g., green).

Polycarbonate: One of the latest greenhouse coverings is polycarbonate. It is much lighter than glass and therefore requires less structural framing. The panels are large and easy to install and have a high impact resistance to hail and vandalism. It is best to purchase coated panels as these show less yellowing over the years. Those with ultraviolet protection will last at least fifteen years. Polycarbonate comes in varying thicknesses; for home greenhouses 8 mm is ideal.

Plastic films: Plastic film coverings are inexpensive and temporary. They are light weight, have good light transmission, and require minimal structural support. Because plastic films come in large widths, often a single piece will cover the entire house, greatly reducing heat leakage. Older plastic films deteriorated rapidly, but now, with new additives, most greenhouse plastic films will last up to four years.

Most greenhouses should be built on foundations of wood or concrete, but plastic greenhouses may be placed on the ground. In warmer climates, where the winters are mild, large concrete foundations are not needed. However, glass and fiberglass houses should have a permanent foundation, which could be nothing more than a wooden sill of 2 × 6-inch boards or a 6-inch concrete footing. The foundation should never be higher than the plant benches and no higher than 10–15 inches if plants are to be grown on the ground.

Before building or buying a greenhouse, select a suitable location. The available space will determine the size of the greenhouse. The greenhouse should be located where it receives maximum sunlight. Remember, it is always easier to shade a greenhouse than it is to increase light intensity after construction. The best available light situation for the greenhouse is when the main axis runs north and south. Determining the location for a lean-to is a little more difficult. A southern or southeastern exposure is the best. The east side would be the second choice, where morning sun is available. Less optimal choices would be southwest or west. If situated in a western exposure, the orchids will probably need shading in summer. North is the least desirable except for tropical foliage plants and African violets.

It is wise to site the greenhouse near sources of water, fuel for heating, and electricity, thereby substantially reducing building costs.

## Shade Houses

Shade houses (fig. 9.4) are best suited for the warmer climates (Hawaii, Florida, California) because they are difficult to heat in the winter. They can be constructed of wood or metal. For hobby houses the upright member can be spaced 6–8 feet on center with the stringers between the posts at least 7 feet above the ground. The stringers can be made of wood, steel, galvanized cable, or heavy galvanized wire, all of which will support the cover. Commercial shade houses usually have their members spaced 12–14 feet on center. Pipe frames in the shape of Quonset huts (fig. 9.5) can also be used for shade houses. In cooler climates, they have the advantage of being easier to cover and heat in winter, as the dome shape easily sheds rain and snow.

The structure is covered with shade cloth. The cloth can be attached by a number of methods. However, it is best to obtain shade cloth with grommets so that it can be attached to the structures with S hooks. This is especially important in

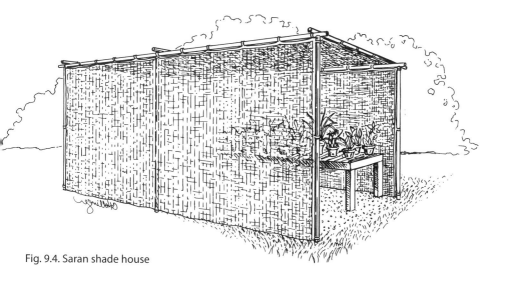

Fig. 9.4. Saran shade house

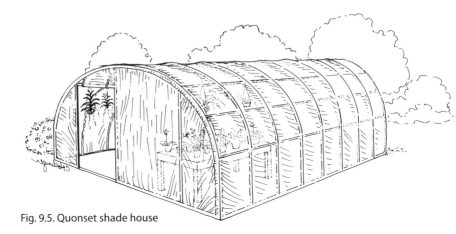

Fig. 9.5. Quonset shade house

Florida and other areas where hurricanes are prevalent, so that the cloth can easily be removed. If lath (1/2 × 2 or 1/2 × 3 inches, usually cypress or redwood) is selected in lieu of shade cloth, the lath should be spaced so that 50% of the area is covered.

Shade cloth comes in a wide variety of light levels, based on the number of threads per square inch. The cloth used for orchid houses, depending on genera grown, will range from 50% to 70% shade. Shade cloth usually needs to be replaced every six to ten years.

Before buying or building any outdoor growing structure, careful thought should be given to size, style, and controls desired. Learn about the problems of people who have greenhouses and check local building codes and zoning laws before starting construction. The more thought given to planning, the more satisfaction will be derived from the structure.

# 10

# Growing Orchids in the Home

It is unfortunate that many individuals have the misconception that orchids coming from steamy tropical jungles need to be grown in a greenhouse. This is not the case, as there are many orchids out there that can be grown as houseplants (fig. 10.1) and they will surprise you with how durable they can be. Although *Phalaenopsis* and *Dendrobium* plants are the most popular and readily available, other genera such as *Oncidium* and its colorful multi-generic hybrids, *Paphiopedilum* and *Cattleya* alliance hybrids, are often found in the marketplace. Once you purchase a plant, grow it, and see it bloom a second time there will be no end to the number of plants in your collection. All one needs to do is follow a few simple cultural steps for success in growing orchids as houseplants. The most important factors to consider are light, temperature, water, humidity and fertilization.

Fig. 10.1. The family cat admires orchids displayed in the home

## Light

Light requirements vary among orchid genera, and for cultivation are broken down into four categories: full sun, partial shade, moderate shade, and heavy shade (see page 196). These are the light levels recommended for best growth and flowering but orchid plants will grow over a range of light levels. However, higher light will enhance flowering.

The best area for growing orchids in the home is by a window facing south or southeast. Northern windows are usually too dark, while those facing west tend to be too hot in the afternoon. The closer the plants are to the window, the higher the light intensity, but never expose the plants to the direct rays of the sun by either moving the plants back from the window or placing a sheer curtain between the plants and the window. Sometimes it takes a little moving back and forth to determine the right light level. Actually, the plants will indicate whether or not they are receiving the proper amount of light. If the leaves are dark green the plant needs more light. Light green leaves indicate the plant is receiving the proper amount of light.

Growing plants in dark areas or in the basement of a home is a little more challenging. If the area is receiving some daylight, then usually a 4-foot shop light with two 40-watt cool white fluorescent tubes spaced 12–18 inches above the plants is sufficient. For those growing in the basement, one simple rule of thumb for lighting orchid plants is for every 4-foot square area use four 4-foot, 40-watt cool white fluorescent tubes and two 40-watt incandescent bulbs suspended 12–18 inches above the plants. They should be lighted 16 hours a day. There are also a variety of grow lamps on the market that can be used in place of the fluorescent tubes.

## Temperature

There are warm, intermediate, and cool growing orchids (see pages 199–200). When selecting plants to grow in the home, the warm (*Phalaenopsis*) and intermediate (*Dendrobium*) are the best suited. Orchid temperature classifications are the minimal night temperatures at which they grow best, although most orchids can survive over a range of temperatures. Most orchids will grow best if the night temperature is 10–15°F below the day temperature to emulate the drop in night temperatures they experience in their native habitats. The temperature in the home at which humans are most comfortable will produce adequate growth in orchids.

## Water

The majority of cultivated orchids are epiphytes and grown in a very porous mixture, usually containing bark, charcoal, and perlite. Hence, unlike soil in which most houseplants are potted, the medium used for orchids dries out much more rapidly. Fortunately, orchid media drain very well, lessening damage caused by overwatering. The best way to water plants in the home is to water thoroughly, applying sufficient water to run out of the bottom of the pot. This ensures the entire medium is moist and also leaches out excess soluble salts. Orchid plants growing in 6-inch or larger pots usually need to be watered once a week in the home, smaller pots may require two waterings per week. During the peaks of the air conditioning and heating seasons, when the humidity is extremely low, more frequent applications may be necessary.

## Humidity

Orchid plants grow best when the relative humidity is between 40% and 60%. Unfortunately, it is often much lower in the home. Homes with air conditioning and forced-air heat can become very dry, hence some method of improving the humidity around the orchid plants will be necessary. In a basement a small humidifier can serve the purpose, but may or may not work for plants on a windowsill, as condensation could damage wood or curtains near the window. Humidity for windowsill plants can be improved by placing plants on water-filled trays of gravel or plastic lattice (the grid sold for fluorescent ceiling fixtures). Keep the water below the level of the gravel or lattice so the bottoms of the plant pots do not touch the water. The trays should be emptied and cleaned weekly to prevent the growth of algae and other microorganisms. Some growers recommend enclosing the area in plastic, but if the plastic inhibits air movement it could be detrimental as good air movement deters diseases.

## Fertilization

Orchid plants growing in the home need to be fertilized once a month with a weak soluble fertilizer. A 20-20-20 or similar balanced soluble fertilizer used at one-quarter or one-half the recommended rate will produce good orchid plants with flowers. Synthetic, controlled-release fertilizers can also be used; apply at half the recommended rate every three to four months.

# Appendix

## Orchid Family Outline

It should be pointed out that several generic names in this outline are no longer considered valid by Dressler and as a result of DNA studies more changes are bound to follow. These genera appear in several books on cultivated orchids or have been moved between genera frequently in recent times so that the names still seem in a state of flux. Two examples are *Acacallis*, also called *Aganisia* (Alex Pridgeon 1992), and *Baptistonia*, also called *Oncidium* (Bechtel et al. 1992).

Apostasioideae: *Apostasia, Neuwiedia.*

Cypripedioideae: *Cypripedium, Mexipedium, Paphiopedilum, Phragmipedium, Selenipedium.*

Spiranthoideae:

Diceratosteleae: *Diceratostele.*

Tropidieae: *Corymborkis, Tropidia.*

Cranichideae:

Goodyerinae: *Anoectochilus, Aspidogyne, Chamaegastrodia, Cheirostylis, Cystorchis, Dicerostylis, Dossinia, Erythrodes, Eucosia, Eurycentrum, Evrardia, Gonatostylis, Goodyera, Gymnochilus, Herpysma, Hetaeria, Hylophila, Kreodanthus, Kuhlhasseltia, Lepidogyne, Ligeophila, Ludisia, Macodes, Moerenhoutia, Myrmechis, Orchipedum, Papuaea, Platylepis, Platythelys, Pristiglottis, Rhamphorhynchus, Stephanothelys, Tubilabium, Vrydagzynea, Zeuxine.*

Prescottiinae: *Aa, Altensteinia, Gomphichis, Myrosmodes, Porphyrostachys, Prescottia, Stenoptera.*

Spiranthinae: *Aracamunia, Aulosepalum, Beloglottis, Brachystele, Buchtienia, Coccineorchis, Cotylolabium, Cybebus, Cyclopogon, Degranvillea, Deiregyne, Dichromanthus, Discyphus, Dithyridanthus, Eltroplectris, Eurystyles, Funkiella, Galeottiella, Greenwoodia, Hapalorchis, Helonema, Kionophyton, Lankesterella, Lyroglossa, Mesadenella, Mesadenus, Odontorrhynchos, Oestlundorchis, Pelexia, Pseudogoodyera, Pteroglossa, Sacoila, Sarcoglottis, Sauroglossum, Schiedeella, Skeptrostachys, Spiranthes, Stalkya, Stenorrhynchus, Stigmatosema, Thelyschista.*

Manniellinae: *Manniella.*

Pachyplectroninae: *Pachyplectron.*

Cranichidinae: *Baskervilla, Cranichis, Fuertesiella, Nothostele, Ponthieva, Pseudocentrum, Pseudocranichis, Pterichis, Solenocentrum.*

Orchidoideae

Diurideae

Chloraeinae: *Bipinnula, Chloraea, Codonorchis, Gavilea, Geoblasta, Megastylis.*

Caladeniinae: *Adenochilus, Aporostylis, Burnettia, Caladenia, Elythranthera, Eriochilus, Glossodia, Leporella, Lyperanthus, Rimacola.*

Drakaeinae: *Arthrochilus, Caleana, Chiloglottis, Drakaea, Spiculaea.*

Pterostylidinae: *Pterostylis.*

Acianthinae: *Acianthus, Corybas, Cyrtostylis, Stigmatodactylus, Townsonia.*

Cryptostylidinae: *Coilochilus, Cryptostylis.*

Diuridinae: *Diuris, Epiblema, Orthoceras.*

Thelymitrinae: *Calochilus, Thelymitra.*

Rhizanthellinae: *Rhizanthella.*

Prasophyllinae: *Genoplesium, Microtis, Prasophyllum.*

Orchideae

Orchidinae: *Aceras, Aceratorcis, Amerorchis, Amitostigma, Anacamptis, Aorchis, Barlia, Bartholina, Brachycorythis, Chamorchis, Chondradenia, Chusua, Coeloglossum, Comperia, Dactylorhiza, Galearis, Gymnadenia, Hemipilia, Himantoglossum, Holothrix, Neobolusia, Neotinea, Neottianthe, Nigritella, Ophrys, Orchis, Piperia, Platanthera, Pseudodiphryllum, Pseudorchis, Schizochilus, Serapias, Steveniella, Symphyosepalum, Traunsteinera.*

Habenariinae: *Androcorys, Arnottia, Benthamia, Bonatea, Centrostigma, Cynorkis, Diphylax, Diplomeris, Gennaria, Habenaria, Herminium, Megalorchis, Oligophyton, Pecteilis, Peristylus, Physoceras, Platycoryne, Porolabium, Roeperocharis, Smithorchis, Stenoglottis, Thulinia, Tsaiorchis, Tylostigma.*

Diseae

Huttonaeinae: *Huttonaea.*

Satyriinae: *Pachites, Satyridium, Satyrium.*

Coryciinae: *Ceratandra, Corycium, Disperis, Evotella, Pterygodium.*

Disinae: *Brownleea, Disa, Herschelia, Monadenia, Schizodium.*

Epidendroideae

Neottieae

Limodorinae: *Aphyllorchis, Cephalanthera, Epipactis, Limodorum.*

Listerinae: *Listera, Neottia.*

Palmorchideae: *Palmorchis.*

Triphoreae: *Monophyllorchis, Psilochilus, Triphora.*

Vanilleae

Galeolinae: *Cyrtosia, Erythrorchis, Galeola, Pseudovanilla.*

Vanillinae: *Clematepistephium, Dictyophyllaria, Epistephium, Eriaxis, Vanilla.*

Lecanorchidinae: *Lecanorchis.*

Gastrodieae

Gastrodiinae: *Auxopus, Didymoplexiella, Didymoplexis, Gastrodia, Neoclemensia, Uleiorchis.*

Epipogiinae: *Epipogium, Silvorchis, Stereosandra.*

Wullschlaegeliinae: *Wullschlaegelia.*

Nervilieae: *Nervilia.*

Cymbidioid Phylad

Malaxideae: *Hippeophyllum, Liparis, Malaxis, Oberonia, Orestias, Risleya.*

Calypsoeae: *Aplectrum, Calypso, Corallorhiza, Cremastra, Dactylostalix, Ephippianthus, Oreorchis, Tipularia, Yoania.*

Cymbidieae

Goveniinae: *Govenia.*

Bromheadiinae: *Bromheadia.*

Eulophiinae: *Cyanaeorchis, Dipodium, Eulophia, Geodorum, Oeceoclades, Pteroglossaspis.*

Thecostelinae: *Thecopus, Thecostele.*

Cyrtopodiinae: *Acrolophia, Ansellia, Cymbidiella, Cymbidium, Cyrtopodium, Eulophiella, Galeandra, Grammangis, Grammatophyllum, Graphorkis, Grobya, Porphyroglottis.*

Acriopsidinae: *Acriopsis.*

Catasetinae: *Catasetum, Clowesia, Cycnoches, Dressleria, Mormodes.*

Maxillarieae

Cryptarrheninae: *Cryptarrhena.*

Zygopetalinae: *Aganisia (= Acacallis), Batemannia, Benzingia, Bollea, Chaubardia, Chaubardiella, Cheiradenia, Chondrorhyncha, Cochleanthes, Dichaea, Dodsonia, Galeottia, Hoehneella, Huntleya, Kefersteinia, Koellensteinia, Mendoncella, Neogardneria, Otostylis, Pabstia (Colax), Paradisianthus, Pescatoria, Promenaea, Scuticaria, Stenia, Vargasiella, Warrea, Warreella, Zygopetalum, Zygosepalum.*

Lycastinae: *Anguloa, Bifrenaria, Horvatia, Lycaste, Neomoorea, Rudolfiella, Teusheria, Xylobium.*

Maxillariinae: *Anthosiphon, Chrysocycnis, Cryptocentrum, Cyrtidiorchis, Maxillaria, Mormolyca, Pityphyllum, Trigonidium.*

Stanhopeinae: *Acineta, Braemia, Cirrhaea, Coeliopsis, Coryanthes, Embreea, Gongora, Horichia, Houlletia, Kegeliella, Lacaena, Lueddemannia, Lycomormium, Paphinia, Peristeria, Polycycnis, Schlimia, Sievekingia, Soterosanthus, Stanhopea, Trevoria, Vasqueziella.*

Telipogoninae: *Hofmeisterella, Stellilabium, Telipogon, Trichoceros.*

Ornithocephalinae: *Caluera, Centroglossa, Chytroglossa, Dipteranthus, Dunstervillea, Eloyella, Hintonella, Ornithocephalus, Phymatidium, Platyrhiza, Rauhiella, Sphyrastylis, Thysanoglossa, Zygostates.*

Oncidiinae: *Ada, Amparoa, Antillanorchis, Aspasia, Binotia, Brachtia, Brassia, Buesiella, Capanemia, Caucaea, Cischweinfia, Cochlioda, Comparettia, Cuitlauzinia, Cypholoron, Diadenium, Dignathe, Erycina, Fernandezia, Gomesa, Helcia, Hybochilus, Ionopsis, Konantzia, Lemboglossum, Leochilus, Leucohyle, Lockhartia, Macradenia, Macroclinium, Mesoglossum, Mesospinidium, Mexicoa, Miltonia, Miltoniopsis, Neodryas, Neokoehleria, Notylia, Odontoglossum, Oliveriana, Oncidium, Osmoglossum, Otoglossum, Pachyphyllum, Palumbina, Papperitzia, Plectrophora, Polyotidium, Psychopsiella, Psychopsis, Psygmorchis, Pterostemma, Quekettia, Raycadenco, Rodriguezia, Rodrigueziella, Rodriguezopsis, Rossioglossum, Rusbyella, Sanderella, Saundersia, Scelochiloides, Scelochilus, Sigmatostalix, Solenidiopsis, Solenidium, Stictophyllum, Suarezia, Sutrina, Symphyglossum, Systeloglossum, Ticoglossum, Tolumnia, Trichocentrum, Trichopilia, Trizeuxis, Warmingia.*

Epidendroid Phylad
    Arethuseae
        Arethusinae: *Arethusa, Eleorchis.*

Bletiinae: *Acanthephippium, Ancistrochilus, Anthogonium, Aulostylis, Bletia, Bletilla, Calanthe, Calopogon, Cephalantheropsis, Eriodes, Gastrorchis, Hancockia, Hexalectris, Ipsea, Mischobulbon, Nephelaphyllum, Pachystoma, Phaius, Plocoglottis, Spathoglottis, Tainia.*

Chysinae: *Chysis.*

    Coelogyneae
        Thuniinae: *Thunia.*

Coelogyninae: *Basigyne, Bracisepalum, Bulleyia, Chelonistele, Coelogyne, Dendrochilum, Dickasonia, Entomophobia, Forbesina, Geesinkorchis, Gynoglottis, Ischnogyne, Nabaluia, eogyne, Otochilus, Panisea, Pholidota, Pleione, Pseudacoridium, Sigmatogyne.*

    Epidendreae I (New World)
        Sobraliinae: *Elleanthus, Epilyna, Sertifera, Sobralia.*
        Arpophyllinae: *Arpophyllum.*
        Meiracylliinae: *Meiracyllium.*
        Coeliinae: *Coelia.*

Laeliinae: *Acrorchis, Alamania, Artorima, Barkeria, Basiphyllaea, Brassavola, Broughtonia, Cattleya, (Cattleyopsis), Caularthron (Diacrium), Constantia, Dilomilis, Dimerandra, Domingoa, Encyclia, Epidendrum, Hagsatera, Helleriella, Hexisea, Homalopetalum, Isabelia, Isochilus, Jacquiniella, Laelia, Lae-*

*liopsis, Leptotes, Loefgrenianthus, Myrmecophila, Nageliella, Neocogniauxia, Nidema, Oerstedella, Orleanesia, Pinelia, Platyglottis, Ponera, Prosthechea, Pseudolaelia, Psychilis, Pygmaeorchis, Quisqueya, Reichenbachanthus, Rhyncholaelia, Scaphyglottis, Schomburgkia, Sophronitis, Tetramicra.*

Pleurothallidinae: *Acostaea, (Baptistonia), Barbosella, Barbrodria, Brachionidium, Chamelophyton, Condylago, Dracula, Dresslerella, Dryadella, Frondaria, Lepanthes, Lepanthopsis, Masdevallia, Myoxanthus, Octomeria, Ophidion, Platystele, Pleurothallis, Porroglossum, Restrepia, Restrepiella, Restrepiopsis, Salpistele, Scaphosepalum, Stelis, Teagueia, Trichosalpinx, Trisetella, Zootrophion.*

Epidendreae II (Old World)

Glomerinae: *Aglossorhyncha, Agrostopohyllum, Earina, Glomera, Glossorhyncha, Ischnocentrum, Sepalosiphon.*

Adrorhizinae: *Adrorhizon, Sirhookera.*

Polystachyinae: *Hederorkis, Imerinaea, Neobenthamia, Polystachya.*

Dendrobioid Subclade

Podochileae

Eriinae: *Ascidieria, Ceratostylis, Cryptochilus, Epiblastus, Eria, Mediocalcar, Porpax, Sarcostoma, Stolzia, Trichotosia.*

Podochilinae: *Appendicula, Chilopogon, Chitonochilus, Cyphochilus, Poaephyllum, Podochilus.*

Thelasiinae: *Chitonanthera, Octarrhena, Oxyanthera, Phreatia, Rhynchophreatia, Thelasis.*

Ridleyellinae: *Ridleyella.*

Dendrobieae

Dendrobiinae: *Cadetia, Dendrobium, Diplocaulobium, Epigeneium, Flickingeria, Pseuderia.*

Bulbophyllinae: *Bulbophyllum, Chaseella, Cirrhopetalum, Codonosiphon, Dactylorhynchus, Drymoda, Genyorchis, Hapalochilus, Jejosephia, Mastigion, Monomeria, Monosepalum, Pedilochilus, Saccoglossum, Sunipia, Tapeinoglossum, Trias.*

Vandeae

Aeridinae: *Abdominea, Acampe, Adenoncos, Aerides, Amesiella, Arachnis, Armodorum, Ascocentrum, Ascochilopsis, Ascochilus, Ascoglossum, Ascolabium, Biermannia, Bogoria, Brachypeza, Calymmanthera, Ceratocentron, Ceratochilus, Chamaeanthus, Chiloschista, Chroniochilus, Cleisocentron, Cleisomeria, Cleisostoma, Cordiglottis, Cottonia, Cryptopylos, Dimorphorchis, Diplocentrum, Diploprora, Doritis, Dryadorchis, Drymoanthus, Dyakia, Eparmatostigma, Esmeralda, (Euanthe), Gastrochilus, Grosourdya, Gunnarella, Haraella, Holcoglossum, Hygrochilus, Hymenorchis, (Kingidium),*

*Lesliea, Loxoma, Luisia, Macropodanthus, Malleola, Megalotis, Micropera, Microsaccus, Microtatorchis, Mobilabium, Neofinetia, Nothodoritis, Omoea, Ornithochilus, Papilionanthe, Papillilabium, Paraphalaenopsis, Parapteroceras, Pelatantheria, Pennilabium, Peristeranthus, Phalaenopsis, Phragmorchis, Plectorhiza, Pomatocalpa, Porphyrodesme, Porrorachis, Proteroceras, Pteroceras, Renanthera, Renantherella, Rhinerrhiza, Rhynchogyna, Rhynchostylis, Robiquetia, Saccolabiopsis, Saccolabium, Sarcanthopsis, Sarcochilus, Sarcoglyphis, Sarcophyton, Schistotylus, Schoenorchis, Sedirea, Seidenfadenia, Smithsonia, Smitinandia, Staurochilus, Stereochilus, Taeniophyllum, Thrixspermum, Trichoglottis, Trudelia, Tuberolabium, Uncifera, Vanda, Vandopsis, Ventricularia, Xenicophyton.*

Angraecinae: *Aeranthes, Ambrella, Angraecum, Bonniera, Calyptrochilum, Campylocentrum, Cryptopus, Dendrophylax (= Polyradicion = Polyrrhiza), Harrisella, Jumellea, Lemurella, Lemurorchis, Neobathiea, Oeonia, Oeoniella, Ossiculum, Perrierella, Polyradicion (= Polyrrhiza), Sobennikoffia.*

Aerangidinae: *Aerangis, Ancistrorhynchus, Angraecopsis, Azadehdelia, Beclardia, Bolusiella, Cardiochilus, Chamaenangis, Chauliodon, Cyrtorchis, Diaphananthe, Dinklageella, Distylodon, Eggelingia, Encheiridion, Eurychone, Holmesia, Listrostachys, Margelliantha, Microcoelia, Microterangis, Mystacidium, Nephrangis, Plectrelminthus, Podangis, Rangaeris, Rhaesteria, Rhipidoglossum, Sarcorhynchus, Solenangis, Sphyrarhynchus, Summerhayesia, Taenorhiza, Triceratorhynchus, Tridactyle, Ypsiloplus.*

Misfits and Problems

Arundinae: *Arundina, Dilochia.*

Collabiinae: *Chrysoglossum, Collabium, Diglyphosa.*

*Claderia.*

*Eriopsis.*

Pogoniinae: *Cleistes, Duckeella, Isotoria, Pogonia, Pogoniopsis.*

*Thaia.*

*Xerorchis.*

## Suggested references for orchid classification

Dressler, R. 1993. *Phylogeny and classification of the orchid family.* Portland, Ore.: Dioscorides.

Pridgeon, A. M., P. J. Cribb, and M. W. Chase (eds.). 1999–2005. *Genera orchidacearum.* Vol. I–IV. Oxford: Oxford University Press.

# Glossary

**Abaxial** (ab-AX-ee-ul) (fig. G.2): The side of an organ, such as a leaf, facing away from the main stem or axis; the underside.

**Acaulescent** (ah-kaw-LESS-ent) (fig. G.4B,E): Stemless, or appearing to be stemless.

**Acuminate** (figs. G.1, G.11A): Having a very sharp apex with long, straight or slightly concave sides.

**Acute** (figs. G.1, G.11B, G.23A,I): Having a very sharp, but not long and tapered, point.

**Adaxial** (fig. G.2): The side of an organ, such as a leaf, facing the main stem or axis; the upper side.

**Adnate** (figs. G.24, G.39M): The fusing together of two plant parts, whether partially or completely.

**Adventitious** (ad-ven-TISH-us) (fig. G.4C): Appearing from abnormal locations on the stem of a plant, in reference to buds and roots.

**Aerial root** (fig. G.6F): A root produced aboveground, along the stem, mainly by monopodial plants. This kind of root usually does not enter the medium.

**Agglutinate**: To glue together.

**Aggregate** (fig. G.14A): To form a dense mass or grouping.

**Albino**: A plant lacking chlorophyll or a flower lacking pigment (e.g., a white flower).

**Alternate** (fig. G.4C,F): Arranged individually at different heights on opposite sides of a stem or inflorescence, in reference to leaves or other plant parts.

**Amorphous**: Having no regular form; formless.

**Amphigean** (am-fih-JEE-an): Any plant distributed in both hemispheres of the Old and New Worlds.

**Anastomosing** (an-NAS-toh-mohz-ing) (figs. G.4E, G.13G,I): Interlacing or running together (e. g., the network of veins on a leaf).

**Ancipitous** (an-SIP-ih-tus): Having two edges and being flattened (e.g., pseudobulbs of *Laelia rubescens*).

**Androecium** (an-DREE-see-um) (fig. G.36): The male portion of the flower (e.g., the stamens).

**Angiosperm** (AN-jee-oh-sperm): A plant with the seed enclosed in a case or fruit.

**Annual**: A plant with a life cycle of one year (i.e., a plant that grows from seed to flower to seed in one growing season).

**Antennae** (figs. G.1, G.34B, G.39G): Slender, elongate appendages (e.g., as on lips of *Phalaenopsis*).

**Anther** (figs. G.35, G.36, G.37): The pollen-bearing portion of the stamen.

**Anther cap** (figs. G.35, G.36Aa, G.37Bc): The covering over orchid pollinia.

**Anthesis** (an-THEE-sus): The period of time when the flower is opening.

**Antipodal** (an-TIP-oh-dal): Growing on opposite sides of the earth.

**Antrorse** (AN-trorse) (fig. G.3C): Growing upward or even forward.

**Aphyllus** (fig. G.4B): Leafless (e.g., *Dendrophylax lindenii*).

**Apical**: At the apex, in reference to a leaf or a bud at the tip of a stem.

**Apiculate** (figs. G.11I, G.23C,F): Ending in a sharp point.

**Asexual**: A form of propagation using vegetative segments of the plant rather than seed to increase the population.

**Attenuate** (fig. G.23H,J): Gradually narrowing to a point.

**Auriculate** (fig. G.1): Having earlike appendages.

**Awl-shaped** (fig. G.11A): Tapering gently from the base to a stiff point.

**Axil** (fig. G.2): The angle formed between a leaf and the stem to which it is attached.

**Axile** (fig. G.40A): Of the axis; a form of placentation in which the ovules are borne on a central axis or on protrusions from it.

**Axillary** (fig. G.19Aa): Arising from a leaf axil (e.g., flowers of some species of *Dendrobium*).

**Axis** (figs. G.6F, G.7): The main stem of a plant.

**Backbulb** (fig. G.2): The older pseudobulbs, usually three, four, or more behind the lead, having lateral buds and sometimes leaves. When severed from the parent, these bulbs usually produce new plants.

**Banded** (figs. G.13C, G.31E): Having strong lines of color, ribs, or similar marks.

**Basal** (fig. G.19Ab): At the base; said of an inflorescence that arises from the base of the pseudobulb (e.g., *Lycaste*).

**Beak** (fig. G.39N): A long, pronounced point, such as the stigma projection that forms the rostellum; a beaklike projection.

**Beard** (fig. G.33Ca,Cb,Ea,Eb): A limited area with hairs, often found on flowers.

**Biennial**: A plant with a life cycle spanning two growing seasons, usually growing vegetatively the first season and flowering and seeding in the second.

**Bifarious** (bye-FAHR-ee-us) (fig. G.4D): Arranged in two rows.

**Bifoliate** (fig. G.4A): Having two leaves.

**Bifurcate** (BYE-fur-kayt) (fig. G.28H): Divided into two branches, forked (e.g., the midlobe of the lip of many orchids but also said of stigma, styles, lip, or some hairs).

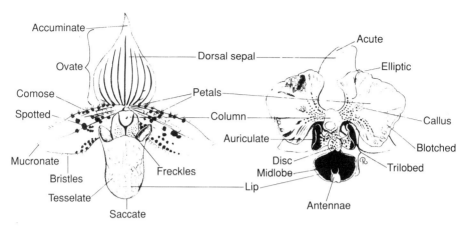

Fig. G.1. *Paphiopedilum lowii* and *Phalaenopsis* × *intermedia* var. *diezii* (right) showing that a variety of terms can be applied to the same part

**Bigeneric**: A hybrid of two genera, such as *Laeliocattleya* (*Laelia* × *Cattleya*).

**Bisexual**: Having both sexes; in reference to flowers having both male and female parts (i.e., stamen and pistil).

**Blade** (figs. G.7, G.8): Flattened, expanded portion of a leaf.

**Bloom**: A whitish gray waxy coating found on some leaves (e.g., *Rhyncholaelia glauca*).

**Blotch** (figs. G.1, G.13C,D, G.31C): An irregular color spot on sepals or petals.

**Boot** (fig. G.26): Pouchlike lips (e.g., flowers of Cypripedioideae).

**Botanical**: Term used affectionately by orchidologists to denote species with small flowers or species not commonly cultivated. Also, having to do with botany.

**Bract** (figs. G.2, G.7, G.17): A leaflike structure that subtends a flower, leaf, or stem.

**Bracteole**: A very small bract; a bractlet.

**Break** (fig. G.2): The point at which a new or lateral bud begins to grow; the lead shoot.

**Bristly** (figs. G.1, G.33Ba,Bb): Having stiff hairs.

**Bud** (figs. G.2, G.17): An unopened flower or an initiated new shoot before it elongates.

**Bulb** (fig. G.2): An enlarged or swollen stem. See **Pseudobulb**.

**Caducous** (ka-DOO-kus): Falling or dropping off early, as sepals or petals.

**Callus** (figs. G.1, G.34): A hard, often waxy projection found on an orchid lip (e.g., *Phalaenopsis*).

**Calyx** (figs. G.17, G.22): The outermost segments of the flower; the sepals.

**Cap** (figs. G.35, G.36, G.37): The removable cover over the pollinia (e.g., anther cap).

**Capsule** (fig. G.41): The fruit of orchids; a fruit from a compound ovary, usually dry and opening at one or more sutures at maturity.

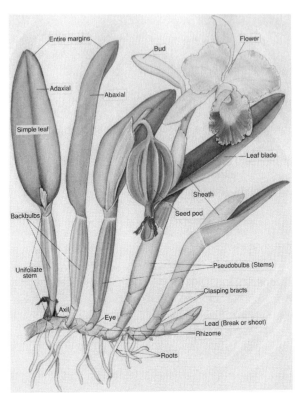

Fig. G.2. A typical orchid plant (*Cattleya*)

**Carpel** (fig. G.40): Basic unit of a gynoecium; cell of a compound ovary.

**Cauda** (fig. G.36D,E): A slender appendage as in *Maxillaria* flowers.

**Caudate** (fig. G.33Fa): Having long, tail-like appendages (e.g., floral parts of *Brassia*).

**Caudicle** (KAW-dik-ul) (fig. G.36E): The stalk of a pollinium.

**Cauline** (KAW-line): Belonging to a stem.

**Cell** (fig. G.40): An opening in the ovary also known as a locule. Also, the smallest unit of plant structure.

**Chlorophyllous**: Having chlorophyll.

**Chlorotic** (klor-ROT-ik): Disease or physiological condition marked by yellowish leaves.

**Ciliate** (figs. G.30B, G.34C): Having stiff hairs on the margin.

**Circumboreal**: Pertaining to the Northern Hemisphere.

**Cirrus** (SEER-rus) (fig. G.34B): Antennae found on the lips of some orchids (e.g., *Phalaenopsis amabilis*).

**Clasping** (figs. G.2, G.4C): Enfolding the stem or pseudobulb, pertaining to a leaf base or a bract.

**Clavate** (fig. G.15): Club shaped with increased thickening toward the apex.

Fig. G.3. Growth habits.
A. Epiphytic (Encyclia *tampensis*);
B. Terresterial (*Cypridedium acaule*). Monopodial: C. *Arachnis*;
D. *Ascocentrum*; E. *Phalaenopsis*.
Sympodial: F. *Cattleya*; G.
*Dendrobium*; H. *Paphiopedilum*

**Clavellate** (fig. G.33Ca,Cb): Club shaped but small.

**Claw** (fig. G.23D,E): Stemlike base of a petal or sepal.

**Clinandrium** (kly-NAN-dree-um) (fig. 1.3): The anther bed; the tissue at the apex of the column under the anther.

**Column** (figs. 1.3, G.1, G.35, G.37, G.39): The waxy structure in the center of the flower. An organ formed by the union of the male and female portions of the flower, also called the **gynandrium**.

**Clone**: A group of plants asexually propagated from one plant.

**Column foot** (figs. G.35, G.39E): An extension at the base of the column, often attached to the lip.

**Comose** (figs. G.1, G.32 right): With hair in tufts.

**Compact** (fig. G.4E): Short or compressed.

Fig. G.4. Growth habits. A. Pseudobulbous orchid. B. Leafless (*Dendrophylax*). C. Reed type with offset (*Dendrobium*). D. Distichous (*Dendrobium*). E. Whorled leaves (*Goodyera*). F. Vine (*Vanilla*)

**Compressed** (figs. G.15C, G.16D,E): Flattened, usually laterally.

**Concave** (fig. G.35): Basin shaped (e.g., many stigmatic surfaces).

**Conduplicate** (fig. G.9B): Folded together lengthwise, pertaining to leaves or other plant parts.

**Conical**: Cone shaped.

**Connate** (fig. G.24C): Joined, said of two similar segments joined at their bases (e.g., the synsepal of the Cypripedioideae).

**Connective tissue**: Tissue that unites the two cells of the anther.

**Constricted** (fig. G.15N): Compressed or drawn together at some point.

**Convex**: Curving upward, the opposite of concave.

**Convolute** (fig. G.9A): Rolled up.

**Cordate** (fig. G.10J): Heart shaped (e.g., leaves).

**Coriaceous**: Having a thick, leathery texture (e.g., leaves).

**Corm** (fig. G.6C): A swollen stem base, usually underground; a storage organ.

**Crest** (fig. G.34D): Raised, irregular toothed area, often found on the lips of orchids.

**Crested** (fig. G.34D): Bearing a crest.

**Crispate** (figs. G.29C, G.30D): Having very strong, wavy margins; the ultimate form of undulate.

**Cultivar**: A horticultural variety often cultivated for its unique characteristics.

Fig. G.5. Growth habits. A. Procumbent (*Dendrobium*); B. Decumbent (*Ludisia*); C. Erect (*Caularthron*)

**Cupped** (fig. G.25F,G): Dish shaped, or resembling a small cup.

**Cylindrical** (fig. G.15J,K): Having the shape of a cylinder; i.e., parallel straight sides, round in cross section perpendicular to its axis.

**Cyme** (SYME): A determinate inflorescence where the central flower opens first; usually a wide, almost-flat-topped inflorescence.

**Cymose** (SY-mohs): Having inflorescences that are cymes or cymelike.

**Deciduous** (de-SID-yew-us): Shedding leaves seasonally and leafless for a period of time (e.g., *Cypripedium*, *Platanthera*, and *Bletia*).

**Decumbent** (fig. G.5B): Reclining, in reference to a stem with the tip turned up.

**Dentate** (fig. G.28T): Having toothlike margins that are usually sharp and coarse (e.g., leaves and petals).

**Denticulate** (figs. G.13J, G.30A): Minutely dentate.

**Determinate** (fig. G.19Ba): Characterized by opening of terminal flower first, with others following in sequence to the base, thus preventing any further elongation of the inflorescence.

**Diandrous** (dye-AN-drus) (figs. G.36Ba,Bb, G.37Aa,Ab, G.38A, G.39Q): Having two anthers (e.g., in Cypripedioideae).

**Dichotomous** (dye-KOT-oh-mus): Continually dividing into twos. Said of branches when they fork into pairs (e.g., *Pholidota*).

**Dimorphous** (dye-MOR-fus): Having two forms. Said of plants (e.g., *Grammatophyllum*) with two forms of vegetative or floral parts.

**Dioecious** (dye-EE-shus): Having male and female flowers on separate plants.

**Diphyllous** (dye-FILL-us) (fig. G.4A): Having two leaves; bifoliate.

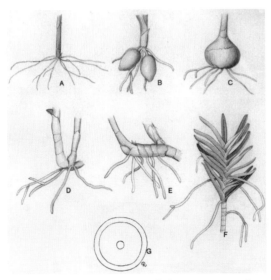

Fig. G.6. Variations in orchid roots. A. Fibrous (*Pogonia*); B. Tubers (*Ophrys*); C. Corm (*Bletilla*); D. Fleshy roots, no rhizome (*Dendrobium*); E. Rhizome and fleshy roots (*Cattleya*); F. Aerial roots (*Aerides*); G. Fleshy root in cross-section showing velamen layer

**Diploid**: Having two sets of chromosomes; the usual complement of chromosomes.

**Disc** (figs. G.1, G.34A): A fleshy structure found on the basal portion of some orchid lips.

**Distichous** (DIS-tik-us) (fig. G.4D): Having flowers or leaves in two ranks, usually on opposite sides of a stem.

**Diurnal**: Active during the day; of flowers, open or fragrant only during the day.

**Dorsal** (fig. G.1): Pertaining to the back (e.g., the dorsal sepal or uppermost sepal).

**Downy** (figs. G.13A, G.33Aa,Ab): Having a dense cover of very soft hairs.

**Elliptic** (figs. G.1, G.10A, G.15G,H, G.23I): Somewhat oval in shape and equally rounded at the base and apex.

**Elongate** (figs. G.15H, G.23J): Very long or drawn out (e.g., leaf or pseudobulb).

**Emarginate** (fig. G.11E): Of a leaf, shallowly notched at its tip.

**Embryo**: The tiny plant found within a seed.

**Endemic**: Restricted to a locality or region.

**Endosperm** (EN-doh-sperm): Carbohydrates usually stored in seed but lacking in orchid seed.

**Ensiform** (figs. G.10G, G.23J): Sword shaped.

**Entire** (fig. G.2): Of leaf margins, not broken, toothed, or serrated.

**Ephemeral** (ee-FEM-er-al): Of very short duration (e.g., flowers of *Dendrobium crumenatum*, which are open for only one day).

**Epichile** (EP-ih-kile): The terminal part of a complex often segmented lip (e.g., the lip of *Stanhopea*)

**Epidermis**: The layer of cells that forms the covering of all plant parts.

**Epiphyte** (EP-ih-fite) (fig. G.3A): A plant that lives on another but does not draw nourishment from the host (e.g., *Cattleya*).

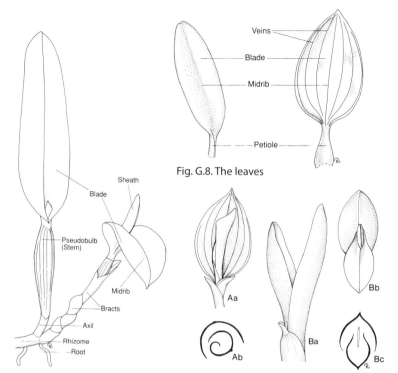

Fig. G.8. The leaves

Fig. G.7. Vegetative parts

Fig. G.9. Leaf emergence. A. Convolute (*Ludisia*): Aa. New leaf emerging; Ab. Cross-section showing inrolled new leaf. B. Conduplicate (*Cattleya*): Ba. Side view; Bb. Top view; Bc. Cross-section showing overlapping

**Equitant** (EK-kwi-tant) (fig. G.4D): Of leaves, overlapping and forming two ranks (e.g., *Psygmorchis pusilla*).

**Erect** (fig. G.5C): Growing upright.

**Erose** (fig. G.11G): Of a leaf tip, appearing to have a torn margin or as if an insect chewed on it (e.g., *Vanda tricolor*).

**Evergreen**: A plant that retains its leaves for more than one year and that does not lose them all at one time.

**Eye** (fig. G.2): The vegetative bud at the base of the pseudobulb of sympodial orchids.

**Falcate** (figs. G.10M,N, G.23F): Sickle shaped.

**Family**: A natural unit in taxonomy comprising one or more genera sharing a number of similar characteristics (e.g., Orchidaceae).

**Fenestrate:** With window-like openings.

**Fertilization**: The fusion of the male (pollen) and female (ovule) that gives rise to the seed. Also, the act of applying nutrients (fertilizer) to plants.

**Fetid**: Having a disagreeable, usually offensive odor.

**Fibrous** (fig. G.6A): Resembling fibers in structure (e.g., roots).

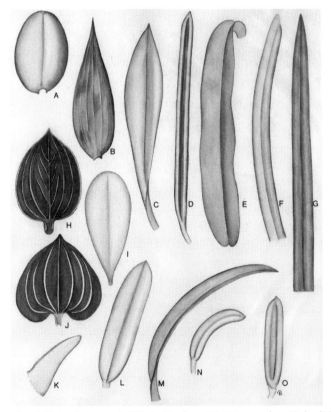

Fig. G.10. Leaf shapes. A. Elliptic (*Sophronitis*); B. Lanceolate (*Sobralia*); C. Oblanceolate (*Gongora*); D. Linear (*Brassavola*); E. Lorate (*Aerides*); F. Ligulate (*Cymbidium*); G. Ensiform (*Epidendrum*); H. Ovoid (*Calypso*); I. Obovate (*Stelis*); J. Cordate (*Pogonia*); K. Triangular (*Lockhartia*); L. Oblong (*Rodriguezia*); M. Falcate and keeled (*Neofinetia*); N. Falcate, fleshy, or thick (*Dendrobium*); O. Lingulate (tongue-shaped) (*Dendrobium*)

**Filament**: The stemlike structure that supports the anther; a part of the stamen, fused into the column in orchids.

**Fimbriate** (fig. G.30E): Having a fringe.

**Fleshy root** (fig. G.6D): A large, thick, succulent root.

**Flora**: All the plants native to a given area or country; also, a book containing descriptions of plants from such an area.

**Floriferous** (flo-RIFF-er-us): Having flowers. Often said of a plant that flowers freely or has many flowers.

**Flower** (figs. G.2, G.17): A stem bearing a pistil or stamens or both generally surrounded by petals or sepals or both.

**Foliage**: Leaves.

**Foot** (figs. G.35, G.39E): See **Column foot**.

**Forked** (fig. G.28E,G,H): Having two or more prongs; of plants, divided into two equal segments.

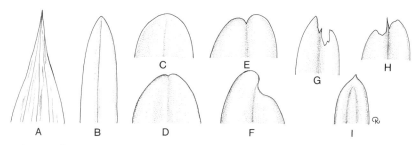

Fig. G.11. Leaf tips. A. Accuminate; B. Acute; C. Obtuse; D. Retuse; E. Emarginate; F. Unequally two-lobed; G. Erose (torn); H. Mucronate; I. Apiculate

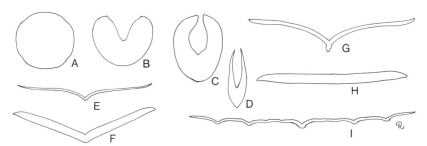

Fig. G.12. Leaf cross-sections. A. Terete; B. Semi-terete; C. Semi-terete, deeply grooved; D. Semi-terete, compressed; E. Thin; F. Thick; G. Keeled; H. Flat, on midvein depression; I. Pleated (or plaited)

**Freckled** (figs. G.1, G.31A): Of petals or sepals, covered with small, usually darker colored spots.

**Fringed** (figs. G.30C, G.39H,Q): Having a border or margin with an edging of fine hairs.

**Fruit** (fig. G.41): The capsule in orchids; any structure that bears or contains seeds.

**Furrowed** (fig. G.15F,G,I): Having long grooves.

**Fusiform** (fig. G.15L,P): Spindle shaped.

**Gamopetalous** (gam-oh-PET-uh-lus) (fig. G.24B): Having fused petals.

**Gamosepalous** (gam-oh-SEEP-uh-lus) (fig. G.24): Having fused sepals.

**Genus** (*pl.* **genera**): A taxonomic subdivision of a family composed of one or more species with similar characteristics.

**Glabrous** (fig. G.2): Without hairs; often misdescribed as smooth.

**Gland**: A secreting organ (e.g., nectary).

**Glaucous**: Having a whitish or grayish waxy bloom on the foliage (e.g., *Ryncho-laelia glauca*).

**Globose** (fig. G.15A): Almost round.

**Glutinous**: Very sticky.

**Gregarious** (greh-GAYR-ee-us): All plants of a given population flowering at the same time, a phenomenon often triggered by an environmental factor such as temperature change (e.g., *Dendrobium crumenatum*).

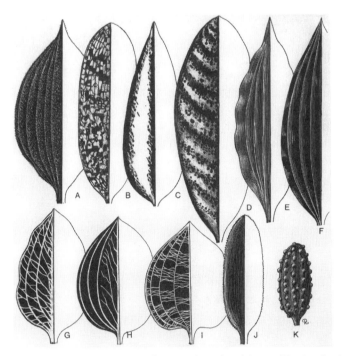

Fig. G.13. Leaf patterns and surfaces. A. Pleated and downy (*Cypripedium*); B. Tesselate (*Paphiopedilum*); C. Irregularly banded or blotched (*Spiranthes*); D. Blotched, spotted, marbled, or mottled (*Phalaenopsis*); E. Undulate (*Calanthe*); F. Pleated (*Eulophia*); G. Netted with oblique webbing (*Goodyera*); H. Veined and striped (*Ludisia*); I. Netted or webbed (*Macodes*); J. Denticulate margin (*Dendrobium*); K. Tuberculate surface (*Dendrobium*)

**Grex**: Collectively the progeny of a given cross; the group of offspring.

**Grooved** (figs. G.12C, G.15F–I,L,M): Having furrows or ridges.

**Gynandrium** (jye-NAN-dree-um) (figs. G.37, G.38): An organ containing the male and female portions of the orchid flower; also called the **column**.

**Gynandrous** (jye-NAN-drus): Having the stamens attached to the stigma and style in one unit.

**Gynoecium** (jye-NEE-see-um) (figs. G.37, G.38): The female portion of a flower.

**Habit** (figs. G.1, G.2, G.3): The form or shape of a plant.

**Habitat**: The environment in which a plant naturally grows.

**Hair**: Threadlike growths on plant parts (e.g., pubescence, beards); see also **Hirsute**.

**Head** (fig. G.18D): Having flowers in a tight cluster at the top of the flower spike; a type of inflorescence; a short compact inflorescence (e.g., *Epidendrum ibaguense*).

**Hermaphrodite** (her-MAF-roh-dyte): A perfect flower (i.e., having both male and female organs).

**Hirsute** (fig. G.33Ba,Bb): Having coarse, usually long hairs.

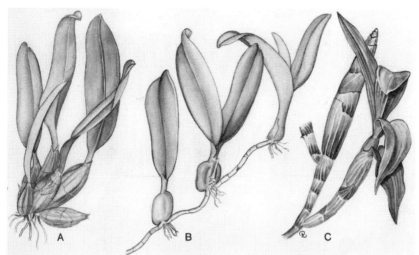

Fig. G.14. Pseudobulb growth habits. A. Aggregate (*Dendrobium*); B. Widely spaced or chainlike (*Bulbophyllum*); C. New pseudobulbs emerging from old (*Pholidota*)

**Hooded** (figs. G.25C–E, G.39F): Bearing floral parts that form a hood (e.g., *Catasetum*).

**Horned** (figs. G.25B, G.39I): Having a hornlike projection (e.g., the lip of *Stanhopea*).

**Hybrid**: A plant that results from the crossing of two varieties, two species, or two genera.

**Hybridization**: The act of producing hybrids.

**Hypochile** (HY-poh-kile): The basal part of a complex, often segmented lip (e.g., *Stanhopea*).

**Imbricate** (fig. G.4D): Overlapping in a shinglelike arrangement (e.g., leaves of *Lockhartia*).

**Imperfect**: Of a flower, having only functional stamens (i.e., male reproductive organs) or functional carpels (i.e, female reproductive organs); cf. **Dioecious, Monoecious**.

**Incised** (fig. G.30E,Fa,Fb): Having a deep, usually irregular cut.

**Indeterminate** (fig. G.19Bb): Said of an inflorescence when the lower flowers open first and the apex of the inflorescence remains vegetative (e.g., *Phalaenopsis*).

**Indigenous** (in-DIJ-en-us): Native to a specific area or country.

**Inferior**: Beneath; i.e., of ovaries, with floral segments attached at the apex.

**Inflorescence** (fig. G.17): A stem bearing a flower or flowers; the flowering portion of a plant.

**Inrolled** (fig. G.26A,B): Having margins rolled in (e.g., the lip in *Cypripedium*).

**Internode** (fig. G.3C,G): The segment of a stem between two leaf nodes.

**Iridiform**: Shaped or looks like iris foliage.

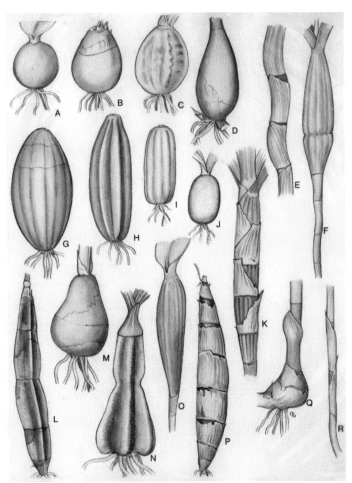

Fig. G.15. Pseudobulb shapes. A. Globose, round, or orbicular (*Sophronitis*); B. Ovoid or ovate (*Neomoorea*); C. Ovoid-compressed (*Laelia*); D. Oblong- or ovate-elongate (*Epidendrum*); E. Jointed (*Dendrobium*); F. Unguiculate (*Schomburgkia*); G. Elliptic (*Grammatophyllum*); H. Elliptic-elongate, sulcate, or furrowed (*Gongora*); I. Oblong-sulcate or furrowed (*Pholidota*); J. Oblong-cylindrical (*Bulbophllum*); K. Cylindrical (*Ansellia*); L. Fusiform-tetragonal or four sided (*Dendrobium*); M. Pyriform (*Epidendrum*); N. Constricted or hourglass shaped (*Calanthe*); O. Obovate, clavate or club shaped (*Cattleya*); P. Fusiform or spindle shaped (*Catasetum*); Q. Swollen base (*Cattleya*); R. Stemlike or reedlike (*Isochilus*)

**Irregular**: Of a flower, where a series of parts (e.g., petals) are not alike.

**Jointed** (figs. G.4C, G.15E): Having very distinct nodes.

**Keel** (figs. G.10M, G.12G): The main dorsal vein (midrib) found on many leaves.

**Keiki** (KEE-kee): See **Offset**.

**Labellum** (lah-BEL-lum) (figs. G.1, G.17, G.22, G.28, G.34): Highly modified petal of an orchid flower; the lip.

**Lacerate** (fig. G.30Fa,Fb): Appearing torn, or cut irregularly.

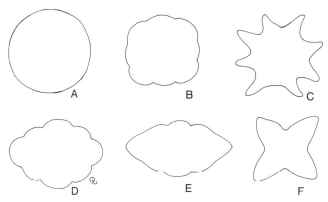

Fig. G.16. Pseudobulb cross-sections. A. Round or orbicular (*Bulbophyllum*); B. Round, lobed (*Pholidota*); C. Round, ridged or furrowed (*Gongora*); D. Slightly compressed, lobed (*Myrmecophila*); E. Compressed (*Laelia*); F. Tetragonal or four-sided or lobed (*Dendrobium*)

**Laciniate** (fig. G.33Ga,Gb): Cut into narrow, ribbonlike segments.

**Lanceolate** (figs. G.10B, G.23C): Lance shaped; longer than broad and tapering toward the apex.

**Lateral** (figs. G.1, G.20): Coming from the side.

**Lax** (fig. G.25A): Having loose, flexible, drooping segments.

**Lead** (fig. G.2): New growth on sympodial orchids.

**Leaf** (fig. G.2): The green, usually flat segment that grows from a stem.

**Leafless** (fig. G.4B): Without leaves.

**Ligulate** (fig. G.10F): Strap shaped.

**Limb** (fig. G.28N): In orchids, the flat, expanded portion of any segment, such as the lip.

**Linear** (fig. G.10D): Long and narrow with parallel sides; of leaves, grasslike.

**Lingulate** (LING-yew-late) (fig. G.10F): Tongue shaped.

**Lip** (figs. G.1, G.17, G.22, G.28, G.34): See **Labellum**.

**Lithophyte** (LITH-oh-fyte): A plant that grows on rocks.

**Lobe** (figs. G.16B,D, G.27F): Rounded projection.

**Locule** (LOK-yewl) (fig. G.40): One of the compartments of the ovary of an orchid.

**Lorate** (figs. G.10E, G.23E): Strap shaped.

**Massula** (MAS-sul-uh): A small group or clump of pollen grains occurring in some orchid genera (e.g., *Vanilla*).

**Medium** (*pl.* **media**): The material in which an orchid is grown. Also, the nutrient solutions, both solid and liquid, used in seed germination and tissue culture.

**Mentum** (MEN-tum) (fig. G.39E): In orchids, a protrusion, often chinlike, at the base of the flower, composed of the lateral sepal bases and column foot.

**Meristem**: The actively growing cell tissue of young stems, leaves, and roots. Also, a vernacular name for a plant derived from tissue culture.

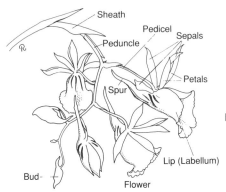

Fig. G.17. The inflorescence and its parts

**Mesochile** (MEZ-oh-kile): The middle part of a complex, often segmented lip (e.g., *Stanhopea*).

**Midlobe**: The center lobe of a three-lobed lip.

**Midrib** (figs. G.7, G.8): The main vein of a leaf.

**Mimicry**: The resemblance of an organism to a completely unrelated organism, in the case of orchids to bring about pollination by deception (e.g., *Ophrys apifera* resembles a bee to attract the bee as a pollinator).

**Monandrous** (mo-NAN-drus) (figs. G.36A, G.37B, G.38B): Having one anther.

**Monoecious** (moh-NEE-shus): Having male and female organs in separate flowers, but both appearing on the same plant.

**Monopodial** (mon-oh-POH-dee-al) (fig. G.3C–E): Literally, having one foot; growing perpendicular to the horizon with strong apical dominance; flowers borne on axillary inflorescences, and terminal buds remain vegetative (e.g., *Phalaenopsis, Vanda*).

**Mucronate** (figs. G.1, G.11H): Having a small, short, sharp tip at the apex of a leaf.

**Multigeneric**: Of hybrids produced by crossing three or more genera.

**Nectar**: The sugary exudate of various glands on a plant that attracts insects and sometimes birds, and helps bring about pollination.

**Nectary** (fig. G.27): The gland that produces nectar, often found at the base of a lip.

**Nerve** (fig. G.8): The small vein of a leaf.

**Netted** (fig. G.13G,I): Forming a connected network.

**Nocturnal**: Active at night; of flowers, open or fragrant only at night.

**Node** (fig. G.3C,G): The point on the stem or pseudobulb where the leaves or bracts are attached.

**Obcordate**: Having heart-shaped lobes at the apex of the leaf (e.g., *Ascocentrum*).

**Oblanceolate** (figs. G.10C, G.23D): Lance-shaped but widest at the apex.

**Oblong** (figs. G.10L, G.15D): Longer than wide.

**Obovate** (figs. G.10I, G.15O, G.23B): Ovate but narrowest at the base.

**Obtuse** (figs. G.11C, G.23B,D,G): Rounded at the tip.

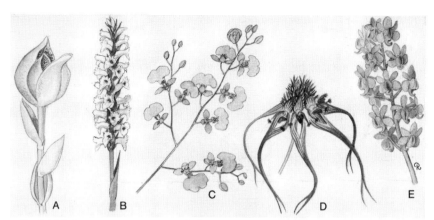

Fig. G.18. Inflorescence types. A. Single flower or uniflorate (*Anguloa*); B. Spike (*Spiranthes*); C. Panicle or spray (*Oncidium*); D. Umbel or head (*Bulbophyllum*); E. Raceme (*Aerides*)

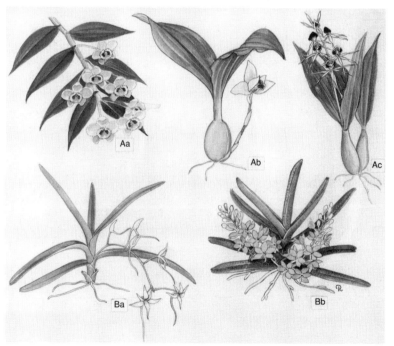

Fig. G.19. Inflorescence origins and methods of flowering. A. Origins: Aa. Axillary (*Dendrobium*); Ab. Basal (*Lycaste*); Ac. Terminal (*Encyclia*). B. Methods of flowering: Ba. Determinate (*Angraecum*); Bb. Indeterminate (*Ascocentrum*)

**Offset** (fig. G.4C): An aboveground lateral shoot that produces roots while still attached to the parent stem, common in some *Dendrobium*, *Epidendrum*, and *Phalaenopsis* species.

**Orbicular** (figs. G.15A, G.16A, G.23G): Round.

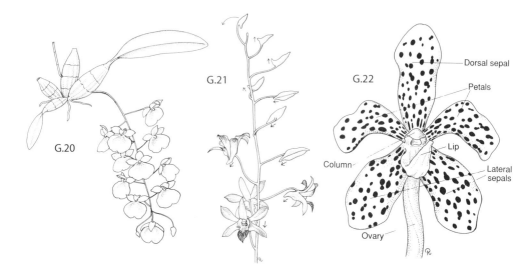

Fig. G.20. (*left*) Inflorescence from the side of the pseudobulb (*Dendrobium*); Fig. G.21. (*center*) *Dendrobium* flower spike showing resupination; Fig. G.22. (*right*) The flower and its parts

**Orchidaceae** (or-kih-DAY-see-ee): The Latin name for the orchid family.

**Orchidist**: A person who is very interested in orchids and their culture.

**Orchidology**: The study of orchids.

**Outrolled** (fig. G.26C–E): Having margins rolled out (e.g., the lip in some paphiopedilums).

**Oval** (figs. G.15G, G.23A,I): Shaped like a thickened ellipse.

**Ovary** (fig. G.22): The basal portion of the pistil containing the ovules; if pollinated and fertilized, the ovary develops into the fruit.

**Ovate** (figs. G.1, G.10H, G.23A): Egg shaped in outline.

**Ovoid** (fig. G.15B,O): Egg shaped as a solid form.

**Ovule** (fig. G.40): A small protuberance in the ovary, capable of forming a seed when fertilized; an embryonic seed.

**Panicle** (fig. G.18C: Having a branched inflorescence (e.g., some *Oncidium* species).

**Papillae** (pa-PILL-ee) (figs. G.32 left, G.34, G.39E): Small pimplelike projections on a surface.

**Parasite**: A plant that derives its sustenance from another living plant.

**Parietal** (pa-RYE-eh-tal) (fig. G.40B,C): A form of placentation in orchids where ovules are borne on the walls or on protrusions of the walls of the ovary.

**Pedicel** (fig. G.17): The stem of a single flower on an inflorescence.

**Peduncle** (PEE-dung-kul) (fig. G.17): The stem of a cluster of flowers or a solitary flower, where the inflorescence is reduced to a single flower (e.g., *Maxillaria*).

**Peloric** (pel-LOHR-ik): Having an abnormal flower form in which the petals resemble the lip or the lip assumes a petal-like form, thus creating a regular appearing flower; not the usual two petals and a lip.

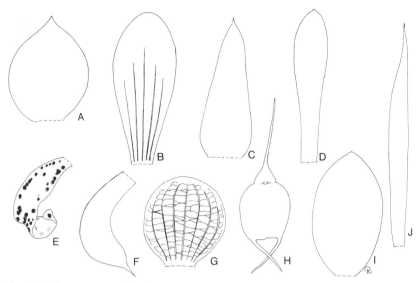

Fig. G.23. Characteristics of sepals and petals, shapes and tips. A. Ovate, acute tip (*Spathoglottis*); B. Obovate, obtuse tip (*Cymbidium*); C. Lanceolate, acute apiculate, obtuse tip (*Vanilla*); E. Lorate, recurved (*Grammatophyllum*); F. Falcate, apiculate (*Trichoglottis*); G. Orbicular or round, obtuse tip (*Vanda*); H. Attenuate (*Masdevallia*); I. Elliptic, acute tip (*Cymbidium*); J. Ensiform, elongate, attenuate tip (*Brassia*).

**Perennial**: A plant with a life cycle that continues for more than two years.

**Perfect**: Of a flower, having both male and female organs.

**Perianth** (fig. G.22): Literally, around the anther; a collective term for the two outer whorls of floral segments (i.e., sepals and petals).

**Petal** (figs. G.17, G.22): The inner whorl of the perianth; the segments, of which in orchids there are usually three with one highly modified; the lip.

**Petaloid**: Having the appearance of a petal (e.g., bracts of *Cyrtopodium*).

**Petiole** (fig. G.8): The stalk of a leaf.

**Pilose** (fig. G.33Ea,Eb): Having a covering of soft hairs.

**Pistil**: The female organ of the flower that produces the seed; a collective term for the stigma, style, and ovary.

**Placenta**: The ovule-bearing portion of the ovary.

**Placentation** (pla-sen-TAY-shun) (fig. G.40): The arrangement of the ovules in an ovary.

**Pleated** (figs. G.3B, G.12I, G.13A,F): Folded as a fan (e.g., leaves of *Calanthe*).

**Plicate** (figs. G.12F, G.15I): Folded (e.g., leaves).

**Pod** (fig. G.41): A rather general term for a dry, dehiscent fruit.

**Pollinarium** (poll-in-AR-ee-um) (fig. 1.5): The entire set of pollinia from a flower including the caudicle, stipe, and viscidium, when present.

**Pollination**: Transfer of pollen from anther to stima; in orchids, act of placing pollinia onto the stigmatic surface of the flower.

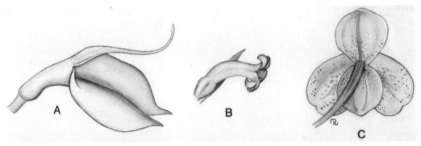

Fig. G.24. Connate flower parts. A. Gamosepalous (*Masdevallia*); B. Gamopetalous and gamosepalous (*Spiranthes*); C. Gamosepalous (*Paphiopedilum*)

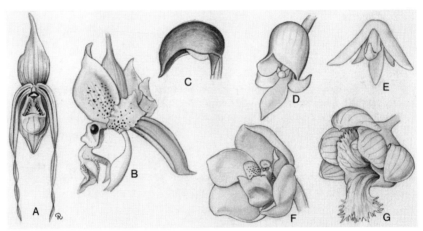

Fig. G.25. Some floral characteristics of orchids. A. Dropping (lax) twisted petals (*Paphiopedilum*); B. Horned lip (*Stanhopea*); C. Hooded, total flower (*Corybas*); D. Hooded, lip (*Schlimia*); E. Hooded, lateral sepals (*Polystachys*); F. Open cupped segments (*Peristeria*); G. Cupped segments (*Catasetum*)

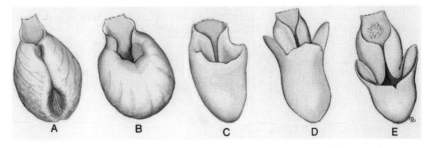

Fig. G.26. Some slipper- or boot-shaped lips. Inrolled top: A. *Cypripedium acaule*; B. *C. calceolus*; Outrolled top: C. *Paphiopedilum concolor*; D. *P. glaucophyllum*; E. *P. insigne*

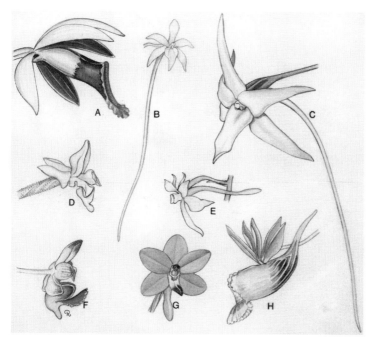

Fig. G.27. Spurs and nectaries. A. *Phaius*; B. *Rangaeris*; C. *Angraecum*; D. *Ludisia*; E. *Platanthera*; F. *Aerides*; G. *Ascocentrum*; H. *Galeandra*

**Pollinator**: Agent bringing about the pollination of a plant (e.g., a bee, moth, bird).

**Pollinia** (*sing*. **pollinium**) (figs. 1.5, G.35, G.36, G.37): Compact packets of pollen found in orchid flowers.

**Polyploid**: Having more than the normal two sets of chromosomes.

**Porrect**: Directed outward and forward.

**Proboscis** (proh-BAH-siss): The long, flexible mouthparts of an insect.

**Procumbent** (fig. G.5A): Lying flat; of a stem, growing horizontally on a surface.

**Proliferation**: The act of bearing offsets.

**Prostrate**: See **Procumbent**.

**Pseudobulb** (SUE-doh-bulb) (figs. G.2, G.7): Literally, false bulb; the aboveground, thickened portion of a lateral branch of sympodial orchids.

**Pseudobulbous** (soo-doh-BUL-bous) (fig. G.4A): Having pseudobulbs.

**Pubescence** (figs. G.33, G.39O): A covering of short, soft hairs.

**Pubescent** (fig. G.39O): Hairy; downy.

**Pyriform** (fig. G.15M): Pear shaped (e.g., pseudobulbs).

**Raceme** (fig. G.18E): An inflorescence with flowers on short stalks.

**Racemose**: Having inflorescences that are racemes or raceme-like.

**Rachis** (fig. G.17): Main stem of an inflorescence.

**Radicle**: Primary root of a germinating seed.

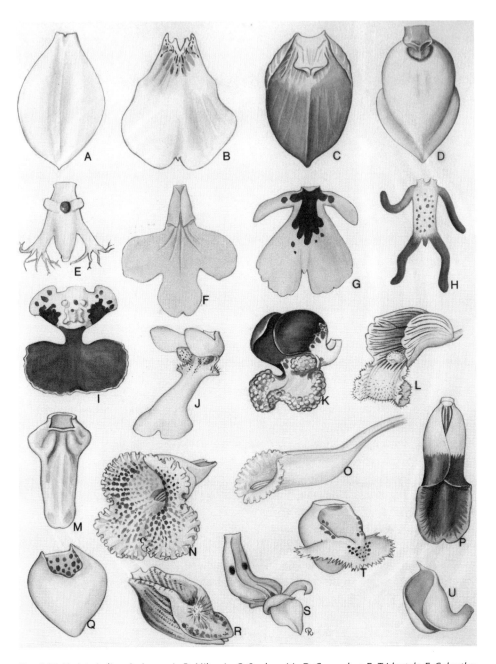

Fig. G.28. Variety in lips. A. *Aerangis*; B. *Miltonia*; C. *Sophronitis*; D. *Cycnoches*; E. *Tridactyle*; F. *Calanthe*; G. *Orchis purpurea*; H. *Orchis simia*; I. *Oncidium*; J. *Spathoglottis*; K. Cyrtopodium; L. *Bifrenaria*; M. *Vandopsis*; N. *Trichopilia*; O. *Vanilla*; P. *Phaius*; Q. *Catasetum*; R. *Calypso*; S. *Stanhopea*; T. *Gastrochilus*; U. *Mormodes*

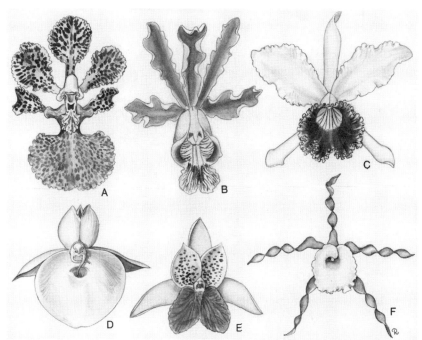

Fig. G.29. Sepal, petal and lip margins. A. Ruffled (*Oncidium*); B. Wavy (*Schomburgkia*); C. Crispate (*Cattleya*); D. Smooth or plain (*Catasetum*); E. Lip bilobed and slightly ruffled (*Cymbidium*); F. Twisted or spiralled (*Trichopilia*)

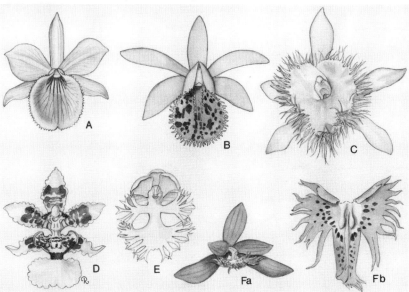

Fig. G.30. Lip margins. A. Finely toothed (*Broughtonia*); B. Ciliate (*Pleione*); C. Fringed (*Rhyncholaelia*); D. Crispate (*Oncidium*); E. Fimbriate (*Platanthera*); Fa. Lacerate (*Epidendrum*); Fb. Lacerate, detail of same

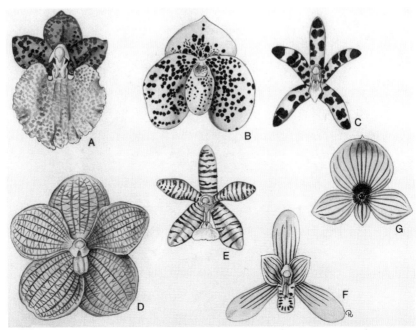

Fig. G.31. Flower markings. A. Freckled or spotted (*Odontoglossum*); B. Spotted (*Paphiopedilum*); C. Blotched (*Ansellia*); D. Tessellated (*Vanda*); E. Cross-banded or barred (*Phalaenopsis*); F. Paralled-striped (*Cymbidium*); G. Curved stripes (*Telipogon*)

**Ramicaul**: Leaf- and flower-bearing stem portion of orchids in subtribe Pleuro-thallidinae.

**Rank** (figs. G.3D, G.6F): Arrangement of flowers or leaves in vertical rows. "Two-ranked leaves" are in two vertical rows.

**Receptacle**: Enlarged apex of a stem upon which some of the floral segments are attached.

**Recurved** (fig. G.34C): Bending backward.

**Reed-type** (fig. G.4C): A type of sympodial orchid with long lateral branches of uniform thickness bearing many leaves (e.g., *Dendrobium*).

**Resupinate** (ree-SUE-pin-ayt) (fig. G.21): Inverted; of some orchid flower buds that emerge upside down and turn 180° to right themselves before opening (e.g., *Vanda*).

**Retrorse**: Pointing backward and downward.

**Refuse** (fig. G.11D): Rounded at the end with a shallow notch in the center.

**Revolute**: Of a leaf, with margins rolled back.

**Rhizome** (figs. G.2, G.6E, G.7): A horizontal stem, either on or just below the ground, with roots and erect lateral branches.

**Ridged** (figs. G.15L,N, G.16C,F): Having strips of raised tissue (e.g., pseudobulbs of *Gongora*).

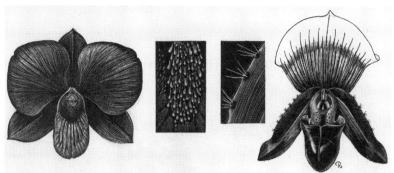

Fig. G.32. Vestiture. Left, papillae on the lip of *Dendrobium phalaenopsis* with detail; right, comose hairs on the petal margins of *Paphiopedilum callosum* with detail

**Root** (figs. G.2, G.6, G.7): A leafless plant segment, usually underground, but often aerial in epiphytic orchids. An underground storage organ in some terrestrials (e.g., *Ophrys*).

**Rosette** (fig. G.4E): Cluster of leaves radiating out from a central axis; characteristic of stemless orchids.

**Rostellum** (ros-TELL-um) (figs. G.35, G.38B,C): Literally, little beak; the sharp apex of the stigma that separates the pollinia from the stigmatic surface; a gland.

**Ruffled** (fig. G.29A,E): Having a wavy margin.

**Rupicolous** (ruh-PICK-oh-lus): Growing on or among rocks, ledges, or cliffs.

**Saccate** (figs. G.1, G.26): Sack shaped (e.g., the pouchlike lip of *Paphiopedilum*).

**Saprophyte** (SAP-roh-fite): A plant that derives its sustenance from the decomposition of old plant parts and that usually lacks chlorophyll.

**Scape**: A leafless flower stalk, often arising from the ground, with or without scales or bracts in place of leaves, and bearing one or more flowers.

**Scapose**: Having flowers on a scape.

**Scarious**: Dry and papery (e.g., bracts).

**Sectile**: See **Massula**.

**Secund**: Having flowers arranged on one side of an inflorescence (e.g., *Dendrobium secundum*).

**Seed** (fig. 1.7): A matured ovule capable of producing a plant.

**Seed pod** (figs. G.2, G.41): The mature ovary containing the mature ovules (seeds).

**Seedling**: Any plant formed from a seed that has not yet attained flowering size. An orchid seedling may be five to seven years old before it flowers.

**Segment**: One of the parts of a plant (e.g., leaf, root, sepal, petal, etc.).

**Semipeloric** (sem-ee-pel-OR-ik): Having an abnormal flower in which the petals have some liplike characteristics.

**Semiterete** (fig. G.12B–D): Said of the leaves of hybrids (e.g., *Vanda*) formed by crossing strap-leaved plants with terete-leaved.

**Sepal** (figs. G.17, G.22): A segment of the outer whorl of the perianth that protects

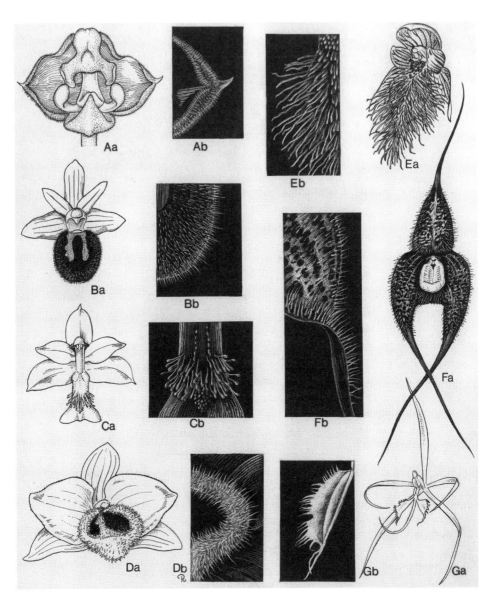

Fig. G.33. Vestiture and margins. Aa. Downy pubescent (*Polystachys*); Ab. detail of same; Ba. Hirsute or bristly or setose (*Ophrys sphegodes*); Bb. Detail of same; Ca. Beard of clavalate hairs (*Calopogon*); Cb. Detail of same; Da. Velutinous or densely pubescent with velvety hairs (*Dendrobium*); Db. Detail of same; Ea. Bearded with pilose hairs (*Calochilus*); Eb. Detail of same; Fa. Villous or long shaggy-haired (*Masdevallia*); Fb. Detail of same; Ga. A finely lacinate margin erroneously described as ciliate by the species name (*Epidendrum ciliare*); Gb. Detail of same

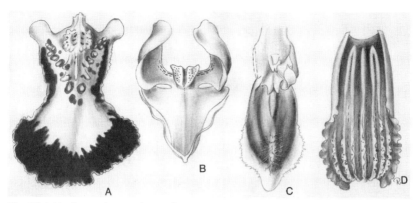

Fig. G.34. Lip decorations and protuberances. A. Lip with ears, papillae and a disc of irregularly lobed tissue (*Oncidium*); B. Trilobed lip with a smooth waxy callus and antennae (*Phalaenopsis*); C. Recurved side lobes, a raised, curved callus, beard of villous hairs and a finely ciliate margin (*Phalaenopsis*); D. Ruffled margins, waxy crests with thickened ridges (*Bletia*)

the unopened flower bud; in orchids the sepal usually is trimerous (i.e., in three parts), with two of the sepals fused in the *Paphiopedilum* group.

**Sessile** (fig. G.7): Stalkless; having the leaf blade attached directly to the stem (e.g., *Cattleya*).

**Sheath** (figs. G.2, G.7, G.17): Any leaflike structure on an orchid that envelops a developing bud and emerging pseudobulb.

**Shoot** (fig. G.2): The new growth of a plant, usually a portion of the stem with its attached leaves.

**Simple** (fig. G.2): Not compound (e.g., a leaf without leaflets or a nonbranched inflorescence).

**Sinus** (figs. G.28E–I, G.29A): The area or space between two lobes of a lip, leaf, or other plant part.

**Smooth** (fig. G.29D): Free of blemishes; not hairy, not rough, and not scabrous.

**Solitary** (fig. G.18A): Having only one flower per inflorescence.

**Spathe** (fig. G.2): A bract or leaf that subtends or encompasses an inflorescence; the sheath.

**Spathulate**: Spoon shaped.

**Species**: A plant or group of plants within a genus, grouped by one or more distinct characteristics and capable of interbreeding.

**Speculum** (SPECK-yew-lum): The central shiny area of the labellum as in *Ophrys*.

**Spike** (fig. G.18B): An inflorescence with sessile flowers; colloquially, any emerging inflorescence on an orchid plant (e.g., our *Cattleya* is in spike).

**Spiral** (figs. G.4E, G.29F): Having leaves or flowers arranged on the stem like a corkscrew.

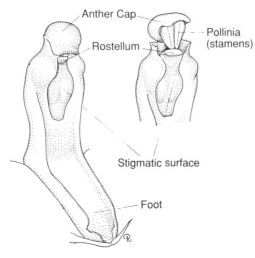

Anther Cap

Rostellum

Pollinia
(stamens)

Fig. G.35. The column

Stigmatic surface

Foot

**Spotted** (figs. G.1, G.28N, G.30B, G.31B): Having irregular areas of color on sepals, petals, or leaves.

**Spray** (fig. G.18C): A general term used to describe all types of inflorescences.

**Spur** (figs. G.18, G.27): The tubular extension found on the lips of many orchids (e.g., *Angraecum*), which usually contains a nectary.

**Stalk**: See **Stem**.

**Stamen** (figs. G.35, G.36B–E): The male portion of the flower composed of a filament and an anther containing pollen.

**Staminode** (STAM-in-ohd): A pollenless or sterile stamen.

**Stellate**: Star-shaped.

**Stem** (fig. G.17): The aboveground segment of a plant. A main axis that bears leaves and that eventually flowers and fruits.

**Stemlike** (fig. G.15R): Appearing like a stem.

**Stigma** (fig. G.39R): The apex of the pistil, often sticky; the receptive portion of the pistil.

**Stigmatic surface**: The sticky area on the underside of the column where the pollinia are placed and the pollen germinates.

**Stilidium** (*pl.* **stilidia**) (fig. G.39K,L): A winglike appendage on the column.

**Stipe** (figs. 1.5, G.36D): A thin stalk that connects the pollinia to the viscidium.

**Strap leaf** (fig. G.11E): A long and narrow leaf (e.g., *Vanda*).

**Striped** (figs. G.13H, G.31F,G): Having lines of color on sepals, petals, or leaves.

**Style**: The portion of the pistil connecting the stigma to the ovary.

**Sub-**: Almost (e.g., subcordate or almost heart shaped).

**Subgenus**: A natural division or group within a genus.

**Substance**: Refers to the thickness and longevity of floral segments.

**Succulent**: Refers to leaves, stems, or other plant organs that are very soft, fleshy, and moist.

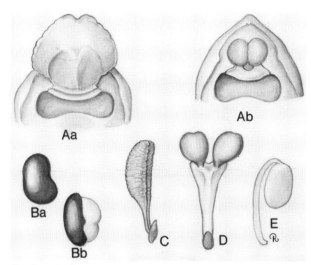

Fig. G.36. Androecium parts. A. Column end (*Grammatophyllum*): Aa. Anther cap in place; Ab. Anther cap removed exposing pollinia. Pollinia B–E: Ba,Bb. Diandrous pollinia, two views (*Paphiopedium*); C. Pollinia (*Ludisia*); D. Pollinia with foot on stipe (*Trichopilia*); E. Pollinia and and plain stipe (*Broughtonia*)

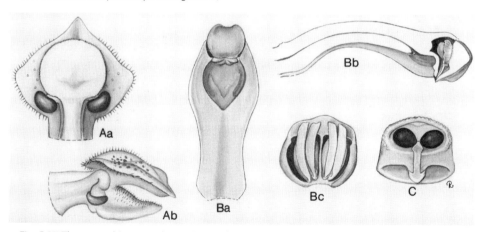

Fig. G.37. The gynandrium or column. A. Diandrous (*Paphiopedilum*): Aa. Column, ventral or bottom view; Ab. Column, side view. B. Monandrous (*Cattleya*): Ba. Column, ventral or bottom view; Bb. Column, vertical section; Bc. Anther cap with pollinia in place; C. Monandrous (*Ascocentrum*): End of column with anther cap removed to show pollinia in place

**Sulcate** (fig. G.15F,G,I,K): See **Furrowed**.

**Swollen** (fig. G.15Q): Larger than other similar parts; distended or enlarged.

**Sympodial** (sim-POH-dee-al) (fig. G.3F–H): Refers to a plant, the main stem of which grows horizontally and has determinate lateral branches; inflorescences are terminal or axillary (e.g., *Laelia*).

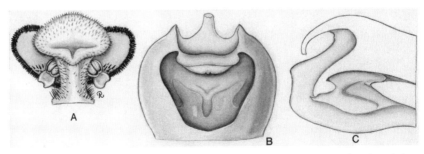

Fig. G.38. Gynandrium. A. Diandrous (*Phragmipedium*); B. Monandrous (*Schomburgkia*); Ba. Stigmatic surface much enlarged, ventral view; Bb. Side view

**Synsepal** (SIN-see-pul) (fig. G.24C): The fused lateral sepals found in the subfamily Cypripedioideae.

**Taxon**: A taxonomic term applying to a related group of plants (e.g., a genus or species).

**Taxonomy**: The science of plant classification.

**Terete** (figs. G.12A): Said of leaves that are round in cross section (e.g., *Brassavola nodosa*).

**Terminal** (figs. G.2, G.19Ac): Refers to a flower arising from the tip of the growth (e.g., *Cattleya*); the uppermost flower or the apex of the stem.

**Terrestrial** (fig. G.3B): A plant that grows in soil or similar medium (e.g., *Phaius*).

**Tessellate** (figs. G.1, G.13B, G.31D): Checkered or evenly netted (e.g., flowers of *Vanda* [*Euanthe*] *sanderiana*, *Vanda coerulea*).

**Tetragonal** (figs. G.15L, G.16F): Four sided.

**Tetraploid**: Having four sets of chromosomes or double the usual two sets.

**Texture**: The surface quality of flowers or leaves (i.e., crystalline, waxy, scaly).

**Throat** (fig. G.28N,O): The basal, usually almost-tubular portion of the lip of an orchid flower.

**Tissue culture**: An asexual method of propagating plants using meristematic tissue to produce like plants. A form of cloning.

**Tomentose** (fig. G.33D): Having a very dense covering of hairs; almost woolly.

**Triangular** (fig. G.10K): Three sided.

**Tribe**: A group of closely related genera.

**Trilobed** (figs. G.1, G.28F): Having three lobes.

**Triploid**: Having three sets of chromosomes; the usual two plus one additional set.

**Truncate**: Said of a leaf that appears to have been cut off at the apex; having a flat apex.

**Tuber** (fig. G.6B): A shortened, thickened stem containing eyes and usually found underground; often misused with orchids. See **Tuberoid**.

**Tubercle** (fig. G.13K): A small tuber not necessarily underground (e.g., a small tuber on a leaf or petal).

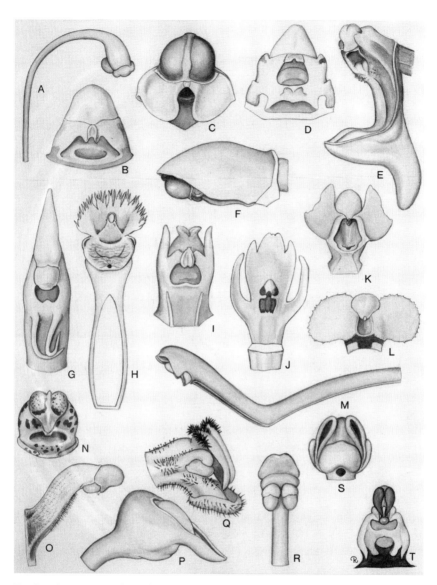

Fig. G.39. Variations in the orchid column. A. Slender, long, curved (*Cycnoches*); B. Short and wide (*Gastrochilus*); C. Flaring "skirt" below cap (*Angraecum*); D. Shouldered (*Vandopsis*); E. Footed, papillate (*Dendrobium*); F. "Hood" over anther cap (*Pholidota*); G. Anther cap pointed, antennae (*Catasetum*); H. Fringed "collar" (*Trichoglottis*); I. Two-horned (*Trichopilia*); J. Two side appendages, large back lobe, tiny anther cap (*Dendrochilum*); K. Winged (*Oncidium*); L. Wide wings (*Lockhartia*); M. Long, perianth parts partly adnate (*Vanilla*); N. Beaked cap (*Rhynchostylis*); O. Pubescent (*Lycaste*); P. Twisted (*Ludisia*); Q. Diandrous, fringed (*Phragmipedium*); R. Large erect stigma, twin anther sacs (*Satyrium*); S. Short with pair of club-shaped pollen masses (*Platanthera*); T. Broad with pair of erect pollinia (*Orchis*)

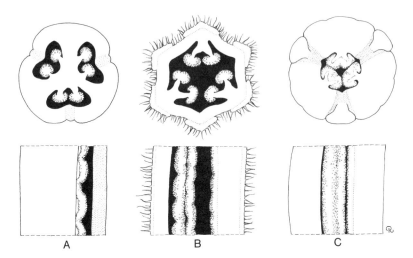

Fig. G.40. Placentation. A. Axile, cross-section and vertical section (*Phragmipedium*).
B. Parietal, diandrous orchid, cross-section and vertical section. C. Parietal, monandrous orchid, cross-section and vertical section

**Tuberoid**: A thickened underground storage organ having both stem and root tissue.

**Tubular**: Having a round cylindrical shape (e.g., fused sepals in some *Masdevallia* species).

**Tunicate** (fig. G.9Ab): Having concentric or sheathing layers of tissue.

**Twisted** (figs. G.25A, G.39P): Having parts that are spiraling or corkscrewlike.

**Umbel** (fig. G.18D): An inflorescence in which the flowers appear to arise at one point.

**Undulate** (figs. G.13E, G.29B): Having an up-and-down wavy margin on a leaf or petal; not waving in and out.

**Unequally two-lobed** (fig. G.11F): Said of leaf tips with unequal apical lobes.

**Unguiculate** (un-GWIK-yew-late) (fig. G.15F): Drawn out at the base, often drawn into a thin stalk or even clawlike.

**Unifoliate**: Having only one leaf.

**Valves** (fig. G.41A,Ea): The segments of a seed pod.

**Variety**: A plant within a species that has a minor, distinct characteristic (e.g., *Laelia purpurata* var. *carnea*).

**Vegetative**: Refers to asexual methods of reproduction (e.g., division in *Cattleya*). Also refers to the leafy portion of the plant.

**Vein** (fig. G.8): Vascular tissue that transports water, nutrients, and carbohydrates throughout a leaf and/or a plant.

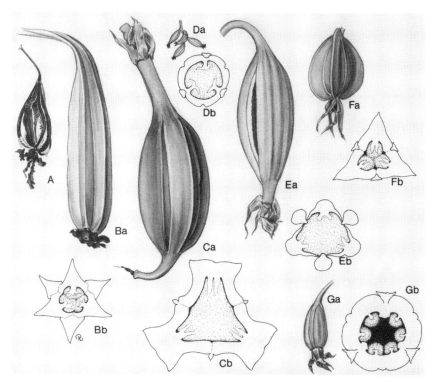

Fig. G.41. Mature seed capsules, habits and cross-sections. A. *Dendrobium* pod split open and seeds disseminated. Ba,Bb. *Vanda* seed pod and crosss section; Ca,Cb. *Cattleya* pod and cross-section; Da,Db *Polystachya* pods and cross-section. Ea,Eb. *Phaius* pod split along one suture and cross-section. Fa,Fb. *Encyclia* pod and cross-section. Ga,Gb. *Dendrobium* pod and cross-section

**Velamen** (vel-A-men) (fig. G.6G): The thick, spongy layer of cells that surrounds the roots of epiphytic orchids.

**Velutinous** (vel-LOO-tin-us) (fig. G.33Da,Db): Having a cover of erect, somewhat-firm hairs.

**Venation** (ven-A-shun) (figs. G.8, G.10, G.13): The arrangement of the veins.

**Ventral** (fig. G.37Aa,Ba): On the lower side, opposite of dorsal.

**Vestiture**: A covering of hairs, papillae, or other protuberances on a surface.

**Villous** (figs. G.33Fa,Fb, G.34C): Having long, soft hairs covering the surface.

**Vine** (fig. G.4F): A plant that climbs.

**Viscid**: Very sticky.

**Viscidium** (vis-SID-ee-um): The sticky disc attached to the pollinia (e.g., *Catasetum*) which adheres to the pollinator to insure removal of the pollinia from the flower and to another flower for cross-pollination.

**Whorl** (fig. G.4E): Three or more plant parts attached at the same point.

**Winged** (fig. G.39K,L): Having an organ with a usually flat projection on one or more sides.

**Woolly**: Having long, soft, sometimes matted hairs.

**Xerophyte**: A plant native to an arid area.

**Zygomorphic** (zye-go-MOR-fik) (fig. 1.2): Capable of being divided into equal halves in one plane only; said of flowers having bilateral symmetry.

# Botanical and Common Name Index

Galeandra: *baueri*, 82; *beyrichii*, 82; *claesiana*, 82; *devoniana*, 82; *lucustris*, 82; *pubicentrum*, 82

Galeottia: *burkei*, 83; *fimbriata*, 83; *grandiflora*, 83; *marginata*, 83

Ghost orchid, 69, **plate 21**

Gomesa: *crispa*, 84; *glaziovii*, 84; *laxiflora.* 84; *planifolia*, 84; *recurva*, 84; *sessilis*, 84; *verbonnenii*, 84

Gongora: *armeniaca*, 85; *fulva*, 85, **plate 25**; *galeata*, 85; *quinquenervis*, 85; *truncata*, 85

Goodyera: *hispida*, 86; *pubescens*, 86; *repens*, 86

Grammangis ellisii, 87

Grammatophyllum: *measuresianum*, 88; *scriptum*, 88, **plate 26**; *speciosum*, 88

Habenaria: *carnea*, 89; *dentata*, 89; *repens*, 89; *rhodocheila*, 89; *splendens*, 89

Holcoglossum: *amesianum*, 90; *kimballianum*, 90; *quasipinifolium*, 90

Holy Ghost orchid, 130

Huntleya meleagris, 91, **plate 27**

Ionopsis: *satyrioides*, 92; *utricularioides*, 92, **plate 28**

Isochilus: *linearis*, 93, **plate 29**; *major*, 93

Jumellea: *fragrans*, 94; *gracilipes*, 94; *sagittata*, 94

Lady-of-the-night, 39

Lady Slipper orchid, 64, **plate 18**

Laelia: *anceps*, 95; *autumnalis*, 95; *cinnabarina*, 95; *flava*, 95; *grandis*, 95; *harpophylla*, 95; *lobata*, 95; *lundii*, 95; *milleri*, 95; *pumila*, 95; *purpurata*, 95, **plate 30**; *tenebrosa*, 95

Lala palusa, 8

Lemboglossum, 119

Lepanthes: *calodictyon*, 97; *escobariana*, 97; *lindleyana*, 97; *obtusa*, 97; *puchella*, 97

Leptotes: *bicolor*, 98; *unicolor*, 98

Liparis: *nervosa*, 99; *nugentea*, 99; *nutans*, 99; *reflexa*, 99

Little man orchid, 84

Lockhartia: *acuta*, 100; *elegans*, 100; *oerstedii*, 100; *serra*, 100

Ludisia discolor, 101

Lycaste: *aromatica*, 102; *brevispatha*, 102;

crinita, 102; *curenta*, 102; *dowiana*, 102, **plate 31**; *leucantha*, 102; *longipetala*, 102; *skinneri*, 102; *tricolor*, 102

Macradenia: *brassavolae*, 103; *lutescens*, 103; *multiflora*, 103

Malaxis: *calophylla*, 104; *latifolia*, 104; *monophyllos*, 104; *ophrydis*, 104; *paludosa*, 104

Masdevallia: *attenuata*, 105; *bicolor*, 105; *caudata*, 105; *coccinea*, 105; *elephanticeps*, 105; *militaris*, 105; *princeps*, 105, **plate 32**; *rosea*, 105; *uniflora*, 105; *veitchiana*, 105

Maxillaria: *acuminata*, 106; *brunnea*, 106; *crassifolia*, 106; *cucullata*, 106; *friedrichsthallii*, 106; *fulgens*, 106; *grandiflora*, 106; *inaudita*, 106; *neglecta*, 106; *ochroleuca*, 106; *rufescens*, 106; *sanderiana*, 106; *sophronitis*, 106, **plate 33**; *tenuifolia*, 106, **plate 34**; *valenzuelana*, 106; *variabilis*, 106; *venusta*, 106

Mendoncella, 83

Mexicoa ghiesbrechtiana, 108

Miltonia: *clowesii*, 109; *flavescens*, 109; *regnellii*, 109; *spectabilis*, 109, **plate 35**

Miltoniopsis: *phalaenopsis*, 110, **plate 36**; *roezlii*, 110; *santanae.* 110; *vexillaria*, 110; *warscewiczii*, 110

Mormodes: *atropurpureum*, 111; *colossus*, 111; *hookeri*, 111; *maculatum*, 111; *rolfeanum*, 111; *sinuata*, 111

Mormolyca: *gracilipes*, 112; *peruviana*, 112; *ringens*, 112

Moth orchid, 133

Myrmecophila tibicinis, 156

Neobenthamia gracilis, 113

Neofinetia falcata, 114, **plate 37**

Neomoorea wallisii, 115, **plate 38**

Notylia: *barkeri*, 116; *bicolor*, 116; *carnosiflora*, 116; *cordesii*, 116; *platyglossa*, 116; *punctata*, 116

Nun's orchid, 132

Oberonia iridifolia, 117

Octomeria: *gracilis*, 118; *grandiflora*, 118; *sandersiana*, 118

Odontoglossum: *constrictum*, 119; *coronarium*, **plate 39**; *crispum*, 119; *lindenii*, 119; *odoratum*, 119; *ramosissimum*, 119

Sarcochilus: australis, 154; falcatus, 154; fitzgeraldii, 154; hartmannii, 154; pallidus, 154;
stenoglottis, 154; virescens, 154
Sarcoglottis: acaulis, 155; grandiflora, 155; metallica, 155; sceptrodes, 155
Schomburgkia: gloriosa, 156; superbiens, 156;
undulata, 156
Scorpion orchid, 30
Scuticaria: hadwenii, 157; steelii, 157
Sievekingia: herrenhusana, 158; peruviana, 158;
reichenbachiana, 158; suavis, 158
Slipper orchid: Cypripedium, 64; Paphiopedilum, 126; Phragmipedium, 135
Sobralia: decora, 159; fimbriata, 159; leucoxantha, 159; macrantha, 159; rosea, 159; virgina-
lis, 159, **plate 57**; yauaperyensis, 159
Sophronitis: cernua, 160, **plate 58**; coccinea, 160;
pterocarpa, 160
Spathoglottis: aurea, 161; ixioides, 161; plicata,
161; ×powelii, 161; pubescens, 161; unguicu-
lata, 161
Spider orchid, 30
Spiranthes: cernua, 162; romanzoffiana, 162;
sinensis, 162; spiralis, 162
Stanhopea: ecornuta, 163; grandiflora, 163;
insignis, 163; oculata, 163; tigrina, 163; wardii,
163, **plate 59**
Star of Bethlehem, 28
Stenia: guttata, 164; pallida, 164
Stenoglottis: fimbriata, 165; longifolia, 165
Swan orchid, 60

Telipogon: nervosus, 166; panamanensis, 166;
pulcher, 166
Tetramicra: canaliculata, 167; elegans, 167;
parviflora, 167

Thrixspermum: arachnitiforme, 168; centipeda, 168
Thunia: alba, 169; bensoniae, 169; marshalliana,
169
Tolumnia: bahamensis, 170, **plate 60**; pulchella,
170; triquetrum, 170; variegata, 170
Toritos, 163
Trichocentrum: albococcineum, 171; carthagenense, 171; fuscum, 171; lanceanum, 171;
leucochilum, 171; panduratum, 171; pfavii,
171; splendidum, 171; tigrinum, 171
Trichoglottis: brachiata, 172; luzonensis, 172;
philippinensis, 172; rosea, 172; sagarikii, 172
Trichoplia: brevis, 173; fragrans, 173; maculata,
173; marginata, 173; suavis, 173; tortilis, 173
Tridactyle: bicaudata, 174; gentilii, 174
Trigonidium egertonianum, 175

Vanda: coerulea, 176, **plate 61**; coerulescens,
176; cristata, 176; dearei, 176; denisoniana,
176; insignis, 176; lamellata, 176; luzonica,
176; merrillii, 176; testacea, 176, **plate 62**;
tricolor, 176
Vanilla: africana, 178; aphylla, 178; barbellata,
178; phaeantha, 178; planifolia, 178, **plate 63**;
pompona, 178

Warrea warreana, 179

Zeuxine strateumatica, 180
Zootrophion: atropurpureum, 181; dayanum,
181; hypodiscus, 181
Zygopetalum: brachypetalum, 182; burkei, 182;
intermedium, 182; mackayi, 182
Zygosepalum: labiosum, 183; lindeniae, 183,
**plate 64**; tatei, 183

# Subject Index

Pfitzer, E., 16
pH, 198
Photoperiod, 197
Physiological problems. *See* cultural problems
Plant shines, 185
Plants in the home, 231
Plaques, 206
Plastic greenhouse, 228
Plastic pots, 206
Pleated leaves, 222
Pollinia, 2, 4
Polycarbonate greenhouse, 228
Postal stamps, 190
Potions, 187
Potting, 207
Practical uses: cooking, 187; flavoring, 188; glue, 187; ice cream, 189; love potions, 187; malnutrition, 187; tea, 187; woven baskets, 67, 187; woven bracelets, 187
Preparing orchids for exhibition: staking and tying, 185
Pridgeon, A., 15
Propagation: asexual, 209; division, 209; flower stalks, 211; keikis, 210; meristeming, 214; seed, 214; sexual, 214; tip cuttings, 212; vegetative, 209

Rasmussen, F., 16
Reichenbach, H., 16
Repotting, 207
Resupinate, 2
Rolfe, R., 16
Root rot, 216
Roots, 185
Rostellum, 2, 4

Salep, 189
*Salepi*, 124
*Salepi dondurma*, 124, 189
Salt deposits, 222
Scale, 219
Schlechter, F., 216
Schultes, R. E., 15
Seed, 2, 5
Selecting an orchid, 185
Sexual propagation, 214

Shade, 196
Shade cloth, 229–30
Shade houses: cloth, 229; lath, 230
Sheehan and Sheehan, 15
Shriveled pseudobulbs, 222
Slow release fertilizer, 201
Slugs, 218
Snails, 218
Soft rot, 215
Soluble salts, 198
Species, 9, 17
Species epithet, 9, 10
Spider mites, 221
Staking, 185
Stipe, 5
Subfamily, 17
Subspecies, 9, 17
Subtribe, 17
Sympodial orchids, 1

Tahitian vanilla, 189
Tea, 187
Temperature, 199–200
Terrestrial media, 202
Thrips, 220
Tip cuttings, 212
Tobacco mosaic, 217
Tribe, 17
Trigeneric crosses, 10

Vanilla, 188–89
Vanillin, 98, 188
Variety, 9, 17
Vegetative propagation, 209
Viruses: *Cymbidium* mosaic, 217; tobacco mosaic, 217
Viscidium, 5

Water: frequency, 199; pH, 198; quality, 198; quantity, 199; soluble salts, 198
Weeds, 222
What orchid names mean, 11
Why orchid names change, 14
Wimder, D., 214

Zygomorphic flower, 2–3

Thomas J. Sheehan is a professor emeritus of environmental horticulture at the University of Florida's Institute of Food and Agricultural Sciences. He authored or coauthored *Orchid Genera Illustrated*, *An Illustrated Survey of Orchid Genera*, *Ultimate Orchid*, and *Florida Landscape Plants*. Sheehan is also an accredited American Orchid Society Judge and has received the American Orchid Society's Gold Medal of Achievement, its highest honor.

Robert J. Black, professor emeritus of environmental horticulture, Institute of Food and Agricultural Sciences at the University of Florida, is the coeditor of *Your Florida Landscape: A Complete Guide to Planting and Maintenance* and coauthor of *Landscape Plants for the Gulf and South Atlantic Coasts*, *Florida Landscape Plants*, *The Florida Guide to Shrubs*, and *Your Florida Guide to Bedding Plants*.

Related-interest titles from University Press of Florida

*Florida Butterfly Caterpillars and Their Host Plants*
Marc C. Minno, Jerry F. Butler, and Donald W. Hall

*Florida Landscape Plants: Native and Exotic, Second Revised Edition*
John V. Watkins, Thomas J. Sheehan, and Robert J. Black

*Landscape Plants for the Gulf and South Atlantic Coasts: Selection, Establishment, and Maintenance*
Robert J. Black and Edward F. Gilman

*Ornamental Palm Horticulture*
Timothy K. Broschat and Alan W. Meerow

*Wild Orchids of the Canadian Maritimes and Northern Great Lakes Region*
Paul Martin Brown with drawings by Stan Folsom

*Wild Orchids of Florida with References to the Atlantic and Gulf Coastal Plains, Updated and Expanded Edition*
Paul Martin Brown with drawings by Stan Folsom

*The Wild Orchids of North America, North of Mexico*
Paul Martin Brown

*Wild Orchids of the Northeast: New England, New York, Pennsylvania, and New Jersey*
Paul Martin Brown with drawings by Stan Folsom

*Wild Orchids of the Pacific Northwest and Canadian Rockies*
Paul Martin Brown with drawings by Stan Folsom

*Wild Orchids of the Prairies and Great Plains Region of North America*
Paul Martin Brown with drawings by Stan Folsom

*Wild Orchids of the Southeastern United States, North of Peninsular Florida*
Paul Martin Brown with drawings by Stan Folsom

*Your Florida Guide to Perennials: Selection, Establishment, and Maintenance*
Sydney Park Brown and Rick Schoellhorn

For more information on these and other books, visit our website at www.upf.com.